PEPÓN OSORIO

PEPÓN OSORIO

My Beating Heart / *Mi corazón latiente*

Edited by Margot Norton and Bernardo Mosqueira

NEW MUSEUM

Contents

Para version en español, utilice el QR code
For the Spanish version, scan QR code

Foreword

—

Lisa Phillips

For over thirty-five years, Pepón Osorio (b. 1955, San Juan, Puerto Rico; lives and works in Philadelphia, PA) has created richly textured sculptures and installations that break through traditional notions of art-making. Known for his sweeping, provocative multimedia installations, Osorio creates fantastical scenes inspired by everyday environments—from home interiors to barbershops to classrooms—that advance critical discussions on topics such as identity, race, gender, and social justice.

Born and raised in San Juan, Osorio studied at the Universidad Interamericana in Puerto Rico and Herbert H. Lehman College in New York, and received an MA from Columbia University in 1985. His artistic practice is directly informed by his background in theater and performance and his experiences as a child services case worker as well as a professor of community art at Tyler School of Art and Architecture at Temple University in Philadelphia. His collaborative process and resulting works are deeply invested in political, social, and cultural issues affecting Latinx and working-class communities in the United States.

"My Beating Heart / *Mi corazón latiente*" is Osorio's most comprehensive exhibition to date, featuring selected works from the 1990s to today. Installed on the New Museum's Second Floor, this show focuses on the elaborate large-scale environments the artist has been creating over the last four decades—often developed through long-term conversations and collaborations with individuals in the neighborhoods they were first shown.

The exhibition features five of Osorio's large-scale installations, the earliest of which, *Scene of the Crime (Whose Crime?)* (1993; pp. 73–83)—included in the 1993 Whitney Biennial—reflects on the social impact of Hollywood's violent representations of Latinx people, depicting what appears to be the aftermath of a murder in a Puerto Rican family's New York City apartment. Other large-scale multimedia installations from the 1990s include: *No Crying Allowed in the Barbershop (En la barbería no se llora)* (1994; pp.

84–105)—originally installed in an abandoned barbershop in New Haven, Connecticut—tackles gender performativity and the perpetuation of machismo; and *Badge of Honor* (1995; pp. 106–27), first shown in a storefront in Newark, New Jersey, investigates the effects of mass incarceration through an intimate conversation between a teenager and his imprisoned father.

The exhibition also includes Osorio's recent project *reForm* (2014–17; pp. 150–67), created in collaboration with students and community members in response to a city-ordained shuttering of a Philadelphia school, and Osorio's new work, *Convalescence* (2023; pp. 168–91), focusing on the difficulties of navigating the US healthcare system and the multiplicity of pathways toward healing. Alongside these installations, the show includes several sculptural works, such as *My Beating Heart (Mi corazón latiente)* (2000; pp. 146–47), a six-foot-tall anatomical heart adorned with a crepe paper technique traditionally used to make piñatas, outfitted with speakers playing the sound of the artist's own heartbeat.

This exhibition offers an unprecedented opportunity to experience Osorio's new projects alongside his most iconic installations for the first time. It also demonstrates the distinctive ways in which he creates encompassing environments that illustrate personal stories and reveal crucial societal concerns. "My Beating Heart/*Mi corazón latiente*" addresses themes that resonate throughout Osorio's practice, including the simultaneous resilience and fragility of human life, the values and desires that propel individuals and communities, and the fundamental urgency to better care for one another.

I would like to thank the curators of the exhibition, Margot Norton, former Allen and Lola Goldring Senior Curator, and Bernardo Mosqueira, ISLAA Curatorial Fellow, who worked closely with Osorio to realize this show and catalogue. Abel González Fernandez, 2022 Bard CCS Curatorial Mentee, provided key early support to the research of the exhibition. This exhibition is the result of the combined efforts of the entire New Museum staff. The show's design, preparations, and installation have been adeptly managed by David Hollely, Director of Exhibitions Management, and his team: Abby Lepold, Senior Registrar; Carlos Yepes, Registrar; Patrick Foran, Chief Preparator; Olivia Biggs, Production Preparator; and Telo Hoy, AV Preparator. The show has also greatly benefited from the on-going support of Isolde Brielmaier, Deputy Director; Diane Vivona, Vice President, Advancement; Mariah Mazur, Director of Development; Dennis Szakacs, Chief Operating Officer; and their respective teams.

We thank the Bronx Museum, the Museum of Modern Art in New York, and the Museo de Arte de Puerto Rico for their generosity in lending significant works to this exhibition. Amy Donghee Oh, Gabriel Osorio-Soto, Miriam Vazquez, and Omar Obdulio Peña, Osorio's studio team, provided invaluable assistance with the planning and coordination of the show.

The New Museum gratefully acknowledges our Board of Trustees and generous sponsors for their support of this exhibition. Major support for "Pepón Osorio: My Beating Heart/*Mi corazón latiente*" is provided by the Mellon Foundation. Artist commissions are generously supported by the Neeson/Edlis Artist Commissions Fund. Generous support is provided by Liza Mauer and Ronald Feldman Gallery, New York, in memory of Ronald Feldman. We gratefully acknowledge the International Leadership Council of the New Museum. Education and community programs are supported, in part, by the American Chai Trust. Support for this publication has been provided by the J. McSweeney and G. Mills Publications Fund at the New Museum.

This catalogue includes an interview with the artist by Norton and Mosqueira, texts by Robert Blackson, Ramón H. Rivera-Servera, and Guadalupe Rosales, and a conversation between Osorio and Rita Indiana. We are grateful to all of the authors for their contributions to this publication. This volume was carefully edited by Sarah Stephenson and designed by Nicholas Weltyk.

Finally, and most importantly, I would like to thank Pepón Osorio for the urgency and complexity of his practice, which brings crucial issues to the fore through multilayered, enthralling artworks. We are honored to have the opportunity to collaborate on this exhibition and work together once more.

— Lisa Phillips, *Toby Devan Lewis Director*, New Museum

El Averigüao

—

Pepón Osorio in Conversation with Margot Norton and Bernardo Mosqueira

Margot Norton: As many of your works refer to childhood, we were thinking of starting from the beginning. How did your experiences growing up inform your artistic practice?

Pepón Osorio: I come from a working-class family. While my mother was a baker and baked cakes for everyone in the community, my father and I would always help with the decorations and layering items on the cakes. We would come up with ideas for putting surprises inside of them, such as rings or objects like hearts—almost like votives or *ofrendras* [offerings]—that were connected to thin ribbons you could use to pull them out. That was the beginning of my understanding of how to surprise people and be generous in the making of things. We all contributed to the making of these cakes for birthdays, weddings, *quinceañeras* . . . I grew up in this extremely inventive family. My parents worked twenty-four hours a day, so a woman named Juana took care of me and my sister. She had all kinds of adornments on her body and always wore beautiful dresses with lots of color and jewelry. It was like a spectacle, an over-exaggerated way of life that charmed me.

I always had a lot of support when inventing new things. Back in the day, when I didn't even know that being an artist was a possibility, I painted my apartment. My friend, artist Awilda Sterling-Duprey, visited one day and said, "Oh! You are an artist!" The truth is that I've never been pleased with flat surfaces—I've always added everything to them and given them three-dimensional treatments.

MN: We recently learned about a particular performance you did with your father and sister about airplane travel. What did this performance entail?

PO: When I was a kid, I was interested in the idea of traveling, moving from one place to another, and experiencing other places. When I was fourteen, I knew I wanted to move to New York City. I developed an obsession with the first person I knew in my neighborhood who traveled outside of Puerto Rico. I remember looking at her shoe soles just to see what the dirt of New York was like. I asked her all the time if I could go to her house and see the shoes, and I would just look at the soles. It was the only way I could see what New York or another place might be like.

My father created the stage, which was like an airport gate, and my sister and I recorded a conversation with a tape recorder, and she would manipulate her Barbies and Kens. This experience unfolded into a lot of other big productions in the house with reams of brown paper . . . nothing was small!

I never knew that art could take an institutional form. I always thought—and still think—you make art for the immediacy, for the people around you.

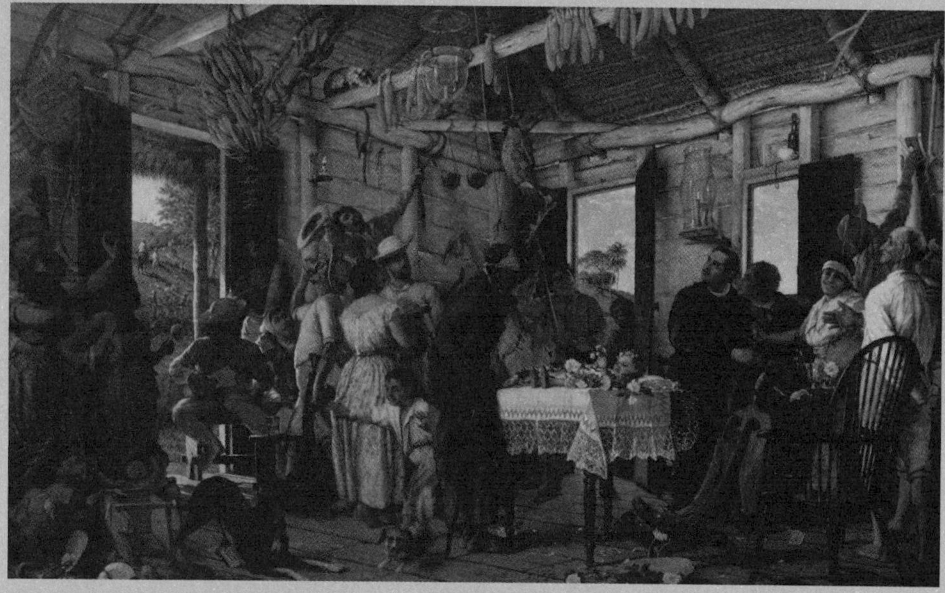

Fig. 1 Francisco Oller y Cestero, *The Wake*, 1893. Oil on canvas, 106 × 162 in (269.24 × 411.47 cm). Collection Museum of History, Anthropology and Art, University of Puerto Rico, Rio Piedras Campus

Bernardo Mosqueira: We also read about your encounter with the painting *El Velorio (The Wake)* [1893; fig. 1] by Francisco Oller when you were sixteen. It depicts the wake of a young child in the middle of a very intense room with people dancing, making out, crying, laughing. There's a priest, kids playing, dogs, chickens, and there's this figure at the center: an older man leaning on a cane. You once said you saw yourself in this figure and also your ancestors . . .

PO: Here lies the secret! There is something about our exhibition that is revealing a lot of information as I look back and come forward. That main figure in Oller's painting was Saint Lazarus for me, a wounded man. What I saw in him was someone healing but also persisting and enduring. I saw myself in him, but also Lazarus, the dead man restored to life by Jesus in the Christian Bible, or Babalú-Ayé, the Yoruba orisha associated with the earth, diseases, and healing.

I also saw a spiritual moment captured by the use of light in that painting. At the time, it was on view to the public at the University of Puerto Rico. I didn't find it by going to a museum. That's why I'm so interested in sharing my work where the majority of people can bump into it.

BM: In the painting, it is really striking that this central figure is the only one actually looking at the deceased child, which is also "decorated"—covered by flowers and light. And there is a remarkable line connecting his eyes and those of the child.

PO: That man resembles the spectators that come to see my work. They know that something is going on. They stand still, observing and watching—perhaps they recognize that they are in front of something that has power and significance. When I see people looking at my work, it brings me back to this memory. Even though my work looks spontaneous, it's intentionally choreographed to bring people to connect with it as outsiders.

BM: It reminds me of something you mentioned earlier today when we were walking in your neighborhood: *el averigüao*—the person or spectator who witnesses an accident on the street or a police car stopping someone and is immediately drawn to watch what is going on, almost in a voyeuristic or perverse way.

PO: *Averigüao*! That should be the subtitle of our exhibition! There is another thing about the figure of the man in Oller's painting: the way he's dressed and his posture make me think he didn't belong to that place. It's as if he comes from somewhere else, and he's just an *averigüao* trying to figure out what the hell is happening.

MN: When we came to visit you in Puerto Rico, we had a great dinner with Awilda, who you mentioned earlier, and you were both reminiscing about when you were roommates in New York. You have been friends for over forty years, and she introduced you to so many people in New York—including your wife, Merián Soto, with whom you also collaborated on performances. Tell us about those early years in New York: What was that time like for you?

PO: I learned a lot about contemporary art with Awilda, and we were, and still are, good friends. When she went to Pratt Institute, I went with her and looked at what she was doing. I would simulate what I saw in her studio without showing anyone. But at some point, I began to open up and make my own work.

I was never satisfied with one medium: I explored painting, collage, printmaking, everything. But, when I saw Mérian's choreographies, it brought me back to a specific memory—I thought, "This sounds like the radio is on at home, the TV is on at the same time, my mother is baking a cake, I'm listening to music, and the next-door neighbor is talking." At that point, I decided that performance was it, and I begged Mérian to let me make costumes for her. She used to live in a very central place in SoHo, and I was in the South Bronx. Every time I came to "New York City"—meaning Manhattan—I always felt displaced, never belonging there. My place of gravity, in terms of ideas and practice, was in the South Bronx.

I started spending more time with Mérian and slowly began to visit different art spaces in SoHo. What intrigued me about some of the artists I was seeing was that they were working big, and I wanted to work big. Because of the restrictions around race in relation to art production, I knew it was almost going to be impossible, but I took the risk.

At that time, I had made some work, but I buried a lot of it in the ground near my studio in the South Bronx. Mérian went to Teachers College at Columbia University to get her master's degree in art education, and I was madly in love with her, as I still am. I told her I was going to get a master's in studio art and asked her what I needed to do to get in. When she said, "Well, I guess you need a portfolio," I responded, "What the hell is that?" And she explained it to me.

I went to the South Bronx with a shovel, dug up the things I had buried, put them in a paper bag, went to Columbia University, knocked at the door, and pulled these things out, covered in dirt. At that time, I made a lot of work that had to do with earth. I was reminiscing about the island of Puerto Rico and missing it a lot, trying to recreate the island in these pieces. The head of the art department at Teachers College looked at me and at the work, and I don't know how, but I was accepted! This was the early '80s.

BM: While you were making stage elements for performances with Mérian and with your performance collective Pepatián, you started to develop your own style, working with small objects important in Puerto Rican vernacular culture. When did you decide to start working with these objects?

PO: There was an exhibition in 1984 at the Museum of Modern Art in New York called "An International Survey of Recent Painting and Sculpture," curated by Kynaston McShine, and the poster for the show was a photograph of tropical fish and toy globes by Neil Selkirk. I immediately loved it, so I took it from the subway. Sometime later, I remember seeing an artwork by an artist whose name I can't remember, which seemed to suggest he was disgusted by a New York family and the numerous toys and objects they had. I was so offended by it I decided to stop working with earth and respond to him. I thought, "If anyone knows about objects, it's me."

From 1985 to 1990, I didn't participate in anything except performance because I didn't want to have anything to do with museums—I resisted the idea of exhibitions. Instead of trying to use mediums dominated by other people, I started to work with, as you say, a Puerto Rican vernacular that surfaced in my childhood memories. That was a turning point in my practice.

MN: Fast-forwarding to 1993, to the Whitney Biennial, you showed a room-size installation called *Scene of the Crime (Whose Crime?)* [1993; pp. 73–83], which was your earliest large-scale piece—and we will be showing it in our exhibition. It was also the first time I saw your work—I still remember that moment so profoundly. You've spoken about how that installation was like taking a piece of the South Bronx and placing it into the Whitney on Madison Avenue. At that time, you were also involved in activism related to the representation of Puerto Ricans and Latinx people in Hollywood. How did the idea for this work come about?

PO: The first activist action I remember participating in was a big demonstration against *Fort Apache*, a 1981 film made in the South Bronx, for its racist depictions of Black and Latinx people. I have always been very curious about how people see others and we see ourselves. With *Scene of the Crime*, I wanted to do a piece about how we Boricuas [Puerto Ricans] are seen in the movies.

I remember making this piece feeling that nothing would stop me, that I had to tell my truth. Up until that point, a lot of people thought I was crazy. But after my 1991 retrospective at El Museo del Barrio, things took a completely different turn, and people started to take me seriously.

I wanted to go into people's homes when crimes had just occurred, and I convinced two detectives to let me sit silently in the back of their car and accompany them as they investigated crime scenes. After I created the piece, I invited one of the detectives to come to the exhibition space to do an investigation as he would at an actual crime scene.

Scene of the Crime was an accumulation of all the different spaces I saw—the objects, personal belongings, and aesthetics. I began to understand that I really wanted to disregard the architecture of the museum and bring in a chunk from the South Bronx, creating tension between those two places. Not only did I feel I wasn't allowed to be part of the mainstream art world until then, but I also felt South Bronx stories weren't allowed to be told. My work looks like I arrange all these objects randomly, but it is very calculated. It comes after months and months of research and careful construction—not for me, but for the work itself, and for the *averigüao,* the viewer.

BM: A few months after the Whitney Biennial, you installed *No Crying Allowed in the Barbershop (En la barbería no se llora)* [1994; pp. 84–105] in an abandoned barbershop in the Frog Hollow neighborhood of New Haven, Connecticut—commissioned by Real Art Ways. Looking at the barbershop as a tragic theater of masculinity, the work illustrates how formative these environments are for Latino men and how they develop their identities and behaviors in them. In a culture defined by machismo, these men are simultaneously victims and perpetrators of gender violence. The work criticizes and confuses gender categories, juxtaposing signals of masculinity and femininity, strength and fragility, pride and vulnerability. I'm particularly curious about how you play, in a very irreverent way, with this proximity between machismo and homoeroticism. Could you talk a little bit about the multiple layers of *En la barbería* and how it came to be?

PO: *En la barbería* came into being around the time I became a father and realized the imposed roles created by machismo and masculinity. I wanted to understand how to prevent myself from falling into the same exaggeration of what it is to be a man. A lot of this construction of masculinity happens in barbershops, in the absence of women, and I wanted to have a conversation with people in the community about it. I wanted women to see what goes on in these spaces that are so sacred to men, and I wanted men to feel their vulnerability by having one of these spaces blown wide open. The Saint Lazarus statue is an important part of this piece precisely because he is a wounded man, a vulnerable man.

With *En la barbería*, I wanted to deal with homoerotic ideas in a way that the viewer would have to check their own homophobia. There is a fine line between machismo and homoeroticism, and I wanted people to begin to look at other possibilities for masculinity and see how locked we are to certain ideas. I put a lot of mirrors up in the work, too, which I also use in *Scene of the Crime* and *Badge of Honor* [1995; pp. 106–27]. I wanted people to be able to look at the installation but also see themselves in the context of the work.

In the process of making the piece, a guy kept telling me he wanted to ejaculate onto the ceiling. When he left, I thought, "I'm just going to silkscreen that whole ceiling with sperm." So when he came to the opening, he looked up and just fell on the floor laughing. We also broke two huge bottles of men's cologne in front of the space. The smell of men was all over the place. The image on the seats of the barber chairs comes from an experience I had when I was in high school. We would draw two hands on the bus seat with a magic marker, and no boy would sit there because, obviously, the intention was that it was like grabbing your ass. As a kid, I would always put my book bag down and sit on top of it. We've come a long way, but we haven't really made that many advances in general. There's still homophobia, and these issues are still so important.

MN: I wanted to ask about your relationship to showing works like *En la barbería* in storefront spaces, with such proximity to the communities you are working with. That close collaboration has been essential to your practice—from *Scene of the Crime* at the Whitney to today.

PO: For *Scene of the Crime*, my next-door neighbor gave me all the photographs in the piece, and that installation was largely based on her apartment. The first review of the Whitney Biennial was in the *New York Times*, with a big image of the piece, and I was very excited. I took the newspaper to my neighbor and said, "Luisa, look! The *New York Times*!" And she said, "Pepón, what the hell is the *New York Times*? Why are you so excited about this?" That was a lesson for me—I just can't bypass the people I'm working with.

From that moment on, I decided to develop my pieces in the context of a storefront space and ask the institution commissioning the work to look for a storefront I could show it in first before moving it to the museum.

I knew from then on who I was committed to. I need to make art that tells real stories of real people during real times.

MN: When you did *Badge of Honor*, did you know you wanted to find a father and son to collaborate with?

PO: No. I begin by having conversations with people, and one thing leads to the other. Merián and I were having a child, and I knew I wanted to have a conversation around fatherhood. I went to different places, and in one group of young kids, I said, "Tell me about your fathers." No one said a word. So I said, "What's up? Are we not going to talk about fathers?" Someone finally came out and said, "Well, my father and many other fathers are incarcerated. So we don't talk about that."

Then I asked the people in the neighborhood and at the Newark Museum, who commissioned the piece, if they could connect me with correction facilities. That's how I met Nelson González, the father in the work. I was impressed when he said he wanted to work with me, and we developed this conversation between him and his son. The work also developed from my experiences as a child. No one in my family was incarcerated, but many elements were similar to what the father was telling me.

MN: Did your methods shift when you were working on more recent projects with communities, like *reForm* [2014–17; pp. 150–67]?

PO: In *reForm*, I became interested in this school that was closed but located in the middle of the community. Little by little, people became familiar with my face around the neighborhood, so when I started to ask questions about the building, they responded. Then I invited people to get together for dinner—we finally gathered about two hundred people. We all sat down with no set agenda; I had no idea what I wanted to do—I just wanted to bring everyone together. After a while, a group of ten kids came around and said, "We want to work with you."

We got together every Saturday and developed a process where we would share information and ideas. At some point, after many meetings, I said, "I want to recreate your classroom. We need to go back to the school, get all the furniture, and bring it here to make an installation." It took me forever to convince the authorities from the Philadelphia school district to allow us to go into the closed school. We picked up the furniture with the parents. People were really excited, curious, and willing to participate. One day, we closed the street in front of the school and invited everyone who went to it to join us there. The former principal and tons of teachers came, as well as people who graduated long ago and the kids! Suddenly, we had a thousand people in front of the school. With the help of the students who were leading this whole event, we made a piñata in the shape of the school district, and they banged it and killed the thing. When all these people were together, we also opened the truck with the belongings—everybody saw them. The principal, teachers, and some of the kids gave speeches. From then on, for about six months, I worked with each of them to develop the installation together.

We wanted to tell the story. Each of them wrote sentiments on the walls of the installation about how they felt, about being betrayed by the school district and missing their school. It was quite beautiful. Then we had an opening, and lots of people from the community as well as the art world came. After that, I was able to secure income for three students to work with me. Also, the students, on their own, went to the school district public hearing and made a position in front of the School Reform Commission and invited them to come to see the exhibition—and they came! They sat and had a conversation with them in the installation. One of them, a brilliant young woman, started to cry, and then one of the commissioners began crying. The students had developed a way of defending themselves, which was what we really wanted to do, and we have been in touch ever since.

BM: It is really fantastic to hear that. If we consider politics as the negotiation of the common, *reForm* is so beautifully political. You created a platform for them to exercise the negotiation of their ideas, their desires, their demands . . .

PO: Thank you. Luis Camnitzer taught in *reForm* one day—I invited him, and he was very moved. He had a conversation with students at Tyler School of Art and Architecture [in Philadelphia] about education. Several other artists came and had conversations; it was quite beautiful. The intention was there, the tables were there, all I wanted was for people to sit down and have a conversation.

BM: In *reForm*, there's also an exercise of mourning, of grief, in relation to the loss of the school. It's like *el velorio*, or the wake, for the school itself. It was an opportunity for people to collectively mourn this loss.

PO: I like what you said because there was a recurring question about whether I was going to bring the school back to them, and I had to make it clear I didn't have the power to do that. I had to convince everyone of my role as an artist. I'm glad you see this as mourning because that's what it felt like to me. As much as I knew it was going to be impossible to reopen the school, I saw the power in these kids. I saw their transformation right in front of me. That was amazing.

BM: Your works often invite us to enter spaces of intimacy, such as among men in a barbershop, between a father and son, and so on. For *My Beating Heart (Mi corazón latiente)* [2000; pp. 146–47], this goes to another level, because it invites viewers to get close to your own heart. The work is a giant piñata in the shape of a heart, the same height as your body, composed of the colors of the Puerto Rican flag, and playing the sound of your heartbeat. When you were talking about *reForm*, you said the kids "killed" the piñata. If piñatas are meant to be beaten and killed, what is it to offer your own "beating heart" as something to be destroyed?

PO: I want spectators of my work to forget they are at a museum. It's an invitation to go somewhere else. My hope is to offer a relationship to the work that goes beyond typical museum practice. This comes out of my own concerns with the architecture of museums—particularly how it relates to people not used to visiting museums.

My Beating Heart is about how I have continued even though I feel I have a broken heart. It's about a heart that has been "killed" but that I have been able to piece back together as an adult, so it can take more of a beating. I'm talking about deceptions of life. Laughter and humor also play an important role in the work as a way of protecting and moving away from that pain.

MN: We were looking at your new piece, *Convalescence* [2023; pp. 168–91], together this morning, and I was thinking about what you called a "veneer" in relation to the humor you described with *My Beating Heart*, as a system of protection or defense. There's always something much deeper that the work is dealing with, but the aesthetics of it can either draw people in or make them confused, perhaps not sure where to place themselves. It might be interesting to speak a bit about *Convalescence* in relation to that and the journey you've had so far with this new project.

PO: *Convalescence* is the closure of my healing journey. Somehow, each work has led me to heal, and I'm very much aware of this now because of the unfortunate health circumstances I started going through four and a half years ago. I'm creating this piece from a place of healing after a process where I had the opportunity to look closely at the healthcare system. It's not a coincidence that I'm developing part of this work in Puerto Rico, where healthcare has collapsed. This work reflects on how the medical field has transformed itself, how health and hospital corporations have transformed themselves, how this affects all of us, and the taboos around our own health. It is about the difficulties of healing within a system that tells us to forget our intuitions about our own bodies and imposes its own way of healing our illnesses.

What I'm doing with this work is creating a space for conversations around what it means to begin to try to heal ourselves—if not physically, then emotionally or spiritually—and to be empowered to listen to our own bodies, as opposed to giving them over to a medical system that has full control of us. The piece will eventually be installed in a hospital in Philadelphia, because, again, I want to go back to the community where it started. It will be accompanied by a series of serious conversations.

This is one of the most complicated pieces I have ever created, and it provides an opportunity for multiple communities to be a part of it—not only Puerto Rican or Latinx communities but also everyone who has been taken advantage of by the US healthcare system. Faith is also a key component in this work. If there is a common denominator in my practice, it is this notion of faith or the belief that there's got to be a way out. That persistence makes you believe things can be different or changed for the best. What I've learned from the group I'm working with for *Convalescence* is that faith plays an important role—in not only the decisions we make but also how we get up every day, move forward, negotiate, and live.

MN: It's interesting that the title of this exhibition, "My Beating Heart," which is also the title of your work, relates to both physicality and the desires and purposes that keep us going—physically, ideologically, and spiritually.

PO: It's about endurance of the heart. You have to make it strong, so it can resist all that might happen to it. No matter what, "My Beating Heart" has to keep beating on a spiritual level.

BM: What do you mean by "a spiritual level"?

PO: I'm beginning to understand there's something spiritual that influences the physical and can somehow keep it alive. The spiritual provides the strength for the physical to keep going. By understanding why and how the spiritual works, we can understand why and how the physical can sometimes give up. I've seen it happen to many people.

BM: There's something interesting in how you talk about spirituality. While faith and a certain idea of spirituality seem to be central to your practice nowadays, you've also said some things directly against religiosity in the past. I wonder if your take on spirituality has changed over time. Is there a difference between how you approach spirituality now compared to a few years ago?

PO: I knew I had cancer way before I was diagnosed. Not because of a physical manifestation but because of a psychic manifestation. I was walking back from the beach in Puerto Rico—we were fixing up the house at that time—and when I got to the gate, I said to myself, "This is the house I'm leaving to my sons." That voice never left me until the day I was diagnosed. Then it just disappeared. That voice came from a place of the unconscious. I began to listen to it; I wasn't worried about it, even though I knew I was dealing with some stuff that scared me. I'm saying all of this because the way I connect with spirituality now is very different from earlier. I thought, in order to be spiritual, you needed to have an intervention with the divine. But now I know I can just connect. I've had revelations similar to this, saying I was going to heal—I don't know how! I am convinced I'm connecting, that I'm bypassing the construct I had around spirituality to actually get to a spiritual space. Lately, I'm becoming more and more certain that spirituality is a way of life and a possibility. I guess it goes back to the broken heart I was talking about earlier—something that has been put together, but it's still broken.

BM: One of the definitions of the word "faith" is "courage to believe"—something that gives you strength to believe even though you have no verifiable reasons. Sometimes living also demands a lot of courage to believe. I see a clear relationship between these ideas of faith and spirituality and your description of "My Beating Heart."

PO: A lot of the people I came across during the process of making *Convalescence* pray, but they all know that's not where I'm coming from. Sometimes I join them and hold hands, but mostly, I wouldn't because I was traumatized by the Catholic Church—but I'm not opposed to people praying. There's something about connecting with hope that makes perfect sense to me.

MN: Something interesting you just touched upon is this simultaneous feeling that something needs to be preserved as part of a culture but also being critical about it at the same time. I feel that simultaneous reverence and criticality are embedded in all of your work.

PO: And not being afraid to do that! In many ways, I relate to most of my work as a little flame in front of me that keeps going. When viewers stand in front of my installations, they might create parallels and connect to aspects of the piece that are also a part of them. I want to believe my work disarms audiences. When I see people looking at the work, I'm always surprised when they connect to it.

BM: I love the idea of the flame. It's not only something that is alive and fighting to be alive because it needs fuel to keep going, but it also illuminates different things for each person. There is something in your work that is so complex and dense; it has so many details and layers, and it is almost impossible to grasp completely. Each person might relate to the work in different ways, and being able to inspire so many different perspectives is powerful. This is especially true for a work that is always presenting and playing with contradictions as they relate to different categories—gender, race, age, geographical origin, etc. What do you think about contradictions in your work?

PO: I perceive the world as a contradiction. Since I was a child, I've always questioned things because nothing makes sense. I spent a lot of time when I was a kid staring at people when they cried and asking them why they were crying. I later found out that my mother told all her friends not to cry in front of me because I would freak out if anyone was crying.

We live in a world of contradiction, a world I have always wanted to be *fair* more than anything else. So when I don't see that happening, it breaks apart this notion of fairness and becomes contradictory. Unfortunately, I don't live in a world that thinks like me, so there's a lot of negotiation that needs to take place. And, out of that negotiation, contradictions come out.

Theaters of Intimacy: On Pepón Osorio's Social Architecture

—

Ramón H.
Rivera-Servera

I walk toward Pepón Osorio's workshop on a recent studio visit at his Cerro Gordo Beach residence in Vega Alta, Puerto Rico. A garage door opens to unveil a recently acquired, flatbed, wooden food cart already in the transformation process as a component of his latest installation. The piece, *Convalescence* (2023; pp. 168–91 included in this exhibition), turns the informal economy platform of the portable kiosk into an altar to the wounded or ailing body. The seemingly intimate scale of the structure opens the door to an embodied exploration of the sociology of healthcare—from its emotional to its material registers—anchored by a Puerto Rican and Latinx iconography of healing.

Osorio's work is known for its signature investment in accumulation and ornamental embellishment as procedure. As I approach the kiosk/object, proximity metamorphosizes the cart from its utilitarian origin into a performative ritual stage. The red and blue wooden *casita*, or house, is overlayed with see-through Plexiglas panels and roof. A display box—built of the same material and typically used to showcase edible goods for sale under a heat lamp—has been turned into a terrarium holding partially buried plastic pill bottles, with their orange tubes and white caps. Red rubber water bags hang above the heat lamp with plastic tubing connecting them to store-bought topsoil that occupies about a third of the enclosure. The effect is that of a closed system of medical nourishment built atop the retail platform. For those familiar with Osorio's work, this cheeky allusion to a closed social circuit is a provocation: it draws spectators in who are, simultaneously, pulled out by the broader social realm activated by his pieces—even when the artwork renders the most intimate of exchanges.

The discreet kiosk architecture leads viewers down multiple associative pathways with larger social referents and consequences. Plastic and glittery sticker fern appliqués and synthetic garlic bulbs partially cover painted signposts, advertising in cursive writing: "big hamburgers," "hotdogs," and "*pinchos*" (or skewers). Centered on the back wall inside the structure, appearing saintlike on a niche, is a life-size medical model of a human torso with removable plastic organs, and a PET-scanned torso is visible from the roof above. This selection of objects begins to open up a broader set of images and practices related to healthcare.

A collection of ceramic doctor and nurse figurines and glass laboratory containers (flasks, beakers, and a pestle and mortar) sit atop a side shelf, anchoring this theme. Most of the statuettes represent Afro-descended health professionals, including a wooden carving of San Martín de Porres—the friar, pharmacist, and herbalist active in Peru in the early seventeenth century. Familiar items are amplified by accumulation and transformed through their positioning in relation to one another: the multiple glass and ceramic objects give a sense of volume, while their fragility signals a history of racial inequality for both patient and healthcare practitioner. Here, the artist indicates that the frail body is aided and supported by systems of care that seem just as precarious, despite their numbers.

The utilitarian structure of the kiosk transforms into a framed, to-be-seen object of art, with any commercial interactions detouring into a sober (though never depressive) exploration of the fragility of the human body and the technologies and agents that sustain it in crisis. The piece holds in tension concepts such as natural versus medical remedies, spiritually grounded or retail-driven healthcare economies, and the racialized sociology of healthcare. The assembled image invokes playfulness while the experience it renders as so palpably real through strategically indulgent artifice provokes viewers. It is both viscerally corporeal and analytically complex, with bodies and healthcare systems cohabiting and colliding in the environment of the piece.

The scene also illustrates two concepts that function as interpretive keys to his practice: intimacy and theater. It is in the interanimation of these two elements, their dynamic, frictional conjoining through extended, accumulated social interaction and object collection and embellishment, where his investment in transformation—of the social as well as the aesthetic—seems most fecund. *Convalescence* is the most recent iteration of a sustained, almost forty-year journey by the artist to house an archive of Puerto Rican and Latinx imaginaries as practices of survival, rescue, and intervention for the viability of Latinx life. This notion of "housing," as a container for sheltering both materials and people, extends to an expanded geography of intimate customs that positions Latinx sociality even in the most hostile of environments.

The traditional wooden *kiosko*—a recognizable icon of the informal economy, both social and commercial—banks on the homeyness of rustic *casitas* common across Puerto Rican communities and their creative practices as symbols of a working-class architectural legacy.[1] They are at once nostalgic representations of an idealized history of inventiveness and survival and animated platforms for new social and economic transactions. Often available as colorful artisanal paintings, ceramics, and wooden plaque collectibles, *casitas* are also deployed as life-size inhabitable structures, especially across diaspora neighborhoods, to house informal social, cultural, and economic exchanges—like the domino game or independent retail ventures. As altar pieces to a Puerto Rican imaginary rendered as architectural archives, the *kioskos* and *casitas*, as well as the expanded collection of interior spaces that characterize Osorio's oeuvre, are containers of histories and catalysts for an emergent sociality.

If the intimate geographies of Puerto Rican and Latinx sociability are central to the spatial logics of Osorio's work, his subject matter and its systemic implications are expansively large-scale. Osorio pursues and builds sites of exchange—whether domestic or public—where the intimate frictions of collective experience take shape. In works like *Scene of the Crime (Whose Crime?)* (1993; pp. 73–83), *El Velorio: AIDS in the Latino Community* (1992), and *No Crying Allowed in the Barbershop (En la barbería no se llora)* (1994; pp. 84–105), Osorio mines spaces that anchor Latinx life. In doing so, he explores the pressure points or domestic dramas that the mantra of coherence as a community might otherwise erase in attempts to deliver a unified, celebratory *Latinidad*. Whether tending to domestic violence (*Scene*), the disproportionate effects of the AIDS pandemic on the Latinx community (*El Velorio*), or the toxic masculinities that both cohere and risk breaking a community (*En la barbería*), Osorio banks on the weightiness of culturally specific Latinx frictions and the sites where they advance (the home, funeral, or barbershop) to stage his inquiries.

In her engagement with Osorio's concept of "social architecture," art historian Jennifer A. González points to the trajectory of socially engaged art "attentive to placemaking" but also imbuing "place with a sense of mobility and exchange."[2] Osorio's inhabiting and rendering of intimate space in the most public of forms—the exhibition—places him in the realm of the theatrical. The *casitas*, portable kiosk, prison cell, living room, barbershop, bedroom, and courtroom all figure as stages for Osorio's imagination. His work is housed in the architecture of memory, which he develops literally as he builds installations with substantial, perhaps even dramatically large amounts of accumulated, intervened objects. Much like the metonymic jump in scale from the singular body to a social collective illustrated in *Convalescence*, his installation work, overall, could be understood as relying on staging intimate relations for larger social activation. This rendition of the personal positions Osorio's work as a particular kind of theater. Intricately embedded in collaborative processes with and in communities—which often constitute the core content of the work and include his own autobiographical experiences—Osorio pursues the particularities of a story while accumulating, amplifying, and activating the presentation through an aesthetic of maximalism.

In the space of an exhibition, an artwork is staged for intended viewers and activated by their spectatorship.[3] And it is now an assumed truism that the relationship between an art object and its audience is theatrical in nature. Osorio's own engagement with the theatrical pushes this basic relationship further as his process-based inquiries—dependent as they are on community engagement—are, in large part, conceived as formally performative. That is, his work often teases spectatorship and activates collaborative participation as it is being developed. Much like the associations that became intimately available to me as a viewer of *Convalescence* (a piece still in process at the time of my encounter), Osorio tends to expose or stage the processes of his art-making purposefully before his intended audiences. Community storefronts, or similar public-facing spaces, are common initial locations for his installations before they are accessioned by and exhibited in formal museums or galleries. Their early exposure to a community of viewers and collaborators exemplifies the theater of intimacy.

The personal relationships Osorio pursues produce content as well as his artistic practice. Casual visitors and more formal engagements with community collaborators build the object and material inventories that accumulate in Osorio's large-scale installations. In this sense, small, familiar items, intimate exchanges about them, and their histories with the artist animate, through collaborative accumulation, large-scale thematic explorations. In a work like *Badge of Honor* (1995; pp. 106–27), this entailed working as a conduit for the intimate communication between a father and son separated by incarceration. It also established his own relationship with them and their families as he deepened his understanding of the circumstances under which their story unfolded. This interweaving of intimacies accumulates in a two-piece stage—one showcasing the prison cell, the other a bedroom. Large-scale video projections on either side of the installation depict the most intimate of conversations atop outsized renderings of the spaces each of the protagonists, father and son, inhabit in real life.

The maximalist aesthetic of Osorio's work is an important indication of his investment in divorcing familiar items from their assumed sociological exactitude. Notwithstanding the emphasis on his culturally specific artistic interventions, Osorio refuses a simplistic interpretation of his work. In a 1999 interview with the late Smithsonian curator Marvette Pérez and anthropologist Yvonne Lassalle, Osorio put pressure on this relationship, describing a tendency to approach his work as "sociology" to the detriment of a rigorous engagement with his aesthetic procedures. The artist explained, "Even though many people think of my work as sociology, and it's okay for me to look at it also in that perspective, I see it first as a work of art. And what's so different about it is that, as a work of art, it brings a discourse. I see myself rather shifting the concept of art, moving it into a different space than that which people are used to finding it in."[4] This productive tension, or frictional intimacy, between the aesthetics of theatrical display and the sociology of his work has been central to interpreting his artistic trajectory since the 1980s.[5]

Osorio's statement that his project "is not so much about ethnography as about shifting the discussion to other places"[6] validates the speculative and imaginative spaces of social architecture he cites and recreates. It achieves an expansive freedom of thought while also marking the historical legacy of these architectural renditions of space and place—which result from an arsenal of cultural practices intended to ensure the survival of Puerto Rican and Latinx communities in contexts of precarity or hostility. This tension between the pursuit and staging of the intimate and its refusal as sociology is illuminating. Osorio started his professional career as a trained social worker and witnessed difficult situations of dispossession and struggle in the communities he served firsthand. Identifying the shortcomings of institutionalized responses and habituated top-down solutions, Osorio migrated toward the arts as a place and set of procedures that allowed more open-ended, collaborative approximations.

"My Beating Heart" and the artworks it presents may be seen as an engagement with the central dynamic in Osorio's work: his intimate proximity to community and the artistic license he takes in rendering it theatrically. It may also be seen as a riff on the common phrase "my bleeding heart." Often advanced with suspicion or mockery when expressing concern for the misfortune of others, "my bleeding heart" opens the wound between the conditions that stress others and the theatrical posturing of those who benefit from showcasing such misfortunes. Those in the political class or disaster capitalists tend to perform such gestures for their own advantage. If opportunistic proximity structures the attitudinal animus to "my bleeding heart," "My Beating Heart" introduces a procedural sincerity grounded on the intimacy of exchange. For those more familiar with Latinx literature,

"My Beating Heart" may also call upon *The Wounded Heart*, the title of Yvonne Yarbro-Bejarano's milestone book on the work of Chicana lesbian playwright and multi-genre author Cherríe Moraga.[7] This collection of critical approximations by an international leading Chicana queer scholar of her accomplished colleague and friend offers a model for pursuing intimacy as a vital practice.

"My Beating Heart" presents the artist as a presence, embodied and sentient. It also announces the central operational dynamic of Osorio's practice: the pursuit of community. Osorio's work stands at the nexus of a provocative publicity, aided by his deployment of a maximalist aesthetic of accumulation and cultivated intimacy with his subject matter—whether through extended community engagement in the research or built out of the work. Pieces like *Convalescence* further clarify another key element of Osorio's oeuvre: deep introspection and autobiographical self-exposure. The beating heart is, thus, an articulation of that presence of self in relation to the sociological realities of the worlds he explores and critiques.

Theater and the social it approximates and seeks to intervene in constitute the crucial tension animating both his monumental multimedia installations and his singular sculptural renditions of embellished objects. Much of this is demonstrated in *Convalescence*, a piece that has evolved since my initial encounter with the food cart and now includes a map of the Puerto Rican archipelago made from collected bottles, which connect to a mannequin overwhelmed by gestures of care—from acupuncture, intravenous supplements, and amplified renditions of their constituent parts in analog and digital forms to the emotional uplift of a "get well" balloon and seashells from Afro-Caribbean ritual healing practices.

Convalescence also returns us to methodologies deployed in previous works. For example, in *Badge of Honor,* Osorio inserts filmed testimonies from participants in the social scene he explores. Embedded in and framed by the maximalist installation, these screened experiences do not stand as simple factual truths but as contextual gestures in a world—or "social architecture," to parse

Osorio's own concept—of Latinx communal life. And in *En la barbería*, the excess of objects builds an emotional crescendo around its thematic focus. Through these aesthetic strategies, we begin to put together a story much bigger than a singular agent. From the testimony on the video screen, we learn that the food cart anchoring this piece was acquired due to the decline in health of its previous owner and his inability to continue his practice. The ensuing communication between Osorio and the last owner also points to the artist's own struggles with chronic illness and his journey of healing and community support. It is additionally a performative act of being present—beating heart and all—in a moment of immense adversity and deploying procedures of art that lift us all into a relationship that is as intimately embodied as it is sociologically immense.

Each piece in "My Beating Heart" brings us, as viewers, into relation with some of the most intimate vulnerabilities and points through the theatrical processes of art. It takes us toward a place of collective possibility, even healing, made possible by the artwork. Pepón Osorio's theaters of intimacy advance social architectures, vital and participatory, connecting the worlds through the resources and practices of art.

1 On the spatial logics of the *casita* as diasporic agency, see Juan Flores, *From Bomba to Hip-Hop: Puerto Rican Culture and Latino Identity* (New York: Columbia University Press, 2000), 63–78; and Luis Aponte-Pares, "Casitas Place and Culture: Appropriating Place in Puerto Rican Barrios," *Places Journal* 11, no. 1 (January 1997): 52–61.

2 Jennifer A. González, "Foreword," in *Pepón Osorio* (Los Angeles: University of California Los Angeles Chicano Studies Research Press, 2013), xi.

3 In Osorio's case, theater and performance have always been central to his practice. From early collaborations with his artistic and life partner, dance-maker Merián Soto, in the 1980s to his design work in support of other artists in the Pepatián Collective, Osorio's objects and environments have always vacillated between static display and performance activations on- and off-stage.

4 Pepón Osorio, in Marvette Pérez and Yvonne Lassalle, "Interview with Pepón Osorio," *Radical History Review* 73 (1999): 4–5.

5 For a discussion on friction as a central component of the intimate publics of Latinidad, see Ramón H. Rivera-Servera, *Performing Queer Latinidad: Dance, Sexuality, Politics* (Ann Arbor: University of Michigan Press, 2012). A more recent theorization of friction anchors Keguro Macharia's arguments in *Frottage: Frictions of Intimacy Across the Black Atlantic* (New York: New York University Press, 2019).

6 Osorio, in Pérez and Lassalle, "Interview with Pepón Osorio," 5.

7 See Yvonne Yarbro-Bejarano, *The Wounded Heart: Writings on Cherríe Moraga* (Austin: University of Texas Press, 2001).

From Observation to Conversation to Installation

—

Robert Blackson

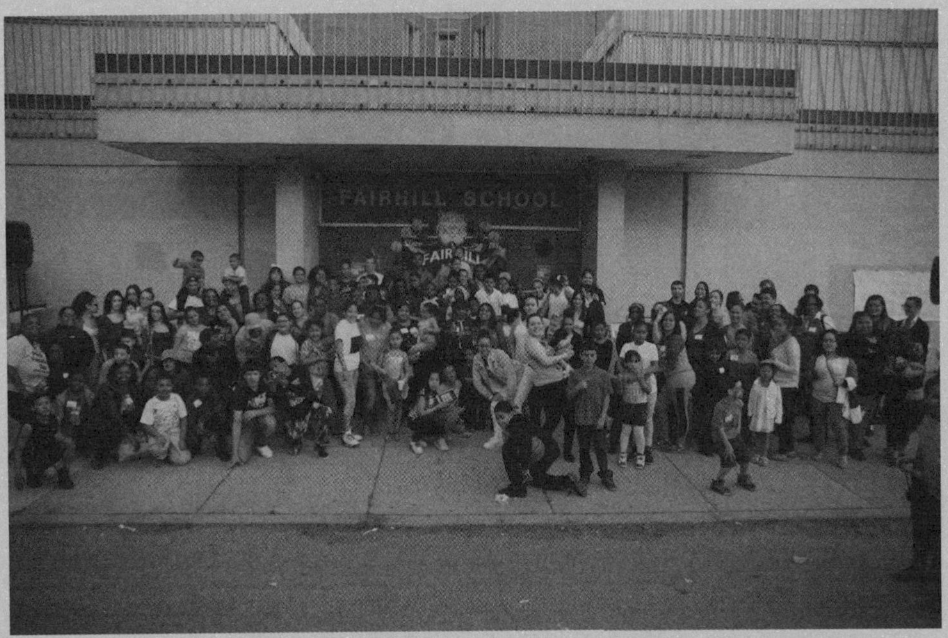

"Fun Day" at Fairhill School in Philadelphia, PA, organized by the students on May 1, 2015.
Photo: Tony Rocco

New York City's Administration for Children's Services (ACS) is one of the largest local social service agencies in the United States. With a $2.6 billion budget and seven thousand employees, it investigates over 55,000 cases of child abuse and neglect every year.[1] This government agency offers a range of support for families in need—everything from counseling services to child placements. With outposts across the five boroughs, ACS strategically locates itself inside dense neighborhoods, in much the same way public schools and hospitals are built to serve in the center of communities. On the frontline of ACS's work are 1,300 investigative caseworkers: men and women who show up at front doors with an accompanying police officer looking for evidence of child abuse and neglect firsthand. It is an exhausting, emotionally draining profession demanding long hours and investigating up to ten or more families at a time. The average caseworker lasts less than three years on the job.[2]

Pepón Osorio was one of these caseworkers. Over his nine years with ACS during the 1980s, he estimates he visited 1,200 families.[3] With each visit, Osorio went into the home, sat down with the family, and attempted to empathetically offer agency services. He did this in the hope that something might help the families cope with their seemingly unmanageable lives and the bureaucratic system Osorio represented—and whose business it was to manage them.

Osorio's beat was up and down Manhattan—from the poverty-stricken Bowery, where the New Museum now stands, all the way up to the affluent sections of Inwood. Primarily, though, he was assigned a heavy caseload of poor Latinx families. After nearly a decade on the job, he knew almost instantly what to expect when a family cracked open their front door. If he saw photographs out on view, he knew it was going to be a relatively stable family. If the dining room looked unused, he suspected instability. Slipcovers over the furniture meant a strong female presence in the home. With each visit, Osorio's eye sharpened.

When he left ACS, he did so with a charged forensic knowledge of exactly what trauma-informed domestic spaces looked like. He would draw from this knowledge again and again to meticulously construct an emotional weight within his installations' domestic interiors. This includes works like *Scene of the Crime (Whose Crime?)* (1993; pp. 73–83), in which he signaled a feminine interior through the careful arrangement of countless framed family photographs. He also dripped cologne in the doorway of *No Crying Allowed in the Barbershop (En la barbería no se llora)* (1994; pp. 84–105), so the unmistakable musk of machismo saturated visitors' first impressions of the installation. And Osorio spent weeks with two families in two neighboring towns of Western Massachusetts, so the contrasting domesticities of *Drowned in a Glass of Water* (2010; p. 58) would emotionally convey their raw disparities.

The trained, sensitive eye that Osorio attained over the hundreds of visits with families in New York was focused again, years later, in Fairhill—a poor, Latinx neighborhood in the lower-northeast section of Philadelphia. He would regularly commute through this part of town on his way to teach at Temple University's Tyler School of Art and Architecture, located about a half mile south of Fairhill. As he passed Fairhill Elementary School, a large blue-and-white "FOR SALE" sign stuck to the side of the building caught his eye. From his days with ACS, Osorio knew how government services were distributed across metropolitan areas—predominantly in poorer areas where they were needed most. Public schools are located in much the same way. Pulling out these services sent a strong message to the community: the system was abandoning them.

Fairhill was not alone. In 2013, the School District of Philadelphia, under the leadership of a state-appointed School Reform Commission, closed twenty-three "failing" schools, predominantly in poor neighborhoods of color.[4] In fact, of the thousands of children directly affected by these closures, only 4 percent were white.[5] From his years working with children forced, through no fault of their own, into traumatic situations, Osorio knew the school closing would be devastating for the Fairhill kids. For starters, the school district's shortsighted strategy to continue educating the children was to bus the majority of them to the closest school still open. This neglected to appreciate the fierce rivalry between neighboring schools and effectively forced the children into daily, potentially violent situations. On top of this is the unwarranted stigma of failure burdened on these children. Fairhill is a proud Latinx community, and its school had served the neighborhood for generations—the parents and grandparents of the children who attended Fairhill when it closed had all gone there. To mark an entire generation of children as those who had "failed" the school was a deeply unfair, shameful weight to load on them. Astonishingly, the district offered no additional counseling services to the kids affected by the closures.

As this dire situation began to reveal itself to Osorio, Tim Gibbon, one of his students at Tyler, shared that he had taught after-school arts programs at Fairhill School, and he was willing to introduce him to some of the children reeling from the closure. With that invitation, Osorio began his artistic process that would later become *reForm* (2014–17; pp. 150–67). He started by meeting with some former Fairhill students that Gibbon initially recommended. This eventually led him to the families, teachers, and the principal. At first, it was not easy; with the closure came fragmentation. As the former Fairhill student Chelsey Velez would later write, “We are now a broken family.”[6] Some students were bussed to Julia de Burgos Elementary (the next closest school), many went to Philadelphia Military Academy, others chose charter schools. Many teachers, defeated by the closure, looked for new careers outside the district. The Fairhill School community had been scattered. But gradually, in what, at times, felt like defiance against the systematic forces that had separated them, the conversations began to expand, much like the concentric layers of an onion: there was the core, which was the students, but growing outward, it included ever-widening relationships and connections.

One of the things Osorio heard over and over as he met with individuals in this scattered community, either in their homes or over the phone, was how much they missed each other. So, before this displaced network that Osorio was connecting to became too big or unmanageable, he decided to invite them all to a simple dinner: nothing fancy, no speeches. It was just a moment to come back together and see each other again. This joyous, emotional reunion was organized in a basement classroom at Tyler. Osorio moved from table to table, sitting amongst the roughly seventy-five students, parents, grandparents, teachers, and secretaries, listening as they ate dinner together and traded stories of their shared time at the school. For Osorio, these conversations were an extension of the work[7] and would inform the eventual installation that many who came to this dinner would create with him in that same room just six months later. Before they left, Osorio laid out a sign-up sheet: anyone who wanted to stay involved and be invited to more gatherings was welcome.

There are numerous artistic and curatorial precedents for mobilizing social purpose in the name of art. In the 1970s, Joseph Beuys’s idealist pursuit of a “social sculpture,” inspired by the teachings of Rudolf Steiner, merged educational reform with city planning. And Osorio’s interpretation of each conversation with participants and their involvement as extensions of the project resemble Nicolas Bourriaud’s curatorial approach to his 1996 exhibition “Traffic” at the CAPC Museé d’Art Contemporain in Bordeaux, France. Bourriaud initiated and operated connections that encouraged interpersonal experiences to be incorporated into the show itself.[8] Unlike these theoretical or directly political examples, however, Osorio's process is motivated by deep empathetic care for the people with whom he creates the work, which can only move forward at the speed of this growing interpersonal trust.[9]

Returning to Osorio's sign-up sheet: by the end of the night, it was full. What became clear to the artist was that a core group of about ten young teens, separated by the school closure, was starting to reconnect. As Osorio began to focus on an installation informed by the stories of the school, he also supported their reconnection. On Saturday afternoons, he began inviting them to meet in the basement classroom, restaurants, or cafés. As the conversations amongst the teens deepened and their shared purpose solidified, they decided to self-identify as the Bobcats, in honor of Fairhill School's mascot. The Bobcats' immediate goal was to continue reuniting the school's shattered community. But, more broadly, they would eventually organize a poetic, multifaceted public attack of the district's callous abandonment. This campaign used news media, protests at the School District of Philadelphia's head office, and speaking at the School Reform Commission's public hearings as catalysts to define what education on the Bobcats' own terms should look like.[10] It was a bold, inspired reversal—refusing the state's education system in order to create their own.

One of the Bobcats' first actions was to reimagine one of Fairhill School's traditions. For years, Fun Day had been a celebration collectively organized by Fairhill's faculty and administration for the students and their families. Spilling over from the school grounds onto the street, live music, food, competitions, and activities joyously signaled the end of the school year and welcomed the upcoming summer vacation. Since Fairhill's closure in 2013, Fun Day had been canceled. But in the spring of 2015, the Bobcats began to strategically organize a new version that would celebrate, honor, and transform the tradition. To call attention to the near absurdity of celebrating the Fairhill School community directly in front of the closed doors, they secured media attention from Philadelphia's local news channels—emphasizing their defiance of the closure—obtained city permits, and launched a door-to-door outreach campaign that inspired over eight hundred community residents (the majority of whom had gone to Fairhill) to attend.[11] Free T-shirts, healthy food, a wall to write commemorative messages, and a social historian recording oral histories[12] of Fairhill were all organized for the day by the Bobcats.

The celebration of Fun Day also doubled as an opportune moment for Osorio and a few of the Bobcats to reenter the closed school and remove select items with which Osorio was planning to build the installation. This sanctioned action by the school district produced an eclectic truckload of Fairhill's fixtures and mementos. Water fountains, floor and ceiling tiles, trophies, posters, clocks, science equipment, and furniture were solemnly removed and taken in a procession back to the basement classroom at Tyler.

As the Bobcats began filling the empty classroom with relics from their school, the significance of this experience made a lasting impression on Osorio—which has shifted his artistic process ever since. As the artist would later recount, "The shift happened when the objects from the school began to show up at Tyler. I saw that I was dealing with objects that had a history, and it was [the Bobcats'] history. So, working with the people who were part of that history shifted a sense of responsibility for me."[13] Before *reForm*, Osorio filled his overflowing installations with items he had found himself. Aside from the direct-to-camera testimonial videos that light up Osorio's installations, the works were layered and stacked with mostly off-the-shelf materials arranged to meticulously portray a situation. But like the museums his pieces were often installed within, they were removed from the traumatic situations they represented.

With this shift, Osorio realized he wasn't making *reForm* for an art museum or its typical audiences; it needed to be built with the Bobcats for Fairhill. Osorio's new approach became an invitation for the Bobcats and the Fairhill community at large to process the closure. The eventual installation was a byproduct of this fractured community reassembling itself. For example, Osorio covered the walls of the basement classroom at Tyler with enlarged, ruled notebook paper. The Bobcats were invited to write directly on it, in larger-than-life handwriting, what Fairhill's closure meant to them. Soon after, Osorio invited the Bobcats' old Fairhill School English teacher, Robert Harris, to read their stories. This quiet facet of Osorio's artistic process transcended the teacher-student dynamic by which Harris and the Bobcats had been previously bound and connected them through the installation to their shared history overshadowed by loss.

As the relationships between the Bobcats, former teachers, and parents grew tighter through Osorio's process, their collective critical examination of the district and the poor decisions[14] that led to the deterioration of Fairhill School and its closure became more informed. These conclusions featured in the installation. It had long been suspected that one of the reasons Fairhill had been closed was because the building itself was dangerously toxic. Signs stenciled above the water fountains warned students (many of which were too young to read) not to drink the water because it was contaminated with lead. Floor tiles removed from the school and chemically tested contained asbestos. The school district's own 2015 report estimated a backlog of necessary expenditures totaling $4.5 billion to remediate and improve toxic conditions across the district's buildings and properties.[15] Evidence of this neglect of the children's health, such as the water fountain and floor tiles, would later be put on full display as part of *reForm*.

As the Bobcats started to recognize their own agency within Osorio's process, they educated themselves on the political and bureaucratic systems that led to the district's decision to close their school. And their self-education spread beyond the confines of the classroom installation. The Bobcats now not only publicly testified about their experiences before Philadelphia's School Reform Commission,[16] but they also created their own needs-based education programs and uploaded the design for their ideal school (complete with cat therapy) onto YouTube. As the Bobcats became more versed in communicating their own disavowal of the public education system and its failures, Osorio began to recognize, through their work, the deficiencies within his own formative education. After this moment, the artist said he could no longer create empathy toward the Bobcats from a place of being "the listener"—a role he had assumed since his time visiting children with ACS. Instead, he became, in his words, "the first person."[17]

This experience precipitated by the Bobcats allowed Osorio to recognize the circumstances within his own life as integral and, at times, even central to the motivation for his work. He now allowed *himself* within the process. This shift continues to drive the unfolding of Osorio's most recent project *Convalescence* (2023; pp. 168–91). Grounded in the artist's recent experience of surviving stage four cancer, the work began with the artist making a "quasi self-portrait" and then casting the sculpture as a narrator for the developing installation. *Convalescence*'s ongoing process now includes multiple families and individuals of color who have lived through or are currently experiencing life-threatening illnesses. The multimedia installation and public program (to be completed in 2024) will be grounded in the fragility of life in communities of color due to the systemic failures of the US healthcare system. The collective goal of this initiative, like so many of Osorio's installations over the past thirty-five years, is to approach healing as a creative act supporting personal and collective change.

1 Wikipedia, s.v. "New York City Administration for Children's Services," last modified February 14, 2023, 02:18, https://en.wikipedia.org/wiki/New_York_City_Administration_for_Children%27s_Services.

2 Abigail Kramer, "Long Hours, High Caseloads: An Ongoing Surge of Cases Weighs on Child Welfare Workers," New School Center for New York City Affairs, accessed February 27, 2023, http://www.centernyc.org/long-hours-high-caseloads.

3 Pepón Osorio, conversation with the author, February 23, 2023.

4 "School Reform Commission Votes to Close 23 Philadelphia Schools, Sparking Anger and Despair for Students, Parents, Teacher," WHYY PBS, last modified March 8, 2013, https://whyy.org/articles/school-reform-commission-votes-to-close-23-philadelphia-schools/.

5 This percentage is from the US Department of Education's National Center for Education Statistics, 2010–11, referenced in Mark R. Warren, "School Closing and Community Openings," in *Pepón Osorio, ReForm* (Philadelphia: Temple University, 2016), 56.

6 Chelsey Velez, "When We Speak You Listen," in *Pepón Osorio, ReForm*, 1.

7 Osorio, February 23, 2023.

8 See "Traffic, Bordeaux, 1996," in *Biennials and Beyond: Exhibitions that Made Art History, 1962–2002*, ed. Bruce Altshuler (New York: Phaidon, 2013), 327.

9 I owe my understanding of this concept to adrienne maree brown's *Emergent Strategy: Shaping Change, Changing Worlds* (Chico, CA: AK Press, 2017).

10 To view the Bobcats' ideal school, visit: "Remodeling Fairhill: Students Re-Envision Our Closed School, reForm Project / Bobcats," Tim Gibbon, posted on December 13, 2015, YouTube video, 2:11, https://www.youtube.com/watch?v=q_avczs5Ez8&t=4s.

11 See Elizabeth M. Grady, "Pepón Osorio: The Impact of *ReForm*," *FIELD: A Journal of Socially-Engaged Art Criticism*, no. 9 (Winter 2018), http://field-journal.com/issue-9/pepon-osorio-the-impact-of-reform.

12 The oral historian was Erin Bernard, Founding Director and Chief Curator, Philadelphia Public History Truck.

13 Pepón Osorio, conversation with the author, March 4, 2023.

14 In 2013, Philadelphia's City Controller, Adam Butkovitz, released a lengthy report questioning the school district's revenue strategies for closing and then selling the shuttered schools. This report highlighted the anticipated catastrophic economic impact on neighborhoods immediately surrounding the schools following the closures if the schools remained unsold. This report estimated that over $1 million worth of lost equity would be absorbed by the Fairhill neighborhood (where median household income in 2013 was $17,400) if the school did not sell. As of this writing, Fairhill School, nearly a decade after its closure, remains vacant and unsold. See Alan Butkovitz, "In Search of Real Dollars and Common Sense: A Preliminary Report on the School District of Philadelphia's School Closure Plan," City of Philadelphia Pennsylvania: Office of the Controller, June 2018, http://controller.phila.gov/wp-content/uploads/2018/06/Controller'sReport_SchoolClosurePlan2013.pdf.

15 See Bill Hangley, Jr., "District's Comprehensive School Planning Process Is Just Getting off the Ground," Chalkbeat Philadelphia, September 18, 2019, https://philadelphia.chalkbeat.org/2019/9/18/22186520/the-districts-comprehensive-planning-process-just-getting-off-the-ground.

16 This commission was mandated by the Commonwealth of Pennsylvania to oversee that the school district voted itself out of existence in 2018. See Kristen Graham, “Notable Moments during 17 Years of Philly’s School Reform Commission,” *Philadelphia Inquirer*, June 29, 2018, https://www.inquirer.com/philly/education/src-timeline-20180629.html.

17 Pepón Osorio, conversation with the author, February 25, 2023.

A Giant Mirror Right in Front of You

—

Guadalupe Rosales

"Coming from a working-class family, being an artist is not an option. It's more of a challenge."
— Pepón Osorio, "Place: Art21 Interview," 2001

When I turned twenty in 2000, I left my hometown of Los Angeles for New York City and cut all ties with friends and family. I started a new chapter in my life and spent fifteen years away from LA. When I look back at all the reasons I cut communication with those I love, I realize I had difficulty sharing my upbringing with friends in New York, fearing I would be misunderstood, stereotyped, or put in a box. Art, however, helped me reclaim and feel empowered by my upbringing, and I could share that part of my life again.

The plan to leave Los Angeles happened overnight, and it could have been because of a survival mechanism. I had never lived outside of LA; I had never visited a gallery or museum—they weren't on my radar; and I didn't know there was such a thing as art school. As a kid, I loved drawing, reading, and sometimes breaking things apart just to put them back together again. I was curious, but I never had the resources or someone in a creative field I could look up to, so being an artist wasn't an option.

In many ways, the neighborhood I grew up in had everything I thought I needed: I saw art on the streets, in my mothers cooking, home decorations, and in the cinematic night sky. The housing projects in Boyle Heights are covered in historic murals that date back to the 1960s, and there was a lot of local pride—that was art for me. In my home, making it past high school was enough, especially in the 1990s when the school district wanted to cut our school budget. This led to teachers losing their jobs, art programs being defunded, and schools not getting adequate maintenance. Students who were supposed to be in school were out fighting for proper education. This was the world I knew.

One of the most important things I learned when I moved to New York was the beauty and complexity of art. Within a year of living there, I became friends with artists deeply involved in the art scene—mostly white, privileged, either in art school or just graduated, and my age. Those who were older, I considered mentors who shared their knowledge—from books to art to films (for this, I am grateful to have found a circle of friends who taught me so much). At the same time, I didn't quite fit in or have a strong sense of belonging—though I didn't see it this way until I got older. These types of things can go over your head, but with time and living in a city like New York, you can start to feel lonely, alienated, and isolated. It also meant becoming more aware of the world around me, with cultural differences, racism, and injustice.

The more familiar I became with the New York art world, the more apparent its gray area was. I was twenty-three when I first walked into a gallery. It was exciting and new, but it was also hard to see myself in that world and feel visible. Art spaces where I hung out had their beauty, where I could imagine and dream—but with limitations. Only so much could reflect back and speak to me. While trying to find my place, not just as an outsider from LA but also as a brown, queer artist, I began to realize how hard it was for someone like me, especially at that time. I also began to miss my family, friends, and home.

In 2013, however, I had a revelation when I went with some friends to see a group exhibition at the New Museum, "NYC 1993: Experimental Jet Set, Trash and No Star." I knew some of the artists in the show, but most I wasn't familiar with. This exhibition changed my view and understanding of the art world. I remember making my way to the second floor, and when I turned to the right, all of a sudden, it felt like I had walked into a telenovela, movie set, crime scene, my home, or all of the above. This was my first encounter with Pepón Osorio's captivating work. Even though *Scene of the Crime (Whose Crime?)* (1993; pp. 73–83) was highly dramatic, I could somehow see myself in this piece. It spoke to me.

"When . . . *Scene of the Crime* was [originally installed] at the Whitney Museum, it almost felt as if I had taken a piece of the South Bronx out of its roots and placed it in the middle of Madison Avenue."
— Pepón Osorio, "Interview: 'Scene of the Crime (Whose Crime?),'" Art21, 2019

It reminded me of my mother's taste in furniture, her home decorations, and color scheme. There are porcelain saints and candles in the room, and the table is covered with a clear plastic sheet to protect the tablecloth. I could almost smell my mother's cooking. The wrought-iron arch hanging above the space was like a relic or reminder of the homes I grew up in and in my Los Angeles neighborhood. At last, through these materials and this immersive art installation, I found a sense of belonging. The work touched all my senses and took me back to the coziness of my family home (regardless of the dramatic scene resembling a telenovela). This is the type of art that makes me curious, think, and ask questions; it gives me both joy and sadness. And I was transported to a place that felt familiar.

I moved back to Los Angeles in 2016, a year after starting Veteranas and Rucas and Map Pointz—Instagram-based, community-sourced digital archives. *Scene of the Crime* inspired me to come back home—it made me feel safe again and embrace the pride I had in being from East Los Angeles. When I first began the archives, they weren't just "ideas." There was an urgency. In many ways, these types of projects or even conversations in public spaces didn't exist yet—not even in institutions or academia—so, as the saying goes, "If it doesn't exist, create it." Here, people (specifically women) who grew up like me get to share stories and reframe history.

At first, it felt like finding missing pieces to a puzzle because so much of our history had been untold, blurred, erased, or demonized/criminalized. And for women, our pride had been challenged or even taken away. I wanted to humanize, reclaim, and celebrate our stories and experiences. I felt the urgency to start conversations around storytelling to make change: a community-generated archive built from the ground up with our collective stories. And when I think of Osorio's work and its impact on the world, or when I get to experience it personally, this is the type of art that creates change. It offers possibility and hope, where many complexities can coexist, where we can feel pride, joy, celebration, and love of who we are while not ignoring the more difficult parts of life, like grief, violence, and tragedy.

In 2017, Los Angeles County Museum of Art (LACMA) invited me to do an Instagram takeover for "Pacific Standard Time: LA/LA," where I posted about art and art events on their Instagram page. I invited my nephew, who was seventeen at the time, to join me on a walk-through of LACMA's exhibition "Home—So Different, So Appealing" (curated by Chon Noriega, Mari Carmen Ramírez, and Pilar Tompkins Rivas). This was my second time seeing Osorio's work in person—and my nephew's first. It was also my nephew's first time at a museum, and I couldn't have asked for a better introduction to the art world and sharing this moment with him. It took me back to my own experience in 2013.

My nephew and I stood in front of *Badge of Honor* (1995; pp. 106–27 for a while and talked. We paid attention to every detail of the bedroom, got close to the work, and stepped back to get a good look at the entire installation. My nephew shared that the work reminded him of his own bedroom—dresser, lamps, baseball cards, posters, trophies, clothes hamper, basketballs, mountain bike, and computer—and, most importantly, of his relationship with his father. So much of this piece felt personal to me and my nephew—a lived experience turned into art. Osorio made a big impact on me and my nephew at different times in our lives, and his work not only gave me hope as an artist but also a sense of belonging.

"As you stand [there], and you're not allowed to come in, then you need to reflect, and you need to confront yourself—almost as if I [placed] a giant mirror right in front of you."
— Pepón Osorio, "Place: Art21 Interview," 2001

The following excerpt from my first LACMA Instagram post sums up the impact of Osorio's practice:

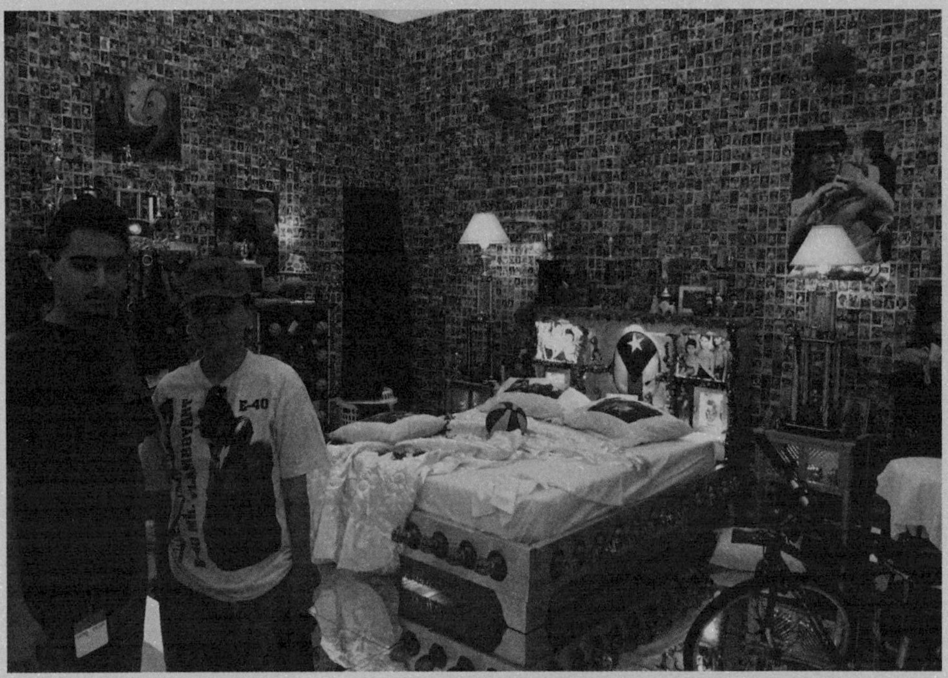

Joseph Mariscal and Guadalupe Rosales in front of Pepón Osorio's *Badge of Honor* (1995) in "Home—So Different, So Appealing," Los Angeles County Museum of Art (June 11–October 15, 2017). Courtesy Guadalupe Rosales

Osorio's work has taught me to value everything I have experienced (every memory [I have had] and place I have been) and to reflect on those experiences because [they have] built the person I am today. [This is] something I come to terms with every day. Osorio wants people to think about who we are in relation to what we have just seen (when looking at his work) and start a negotiation not only with the artwork but [also] with the public at large—who we are and where we stand.

Perhaps Atomic

—

Pepón Osorio in Conversation with Rita Indiana

Rita Indiana: I have this obsession with childhood. I think it's fundamental—a critical moment of formation for artists. So I must ask: How did *that* Pepón Osorio observe the world? How did he perceive time, the spaces he inhabited, the objects that inhabited his home, the home of his grandparents, or his school? In other words, can you describe your perception or vision as a child?

Pepón Osorio: I've always used my process and practice to stimulate looking backward and forward at the same time. That experience of reliving my childhood, which is my center, the axis of my practice, always helps me share my realities with my collaborators. My work's creation is a process where various realities converge—mine and those I work with. After a certain point, it is constructed to arrive at a "happy medium" between these realities, and it develops on its own, in the swing and sway between how I and others see. My work always begins with a personal preoccupation, and the journey to understand that preoccupation brings me to others with whom I can enter into a dialogue. This dialogic process reveals intersections and parallels that transform into images later incorporated into the installations.

It's a rather complicated process. How can I make it clearer? In that moment of conversation, the work or the art isn't at the center. What is most important is the human connection and the construction of images that then influence the installation. They add class, race, and other social layers that intervene and climb atop one another. In the end, the imagined reality we've constructed almost always crumbles apart by the same means. For me, it's a coming and going through time. At any moment, I can be in the present, future, or past.

RI: In that regard, there are two pieces we might be able to use as examples for what you're describing: *Drowned in a Glass of Water* [2010; fig. 1] and *Badge of Honor* [1995; pp. 106–27]. I think of these pieces almost like science fiction!

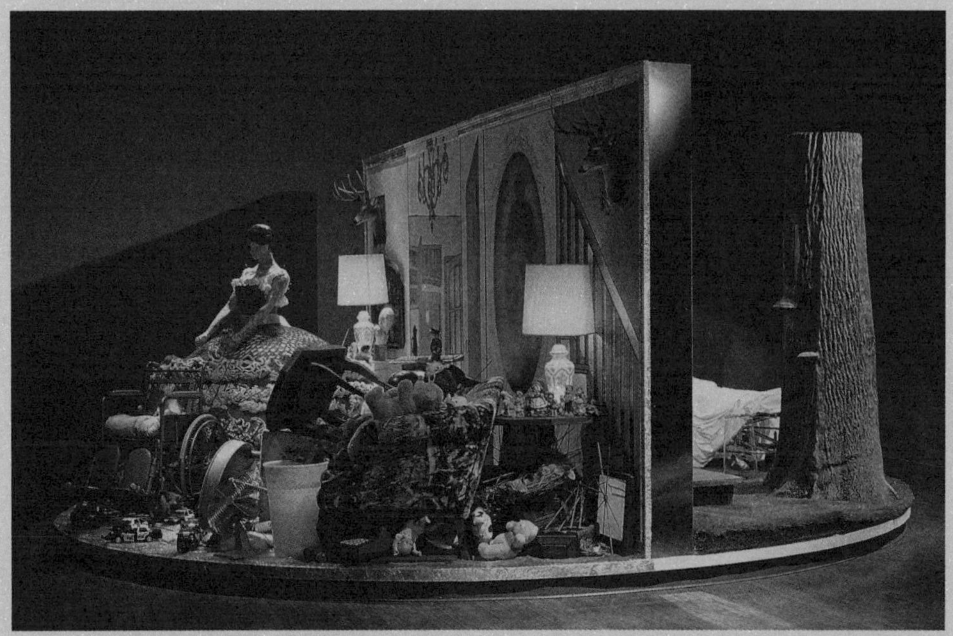

Pepón Osorio, *Drowned in a Glass of Water*, 2010. Mixed mediums, dimensions variable. Courtesy the artist

In the case of *Badge of Honor*, it's as if an invisible time machine—you!—unites these two temporalities, these two spaces. That time machine is also affect, which interests me a lot in my work as well: affect as the power of emotions to invoke time, space, objects, and memory. Like an instant that contains everything, that contains the perfect film. In *Badge of Honor*, you arrived at the idea of locating two spaces, one next to another, and all that's emotionally contained in them. Maybe you could start by talking about the referents and influences contained in your work.

PO: I come from a family that would talk to the television. My parents and Juana, the person who raised me, had a very particular relationship with TV. As a young boy, it seemed strange to me that Juana thought this instrument had life. She would yell at the television, at the characters on the shows. She would laugh and have conversations with them. At an early age, I was impacted by how an instrument could be manipulated to create another reality. I understand video as an opportunity to humanize, escape, and negotiate.

Before I created *Badge of Honor*, Merián Soto and I had our first son, Marcelo. I didn't have a single clue about how to raise a child. I've always rejected machismo and hypermasculinity, and once Marcelo arrived, I began to question what it meant to be a father—particularly in relation to my parents' traditional values and definitions.

I began taking a slide carousel of images of my pieces around and talking with different groups about my work, looking for people with whom I could share my preoccupations. While talking with some young people in Newark, New Jersey, there was a deathly silence when I asked them, "And your fathers, where do they live?" No one responded. It turned out that most of their fathers were in prison. From that point on, I took my slides and carousel to the prisons in search of ways to have conversations with these men who had been denied the opportunity to build their own lives and develop as fathers. The system was defining their behavior: prison was defining not only their future but also who they were.

That's where I entered, and with some luck, after one of those sessions, I began a dialogue with one of the men, and we eventually collaborated. All the images from *Badge of Honor* came from those conversations. The installation is like the algae that remain after the process. From those conversations, memories of television and Juana talking to the TV started coming back to me. I began understanding a series of things and tried to translate all this imaginary language into an object. Most of my work is like this. It's simply trying to contextualize conversations I have with people in a material and metaphorical form; that's how I develop the work. It's complicated because the conversations are complicated. One of the most interesting things I notice when I see the audience in front of my work is that it transports them to a personal space that's also complex.

RI: We also come from a culture of extreme spectacle. Even our DNA is ostentatious! It's impossible to reduce it to the minimal. Like one of my teachers, the Dominican artist Raúl Recio, says, "The minimal is cruel."

PO: True, true!

RI: Since you're talking about spaces that you, in some way, penetrate, like the prison—places where it isn't assumed the artist can enter, but the activist or artist disguised as an activist enters—how is your emotional state when you enter the space of social work, when you begin a relationship with these people that sometimes concludes in art? At times, I imagine that these relationships don't, in fact, end in art. What I mean is—what is it like coming together with people who bring so much to the work?

PO: I have an unusual career path because I didn't train as an artist but as a social worker. It wasn't until after becoming a social worker that I became interested in cultural production. I don't think social work is successful—it's too controlled by the institution, and those who receive the services aren't heard. To a certain point, art is controlled as well—although, as an artist, I have a lot of freedom.

What interests me in my practice is entering unusual spaces. I never contextualize the work with a gaze toward the exhibition space. I enter spaces where I'm not seen as an artist, and I connect like a human being, like a citizen—even though, in the end, I identify as an artist. I seek exchanges and sensations of life that we can share. I understand clearly, upon entering and leaving these spaces, that the three-dimensionality allows me to see and understand myself, within and outside my work. I recognize that I enjoy some privileges as an artist that maybe others don't.

How do I flex and conserve all of that emotional energy in order to create from there in the future? When I'm finished with the installation processes, I'm left totally devastated. I feel as though I've run a marathon! Those worlds, those environments I enter, drain me. When I enter the space of the exhibition, I recognize that some comforts in that world don't exist elsewhere, and those contradictions exhaust me!

For *Badge of Honor*, alongside the cinematographer Irene Sosa, I spent three weeks visiting the son and father daily. In the morning, we visited the father in prison, and in the evening, we went to the young boy's home. Sosa documented it on video while I constructed a dialogue between the two utilizing a single word. Eventually, through presenting the footage of the previous session, a long-distance conversation between the two began to develop. I was a witness to a deep exchange. Eventually, two worlds developed, two spaces of "coming and going." I started to realize the . . .

RI: . . . the chasm?

PO: Precisely! A chasm existed between these two worlds, inside and outside prison. You can already imagine the sensation of guilt and fragility that man had when I went to visit him. Emotions were running high when I interviewed him and his son. Obviously, Sosa and I were consumed by that energy. We experienced a few intense, real moments. I couldn't even speak after finishing that installation!

RI: At the start of our conversation, you mentioned the overlap of time and space, and considering what you're describing now, we can talk about the labor taken on to produce the piece. We inhabit two worlds, like those you encountered, to create a work that is more than just artistic; it is also spiritual labor, something emotional. Within that space, there is intangible emotional work. You can sense it, perhaps, in the atmosphere of the piece, but it's the individual that's left with the impact. That's the labor I'm referring to when I'm talking about the machinery; that time machine—that's you. You're the one doing the work of joining those two worlds! And it is a labor.

PO: It's a colossus, Olympic even!

RI: Exactly—perhaps atomic! Sometimes when you finish, you almost want to die! I've thought a lot about *Ahogado en un Vaso de Agua (Drowned in a Glass of Water)*. I say it in Spanish because I like it more in Spanish. Within that piece, there are themes that interest me a lot: mental health and death. I also think about the difficulty we experience dismantling the grand bewitchment that is the "division of classes," which is a type of insanity. That piece also spoke to me in terms of the invisible limits between the bodies within the same family. Who's the richest? Who has less? Who has more? Who is darker? All these structures and classifications only end up alienating. So, I wanted to ask you about your interest in mental health, which is extremely evident in your work.

PO: Yes. Health, or the lack of access to health resources, is always evident in my work. In each of my pieces, you'll encounter, in some shape or form, a confrontation with death or the rupture of health or care. The truth is, I don't produce a lot. I'm not like other artists who are constantly producing and exhibiting work. I don't have that capacity because I have to take care of myself. My work begins with the alignment of the spiritual, the physical, and the mental. If these things aren't aligned, I can't work; I can't do anything. Also, the work takes me a long time.

My concerns with health come from a traumatic experience I had when I was young. When my grandfather, from my mother's side, had a stroke, he became the center of my whole family's attention for a long time. Everyone else was pushed aside; they had to take turns being cared for. Recently, I realized that, in one form or another, I end up introducing references to health, particularly mental health, in my work. It's a well-defined yet unconscious thread.

I use the tension between two spaces, which are also always present in my work, like a magnet to wrestle with and unify the irreconcilable. I create two spaces but one scene. *Ahogado en un Vaso de Agua*, which is not included in this exhibition, has to do with our realities and traumas. We think that problems are bigger and more overwhelming than they really are. At the same time, we feel defenseless. The piece is constantly turning; it's a cyclical issue. So, you are in front of these two realities, and you see that they're yours, and you've refused them. The piece begins to awaken you or that which you have tried to deny all along.

RI: I have thought a lot about "The Zahir," Jorge Luis Borges's short story, which I've visited in a song, too. It's the story of a man obsessing over a coin he's given in a bar because he can see both sides at the same time. I also think about class complexes as histories, like recordings, loops that are repeated over and over. The story similarly turns and turns, and after ten years of therapy, things return, like cassettes constantly revolving.

Speaking of which, your work *Scene of the Crime (Whose Crime?)* [1993; pp. 73–83] is, in a way, contradictory in its strategy. In that piece, the spectator isn't permitted to enter the space. It is static like a photograph—you're unable to penetrate it; you can't move through it. There are some ways to look at it, which you control. It's a work that speaks to me a lot after living in Puerto Rico for fourteen years. There's also a subject that perhaps isn't obvious—blood. The blood behaves like a messenger, like spiritual nourishment. Seeing all the religious figures and the photos of family, I think of a future Puerto Rico that no longer depends on a territory but on a cultural DNA that *isn't* only blood.

In the book you sent me, I read that the police arrived to investigate the scene, and they looked for traces of DNA—what the blood in the work contained. I wanted to talk about that genetic information: What does it signify for you to be Puerto Rican? What does the idea of Puerto Rico signify after the hurricane, with climate change and the imminent disappearance of the Caribbean Islands looming? And what does that piece signify now?

PO: I always collect objects thinking about the people I've collaborated with in the construction of the installations. In *Scene of the Crime,* I collaborated with a specific family. The objects are nearly identical to those in the home of the women with whom I collaborated. In fact, the photographs on top of the table are photos of her family. I walked through all of New York looking for objects that looked like they were hers. The tearing of space appears—the white and red side of the installation. And there are the saints with skin painted black—I always begin by referencing spirituality. It's important to understand that those objects have a limited shelf life in the market. After a few years, they aren't easy to find.

Today, you can read *Scene of the Crime* like a monument to the victims of femicide. The high heel, which you almost don't see, evokes femicide, but back then, no one spoke of that.

And how do I feel being Puerto Rican? I've always seen myself as a hybrid Puerto Rican. I'm not rich, but I'm not poor. Nor am I able to enter the parameters of what's expected of the middle class. I flow between the three classes. In political terms, I always believe in the possibility of an independent Puerto Rico. We have the ability to be responsible for ourselves, but instead, we've had a dependence imposed on us that is often reflected in our behavior. Ideologically, I'll always critique the establishment. It's necessary to always resist the system that prohibits us from reaching our potential. Like my work, I'm a complex person with the gift of making you see what you don't want to recognize.

In *Scene of the Crime,* the classic, obvious issues of the Puerto Rican flag, femicide, saints, and the viewer converge. I'm interested in the obvious because it permits us to self-reflect and reposition ourselves in front of what is ours and what we reject. When I read your novel *La Mucama de Omicunlé,* that sensation caught my attention because there were a number of spaces I couldn't enter. I was reading the book and understanding the complexity of that world from the outside—with you. Now, I'm interested in looking at the museum and the spectator in a different way. The installations are real, in a sense, but very few people can see and understand the real.

I'm also interested in the spaces we can enter and the ones we can't. The space in *Scene of the Crime* is sacred, although there is no such thing as the sacred, because to remove yourself from your own environment, to become exposed, is to be no longer sacred. I allow you to stand at the edge of the installation, but you *do not* enter. You can enter *No Crying Allowed in the Barbershop (En la barbería no se llora)* [1994; pp. 84–105] because machismo is an issue that affects us all. But when the installations are about specific people, the spaces are not admissible; you have to respect that.

RI: All of the world's magic traditions discuss objects having a particular charge to them. Some are charged intentionally through ceremony and converted into magical tools; others are charged accidentally by coming in contact with some form of energy. So when you talk about looking for objects for *Scene of the Crime,* I imagine you like a saint on a pilgrimage in search of them. How do you provoke that charge within the objects—the charge that is also in your work?

PO: In the installation, there was a chronology for what I was using and invoking. I come from a family that has almost a tradition of adoring objects: baby Jesus, my umbilical cord in a bottle of alcohol. In fact, they would bring the Virgin of Guadalupe to my house each month on an altar—the altar moves from home to home. I've always spoken to objects. In my personal space, I utilize many objects. They arrive with a history, and when I collect them, it's as if they were a chronology of my life!

In my work, the objects are positioned so they can speak to one another. They live, like you say, charged; they come into my hands with a history, and I don't want to sanitize them of that. Instead, I want to layer more on them. Since I was a young boy, I would speak to the objects in my house. It was also a sensation of faith. I'm not talking about religious faith, but the faith of creating yourself out of what's possible. It's part of my psyche and, as you say, my DNA.

RI: This interests me a lot. Now that we're talking about transforming into an oracle or intervening like an oracle, trying to disrupt chance, I want to understand what you do with the personal objects on your table, your practice of always creating relationships between them. It makes me think of little children picking up toy soldiers as they prepare a battlefield.

Also, one of the strengths of your work is precisely that it erases the museum. Your installations aren't within the white box where one continues to see its frame. You make the museum disappear as we enter another dimension, time-space, social class, register. There is no trace of the museum; it's super potent.

And on a different note, as a woman, desire is part of the history of my community. How did the AIDS epidemic impact you? How did it make you become the artist you are today?

PO: Thank you for that question! I lost many friends during the AIDS epidemic. It was a time of much speculation and uncertainty. It was a crucial moment that impacted me greatly: spiritually, physically, and mentally. It revived the trauma of my grandfather, of seeing a person totally incapacitated and fragile. I saw that in my friends. I find it difficult to see a person in their final days; it puts me out of order, removes me from the alignment I need. I lived that constantly with people very close to me. I began to develop an awareness for activism and how we could take these conversations beyond the casual and toward a form of resistance. I started to doubt institutions and understand our reality as Puerto Ricans—who are given very little, very late—and I created *El Velorio: AIDS in the Latino Community* [1991]. *El Velorio* was the first installation where I invited the public to sit within the work. I did it as political resistance more than anything else and because I got tired of continually being offered exhibition opportunities in small spaces.

RI: How did Pepón survive in New York? What did Pepón do to eat, live, have a roof over his head? How did Pepón search when he was just starting out?

PO: I always searched. I've been very fortunate. And I've always had work. I worked as a social worker in New York City's Department of Human Services for a long time as I developed my practice. After leaving there, I worked in El Museo del Barrio for many years as an artist-in-residence. From there, I had a series of residencies and other opportunities. I had an apartment in the South Bronx where the rent was $150 a month, and I was part of a network of people that looked out for one another—within that network were some of the friends I lost. I'm the type of person that doesn't know where they're headed but always sees it to the end!

RI: You're optimistic!

PO: Yes! When I see the end, I think, "Aha! Cool, now how am I going to get there?" In fact, I'm an anomaly within the art world. I was a latecomer to gallery representation. I never thought about the commercialization of my work. Opportunities and exhibitions always arrived eventually. No one stops me. I once heard the great Jorge Pineda say, "*Saludos* to those who love me, and *saludos* to those who don't love me, too." I'm still here, and I'm still down!

RI: "To those I don't love so much but who I also love."

PO: Exactly! My attitude is that of a person who has been marginalized for a long time. At a certain point, I got up and said, "Enough with colonization!" I'm not afraid of failure. I've created so many terrible pieces—I see them, understand them, and continue onward.

RI: If you had all the resources in the world—all the time, all the good health—to make one project, the ideal project you've always wanted to make, do you have one? Or is the project a process?

PO: If I had all the resources in the world, I wouldn't use them. Because my work truly emerges from both personal and collective fragility. In fact, it's notable throughout the videos. The images within my videos are not perfect, nor are they technologically advanced. I'm not looking for perfection or the cutting edge. As I said before, I want to create work that surges from spiritual, emotional, and physical alignment. If I had all the resources in the world, I would become misaligned. I wouldn't be able to create work. I know myself well enough to know that!

RI: Each of your works of art, for many artists, would be a dream in terms of resources. They're all grand, monumental pieces that demand all kinds of resources. But an artist always has a work in the back of their mind that they've never made but have always wanted to. For example, I always have that one novel. It's a thousand-page book that, one day, I'm going to write. But it never happens because my format is the short novel. It's like an obsession that's always there, lingering in the background!

PO: It has to do with a matter of entering a circuit that isn't mine. I'm very aware of where I belong. That same certainty allows me to wrestle with the issue of hybridity.

RI: As the Caribbeans that we are, we spoke in the beginning about the issue of climate change, of the eventual disappearance of the islands we come from. Has this affected how you think about your materials, space, and how you imagine the relationship between bodies and the environment? Has your way of thinking as an artist, an activist, a Puerto Rican, a human shifted?

PO: I'm in Puerto Rico now, and there's a frigid cold. People are wearing coats. People like to wear that kind of clothing because it makes them feel like gringos—but it scares me. Climate change affects all of us. It affects our mental health. I'm not talking about a clinical madness, but human disorderliness, a lack of focus on what's happening. And at the same time, there is resilience, especially within nature.

I'm also aware that new layers are building within layers that already exist. Puerto Rico is a very difficult country—it's an uphill battle twenty-four-seven. Things will get even steeper, more difficult than they were before. People are scraping by, and the personal is converting more and more into the public. When we sit on the bus, we can hear the life of the whole world talking on their cell phones. This tells me a lot about the ethics of my work. How do I expose the personal in the public?

I also think corporations are imposing a formula for "the new Puerto Rican" in Puerto Rico that isn't real; it's an invention. They aim to mold who we should be, a construction viewed through a reality that isn't ours. It feels like schizophrenia. In Puerto Rico, you can see the years collecting on top of people, crushing them, but they're also resisting. They can't give much more, but they keep on. At the same time, that vulnerability creates opportunities for others with money to enter and take everything. This reality that we are building—within and outside the island—breaks from this same effort.

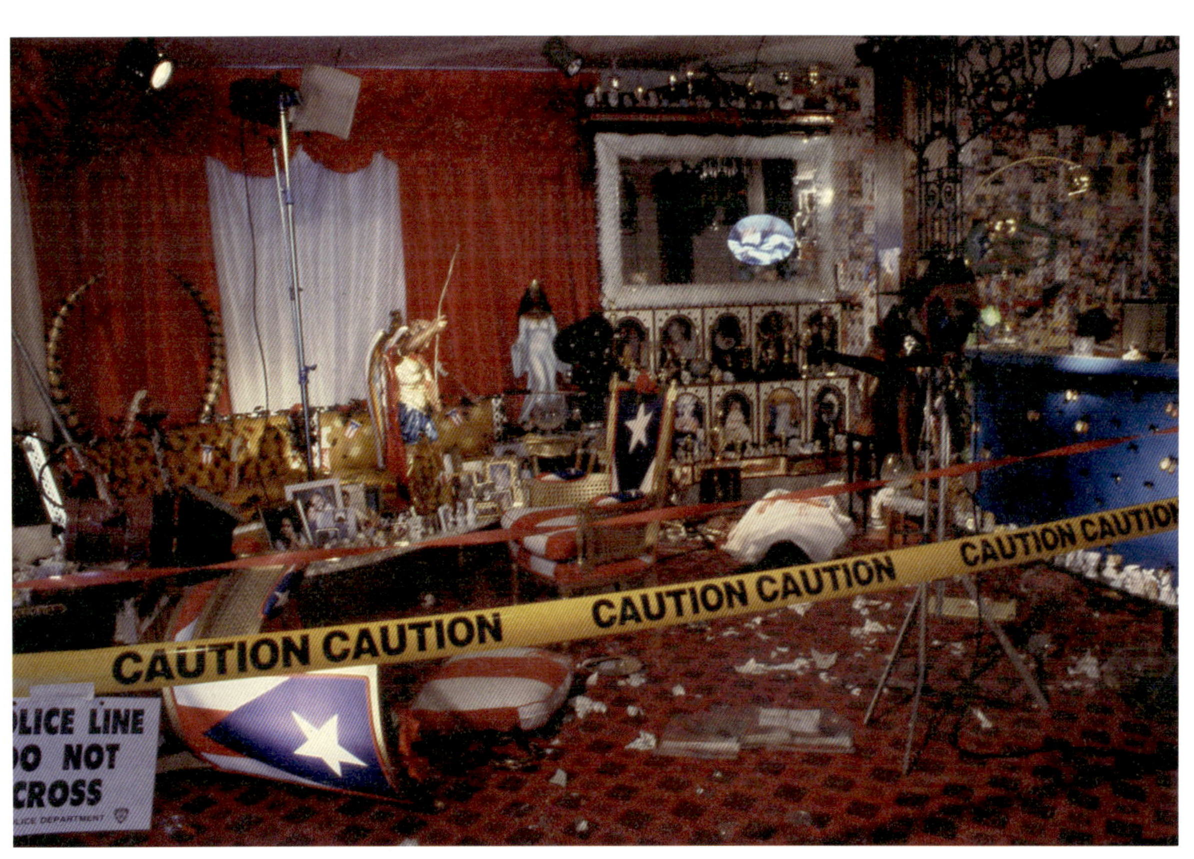

Scene of the Crime (Whose Crime?), 1993

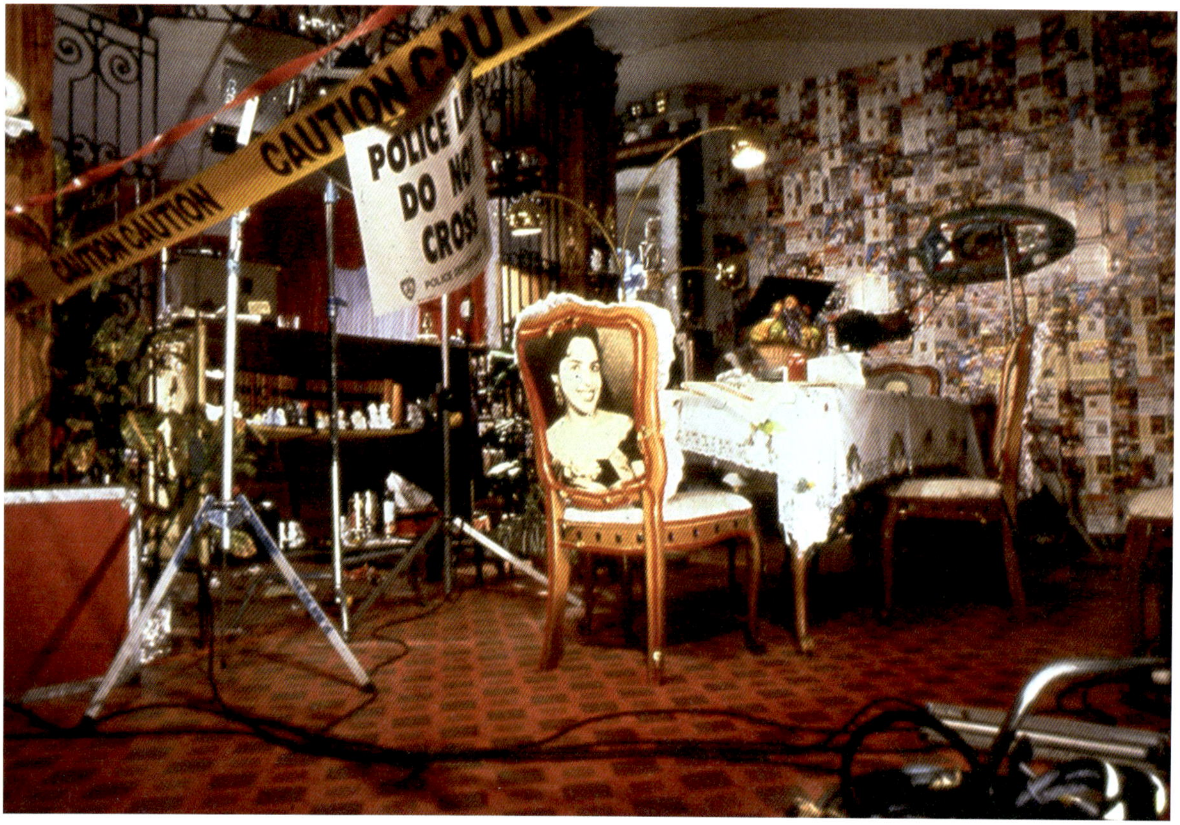

CAUTION CAUTION
CAUTION CAUTI
POLICE LI
DO NO
CROSS

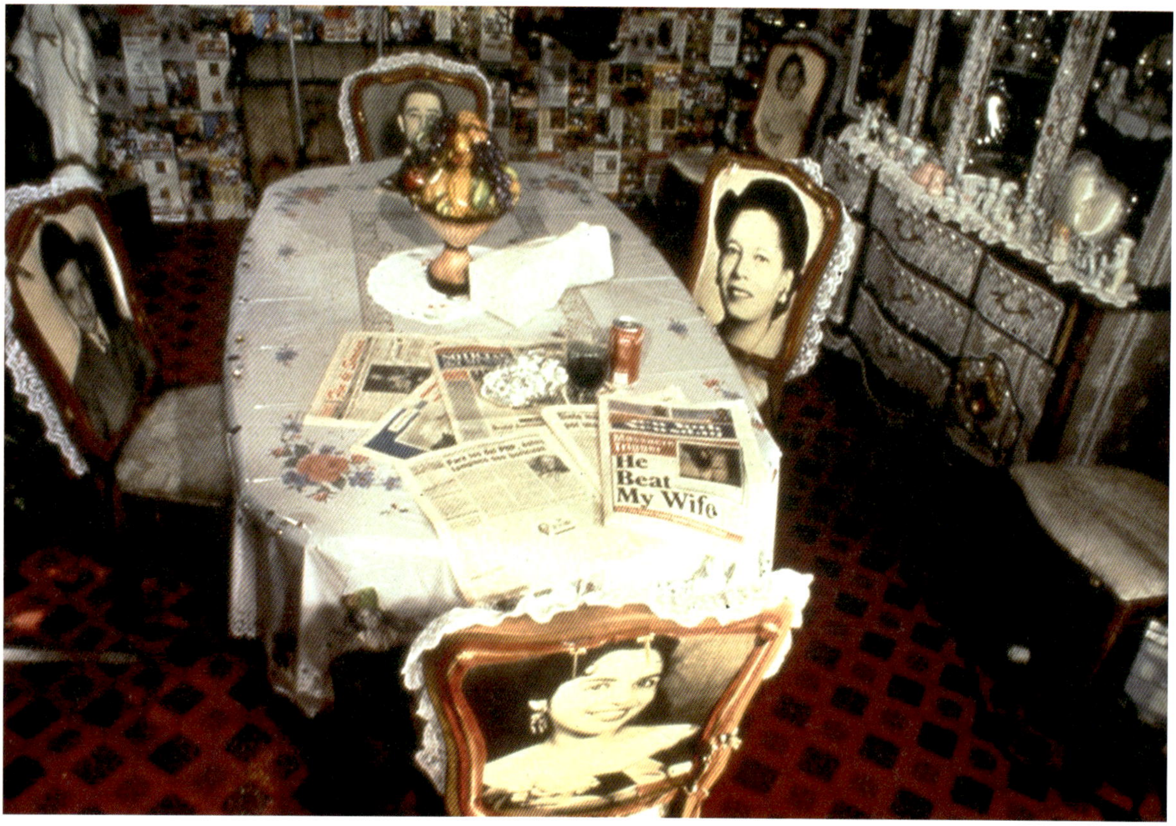

He
Beat
My Wife

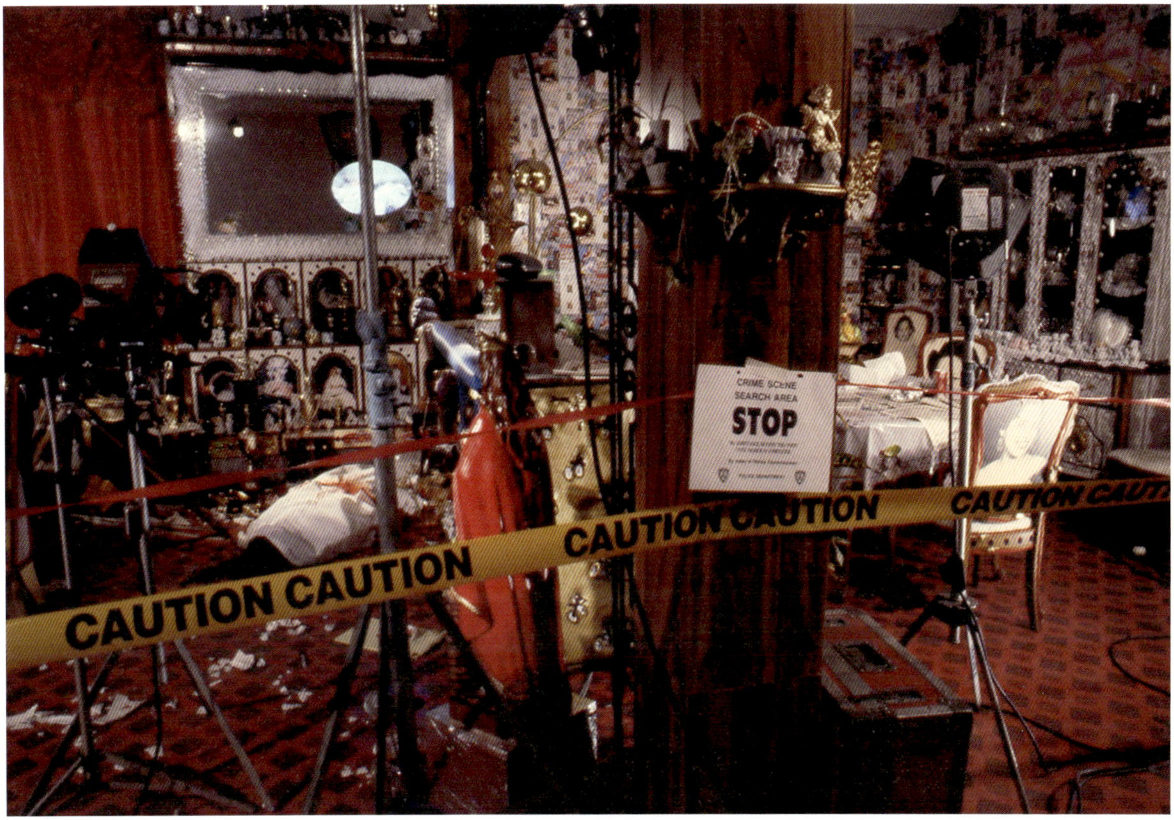

CRIME SCENE
SEARCH AREA
STOP
CAUTION CAUTION
CAUTION CAUTION
CAUTION

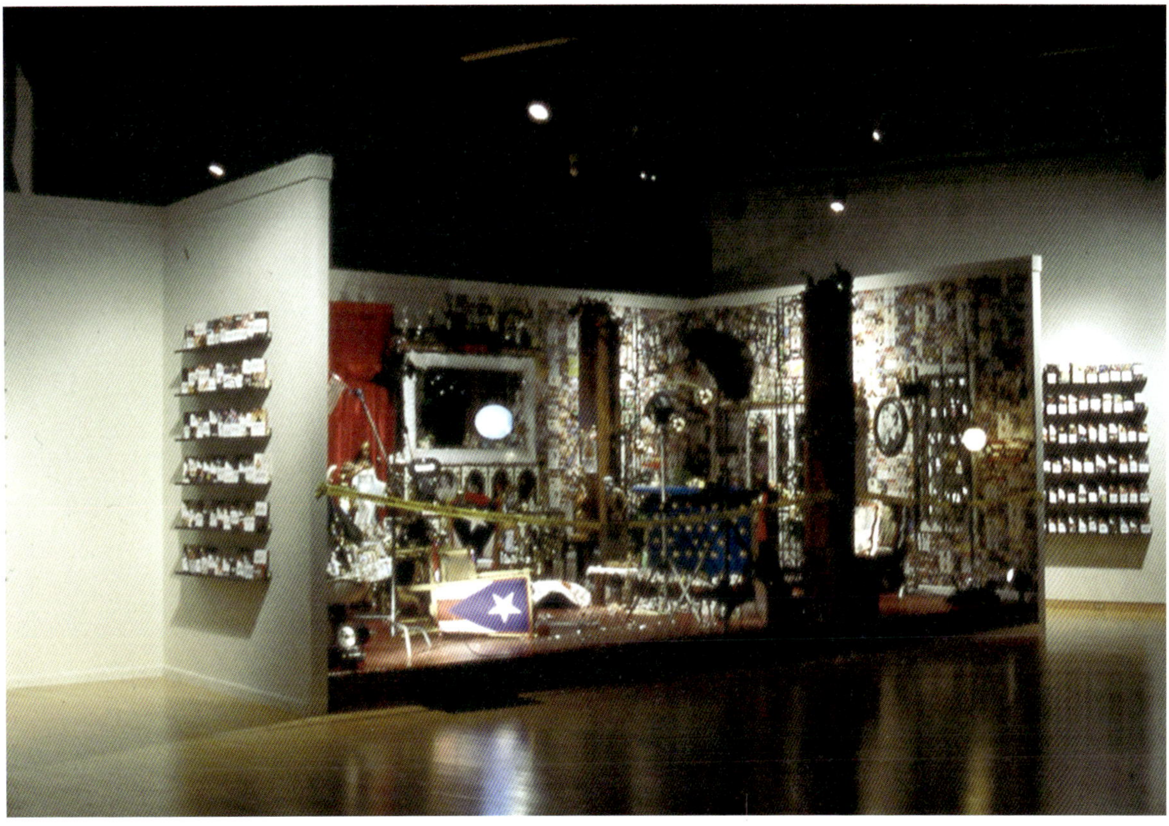

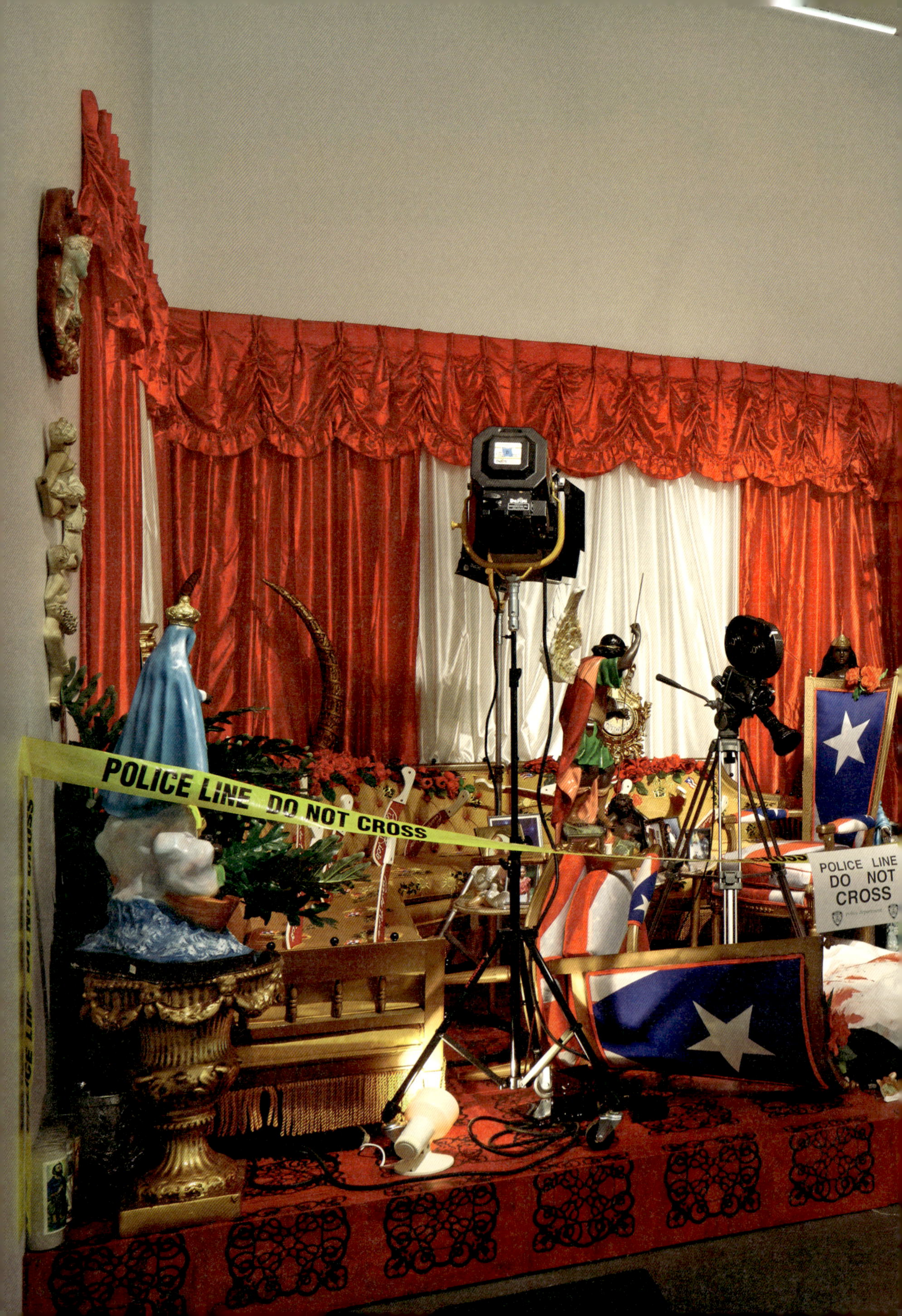
POLICE LINE DO NOT CROSS
POLICE LINE
DO NOT
CROSS

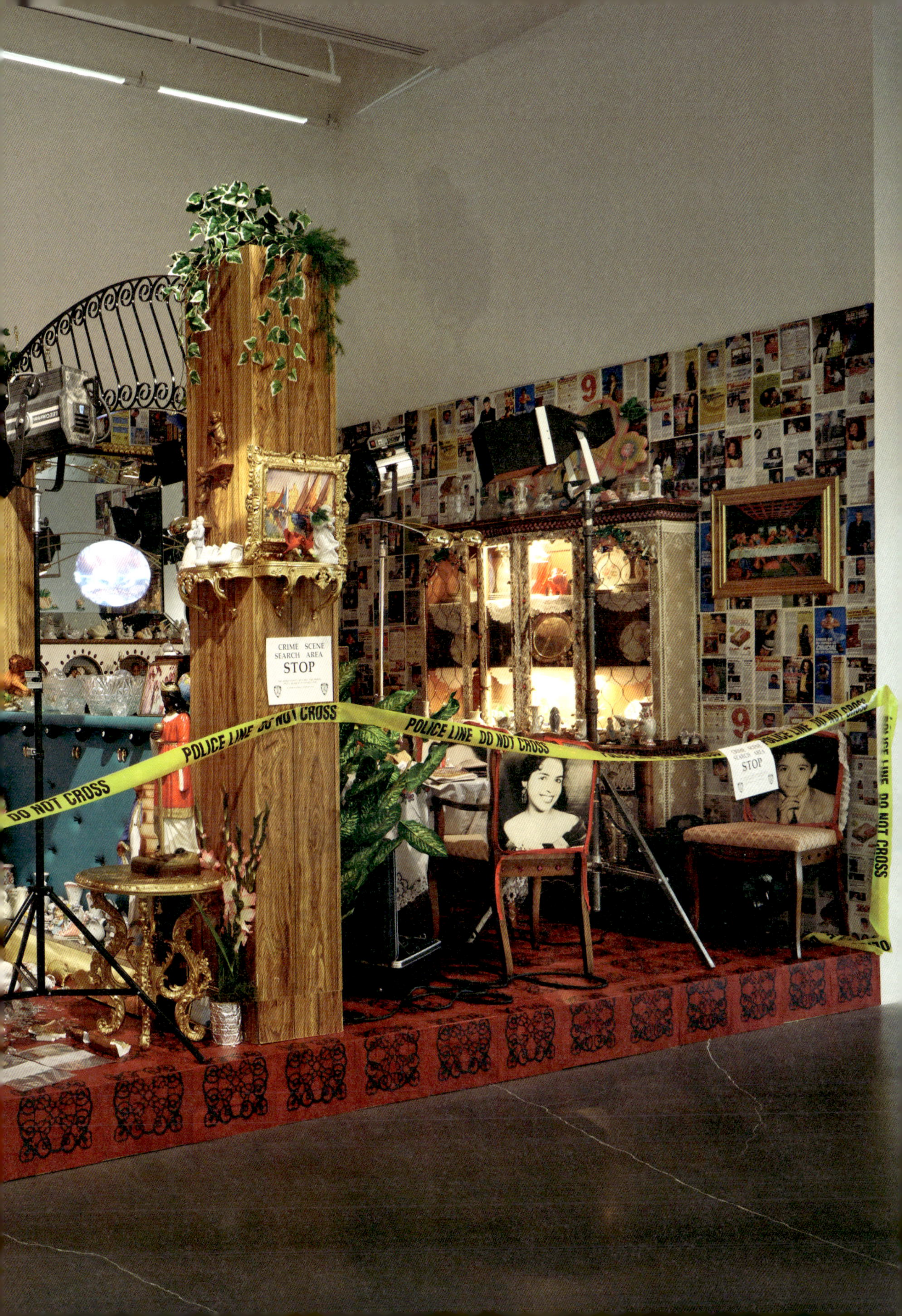
CRIME SCENE
SEARCH AREA
STOP
DO NOT CROSS
POLICE LINE DO NOT CROSS
POLICE LINE DO NOT CROSS
STOP

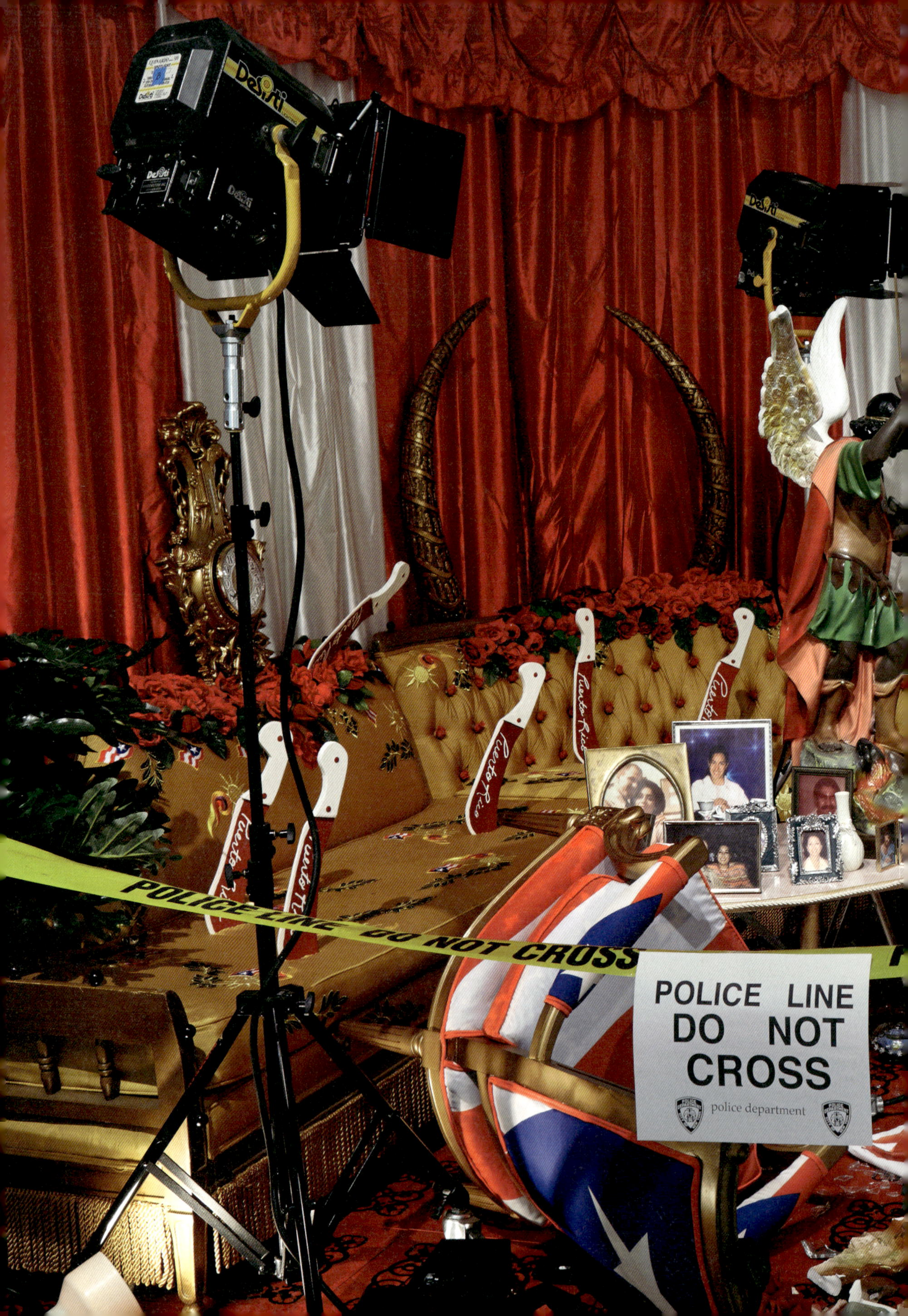
POLICE LINE DO NOT CROSS
POLICE LINE
DO NOT
CROSS
police department
DeSisti
Puerto Rico

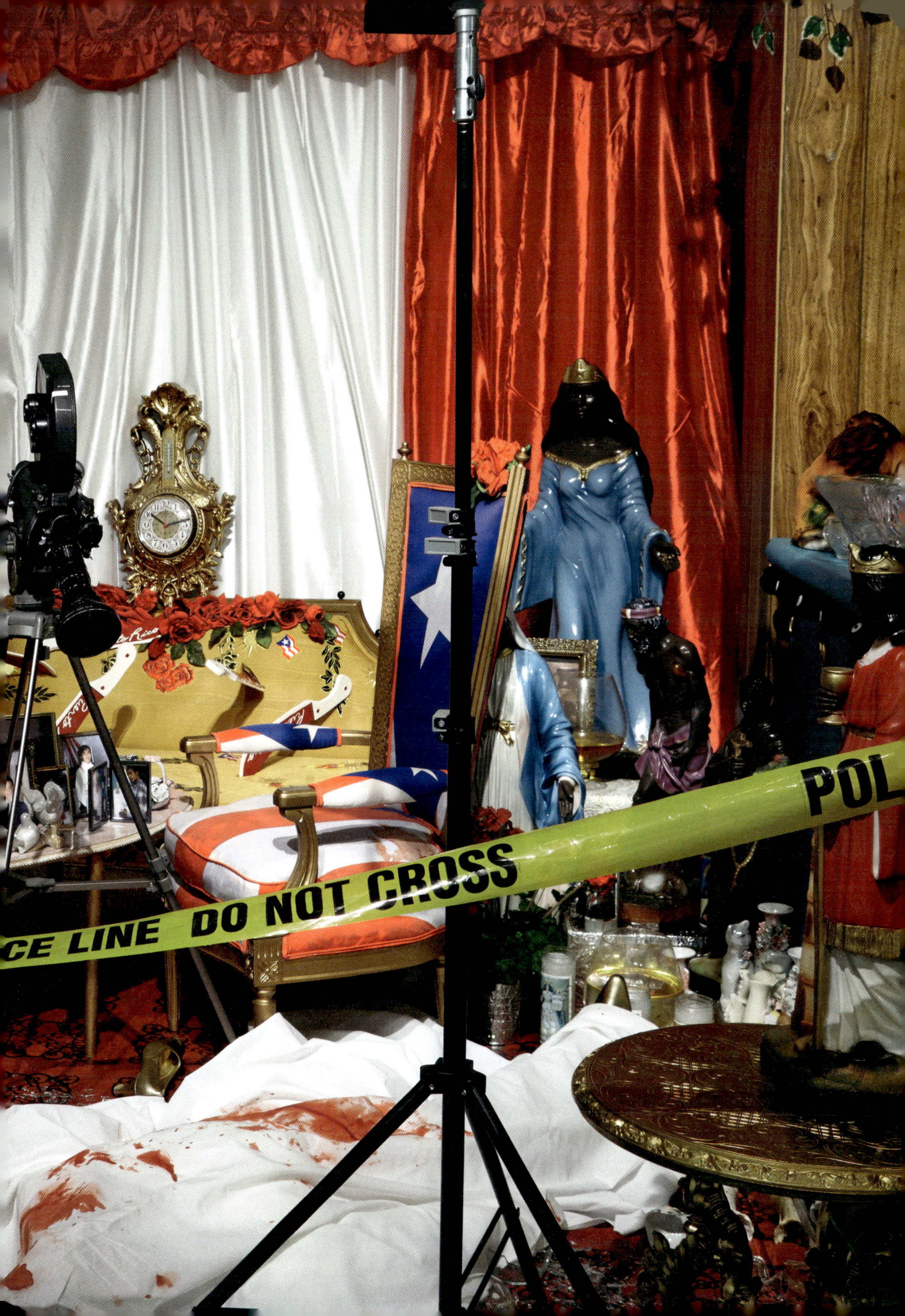
CE LINE DO NOT CROSS
POL

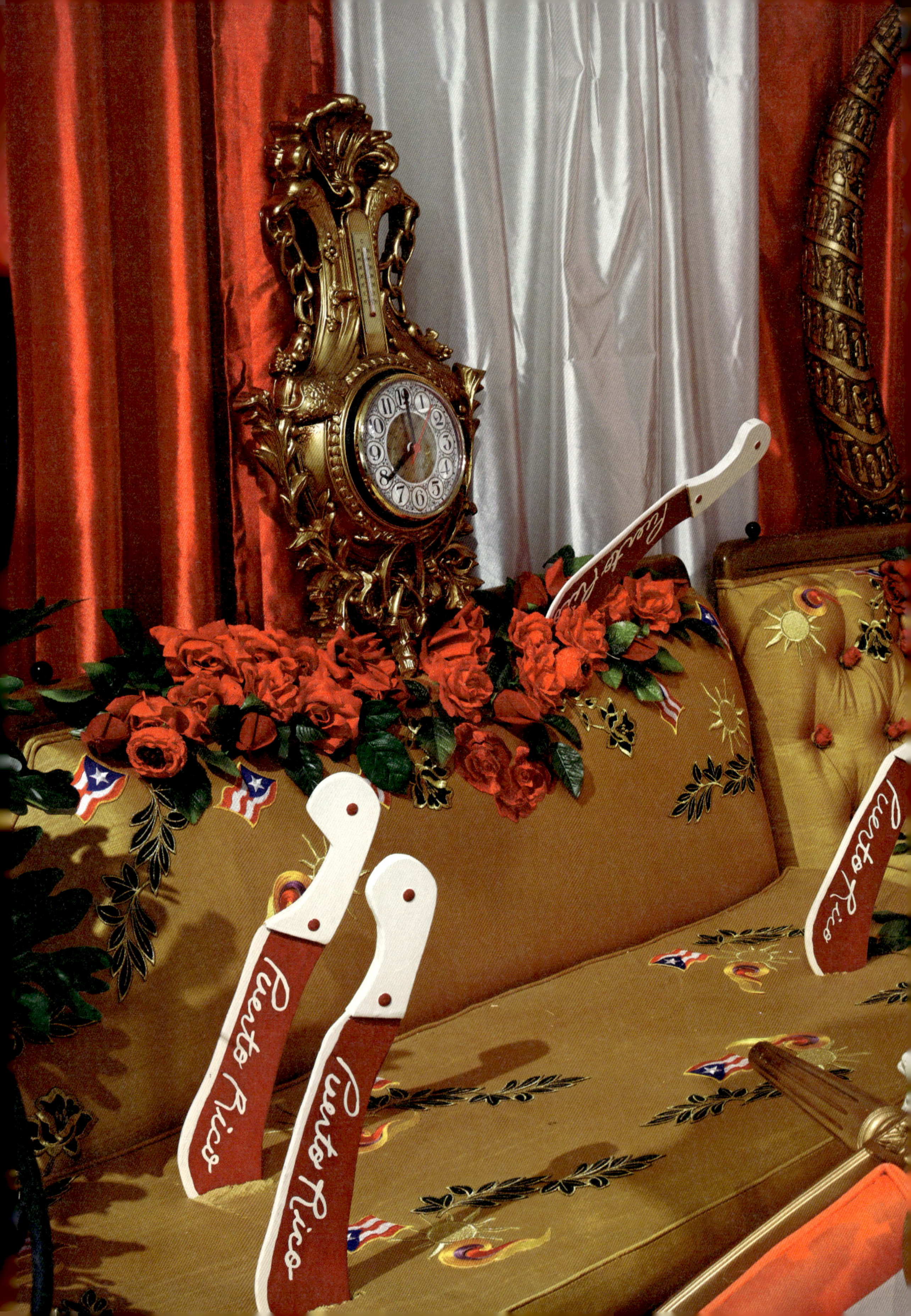
Puerto Rico
Puerto Rico
Puerto Rico

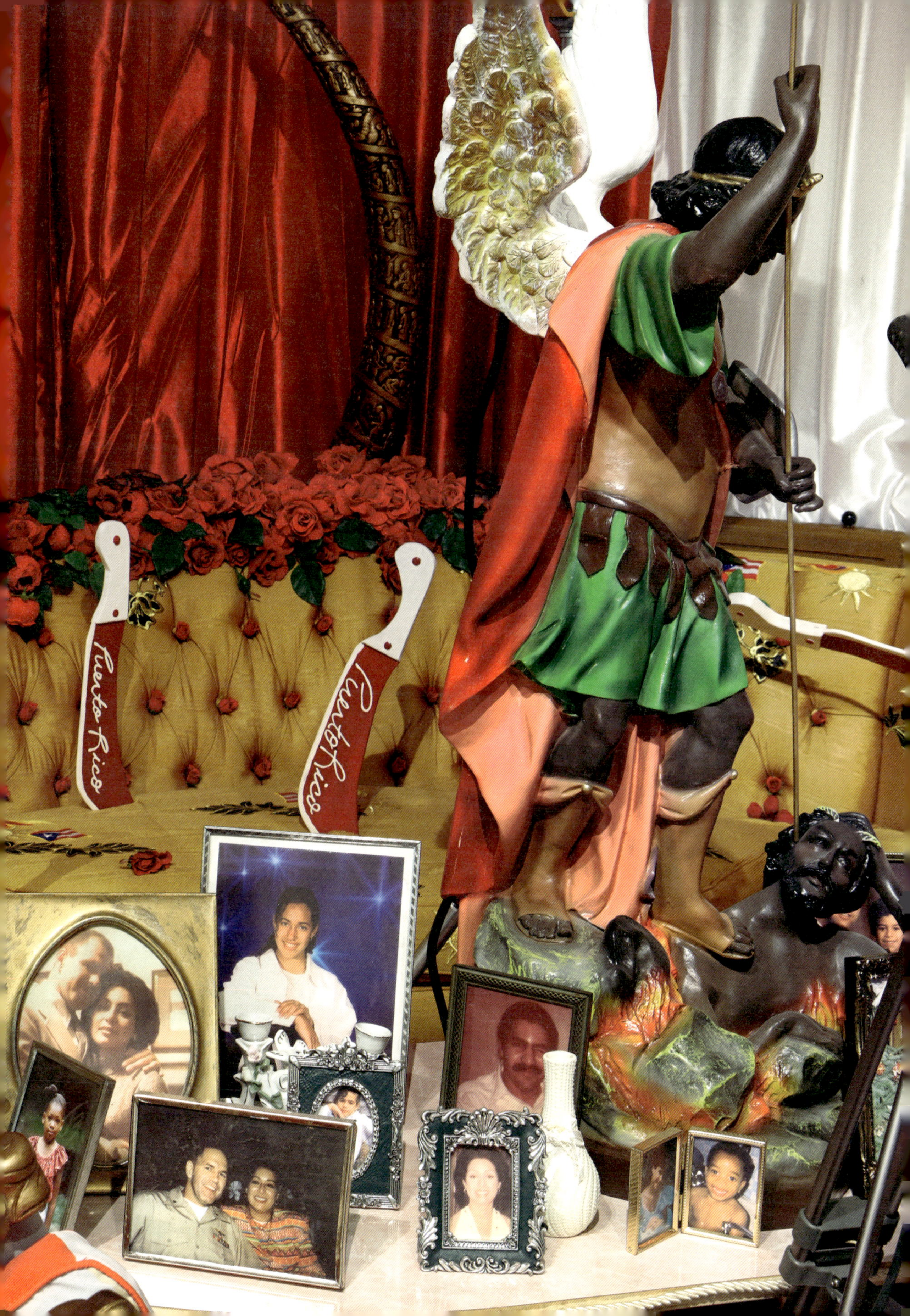
Puerto Rico
Puerto Rico

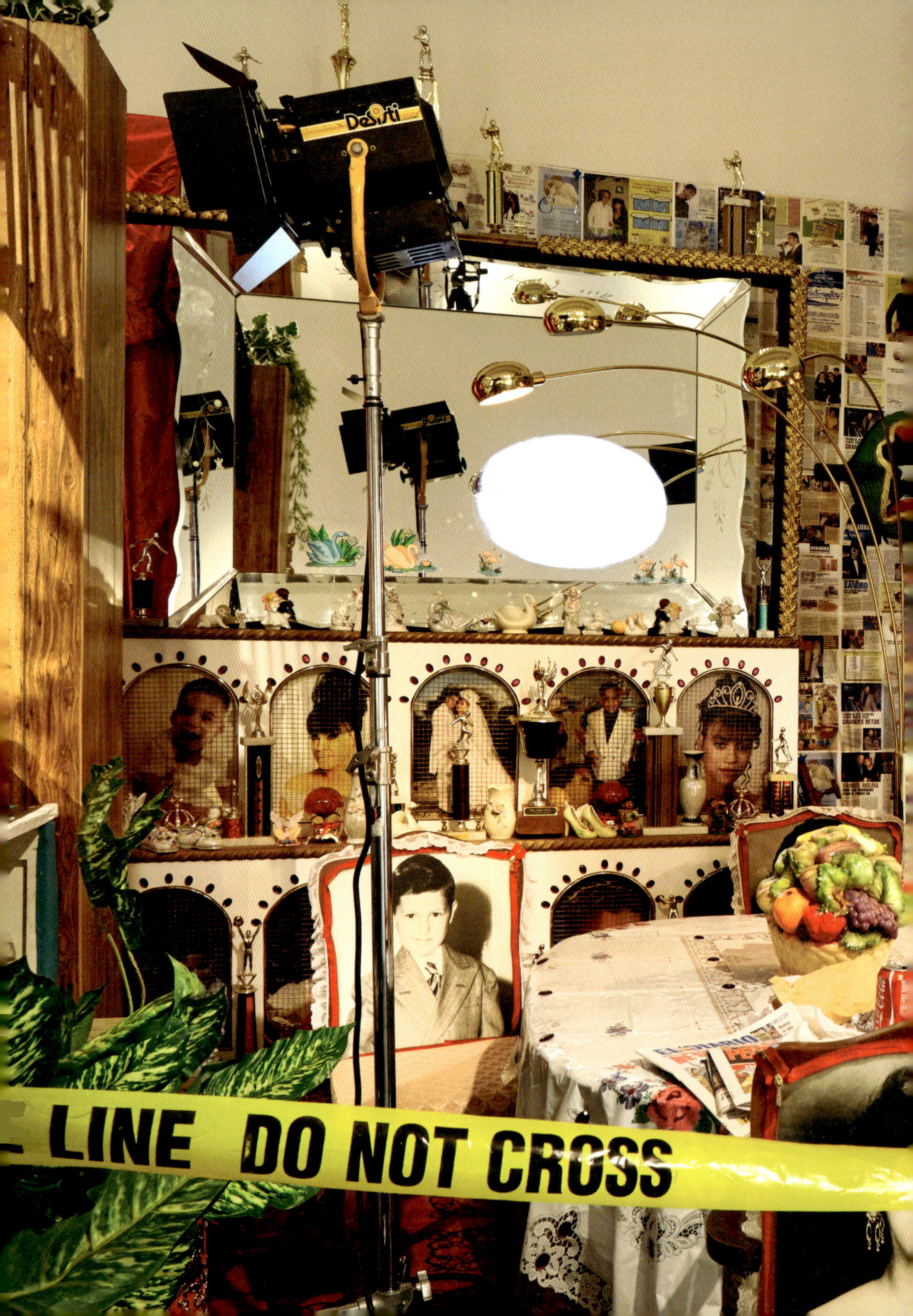
DeSisti
LINE DO NOT CROSS

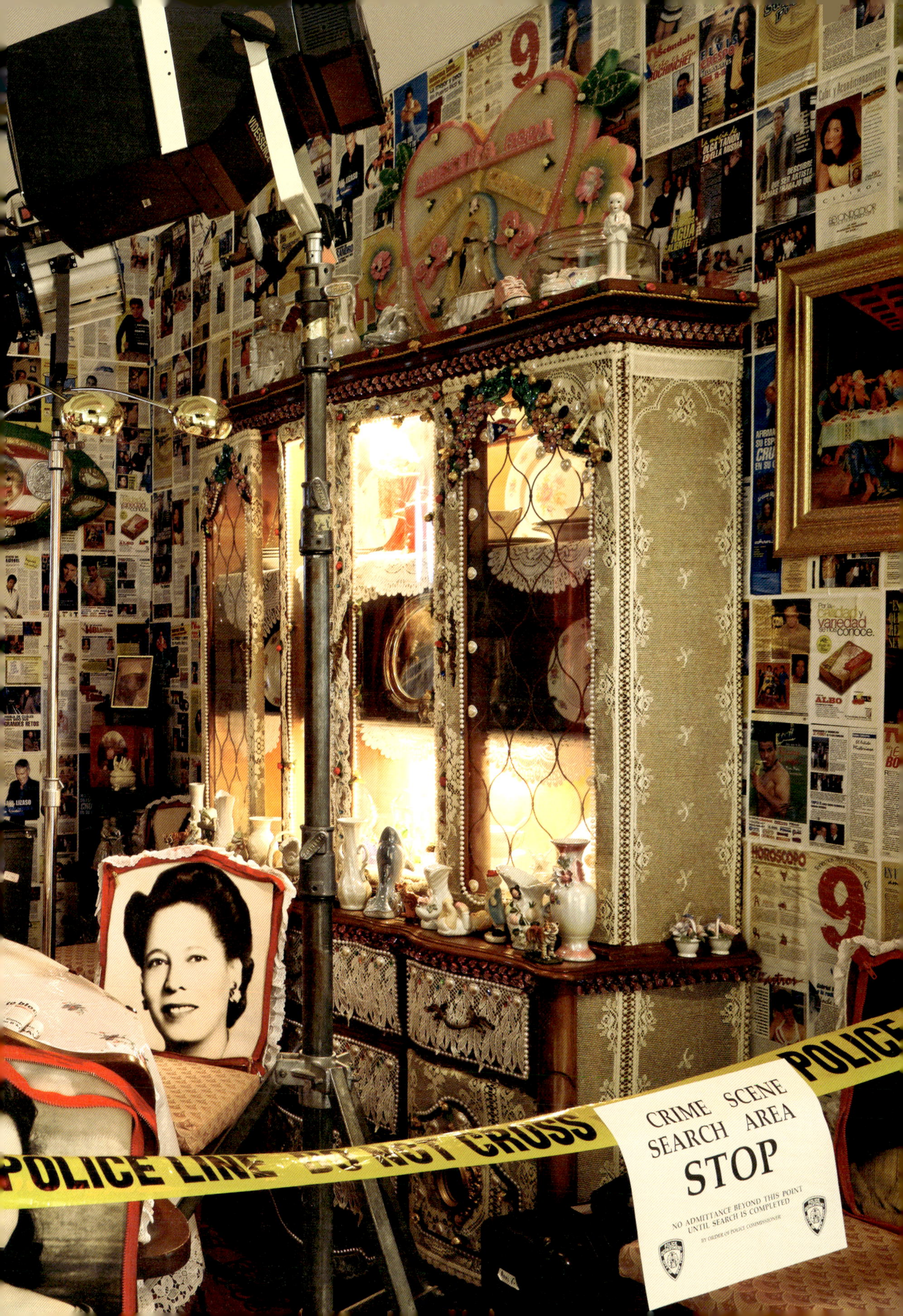
POLICE LINE
POLICE
CRIME SCENE
SEARCH AREA
STOP
NO ADMITTANCE BEYOND THIS POINT
UNTIL SEARCH IS COMPLETED

No Crying Allowed in the Barbershop (En la barbería no se llora), 1994

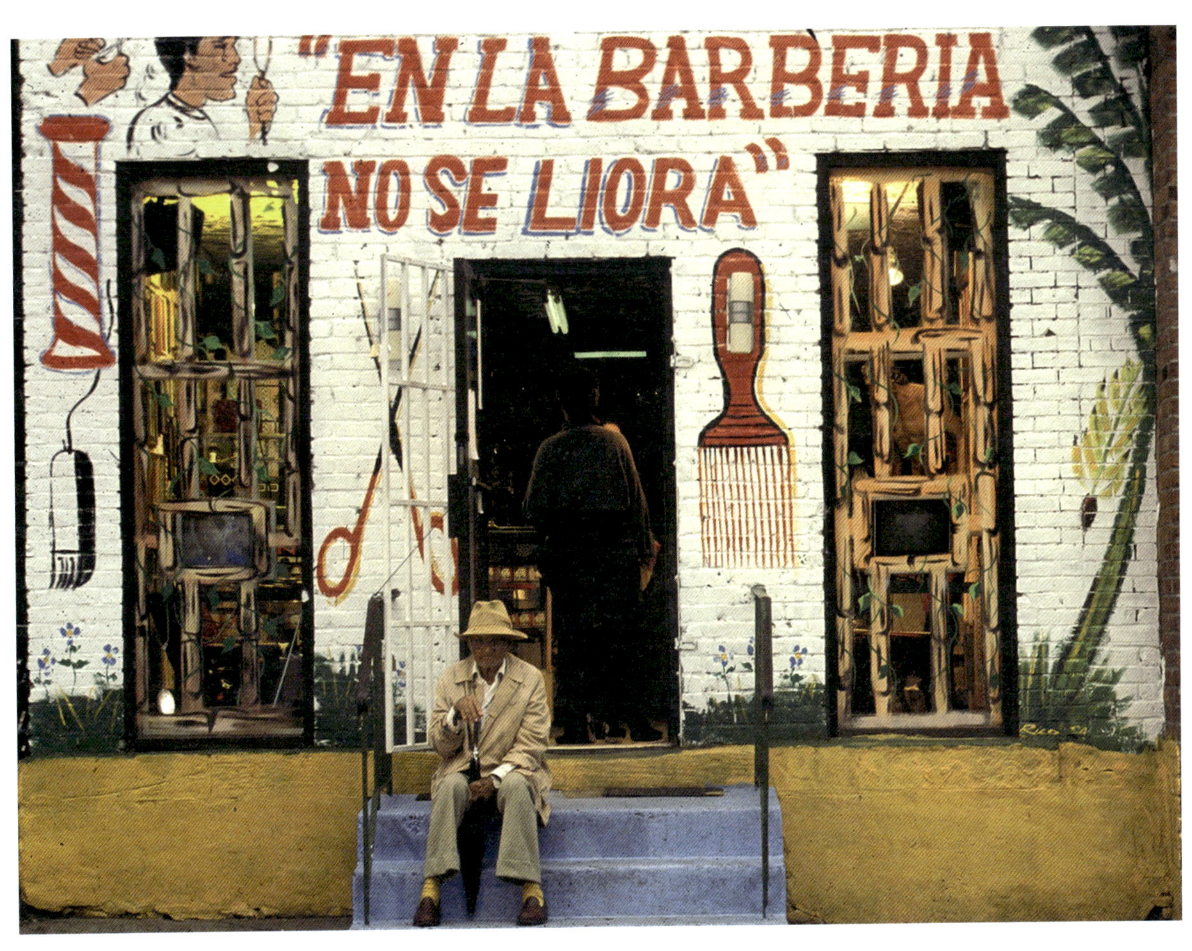
"EN LA BARBERIA
NO SE LIORA"

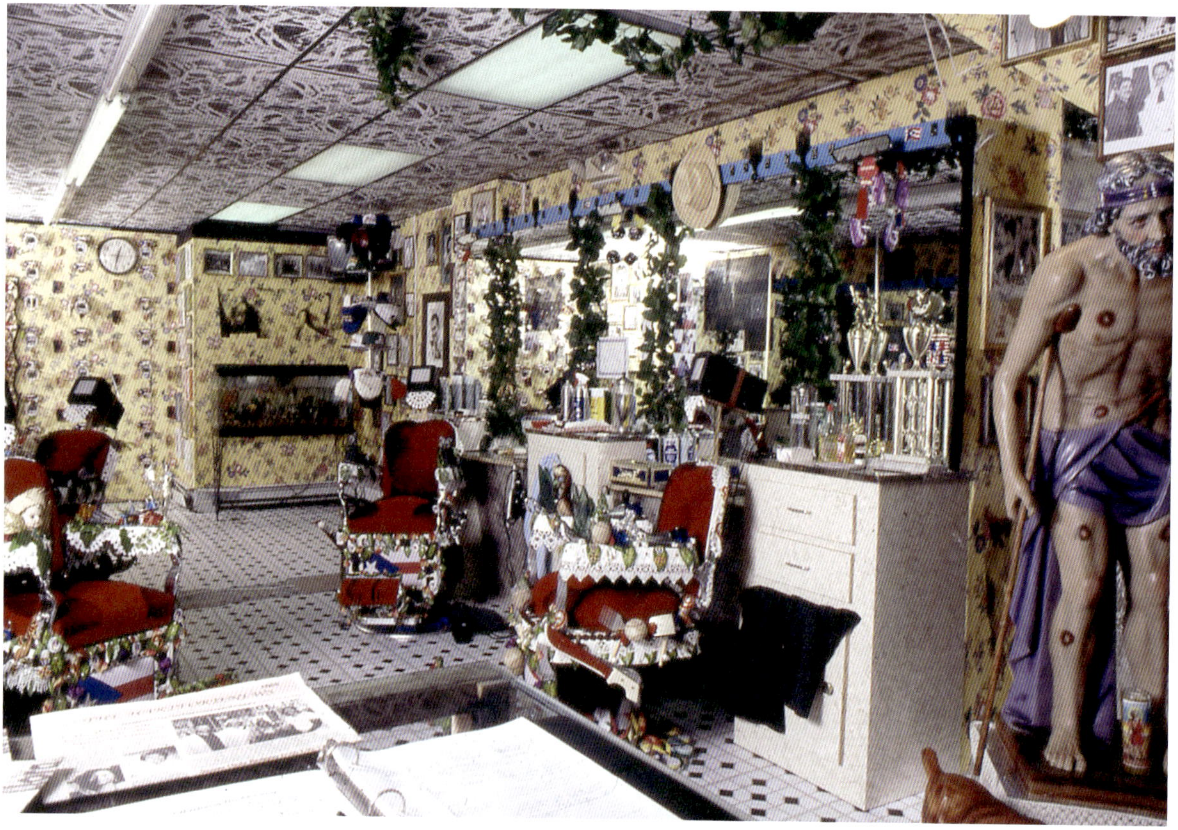

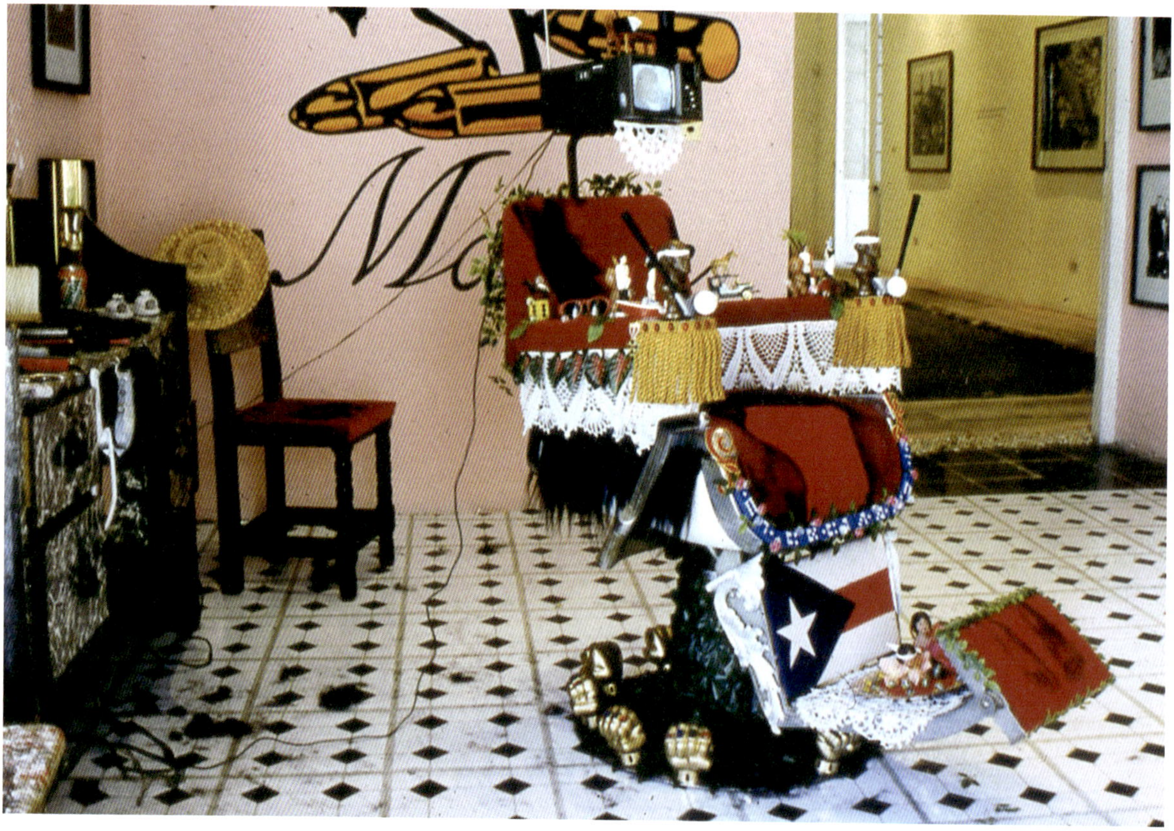

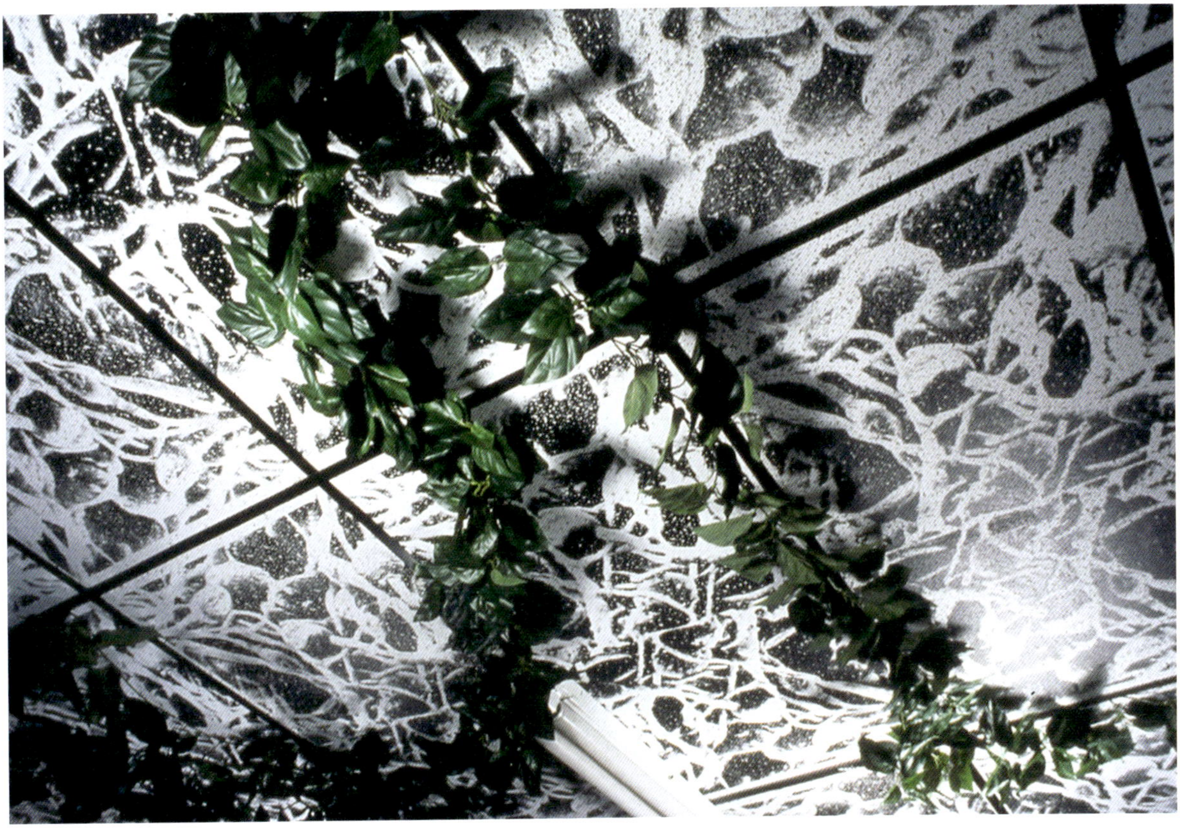

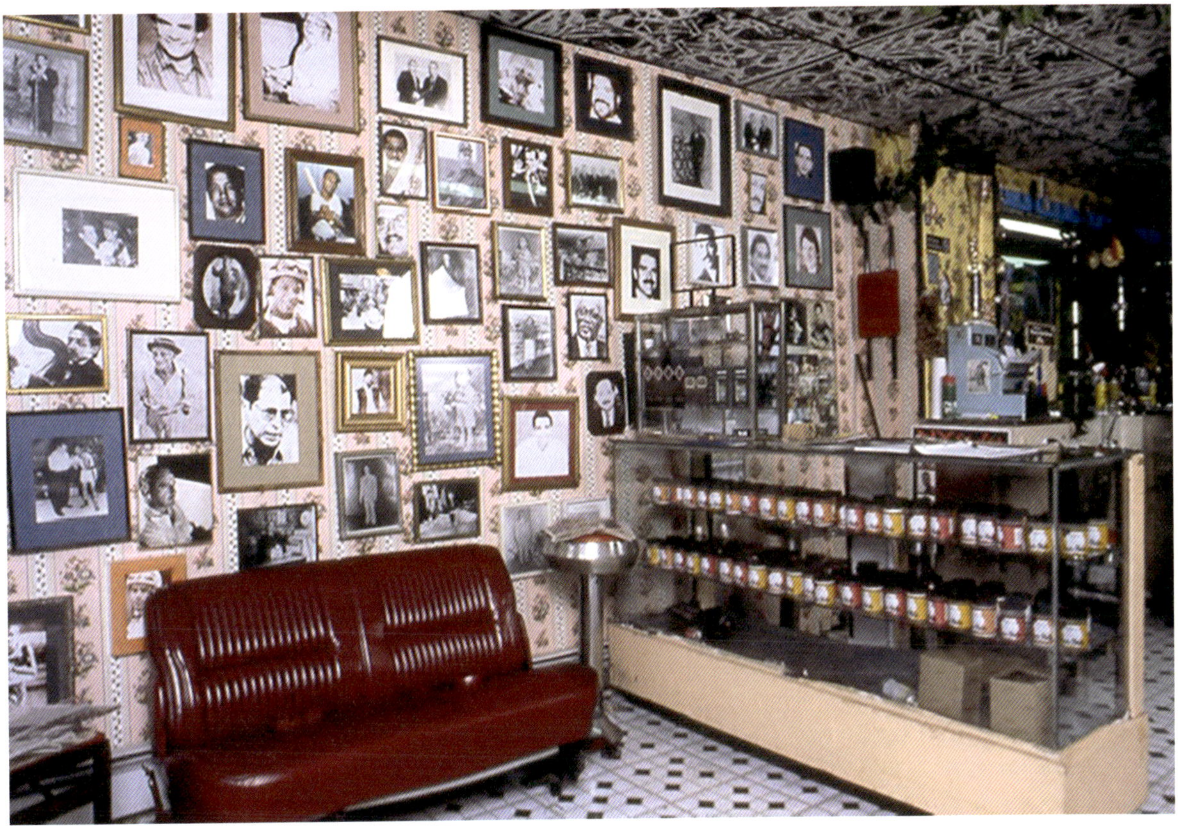

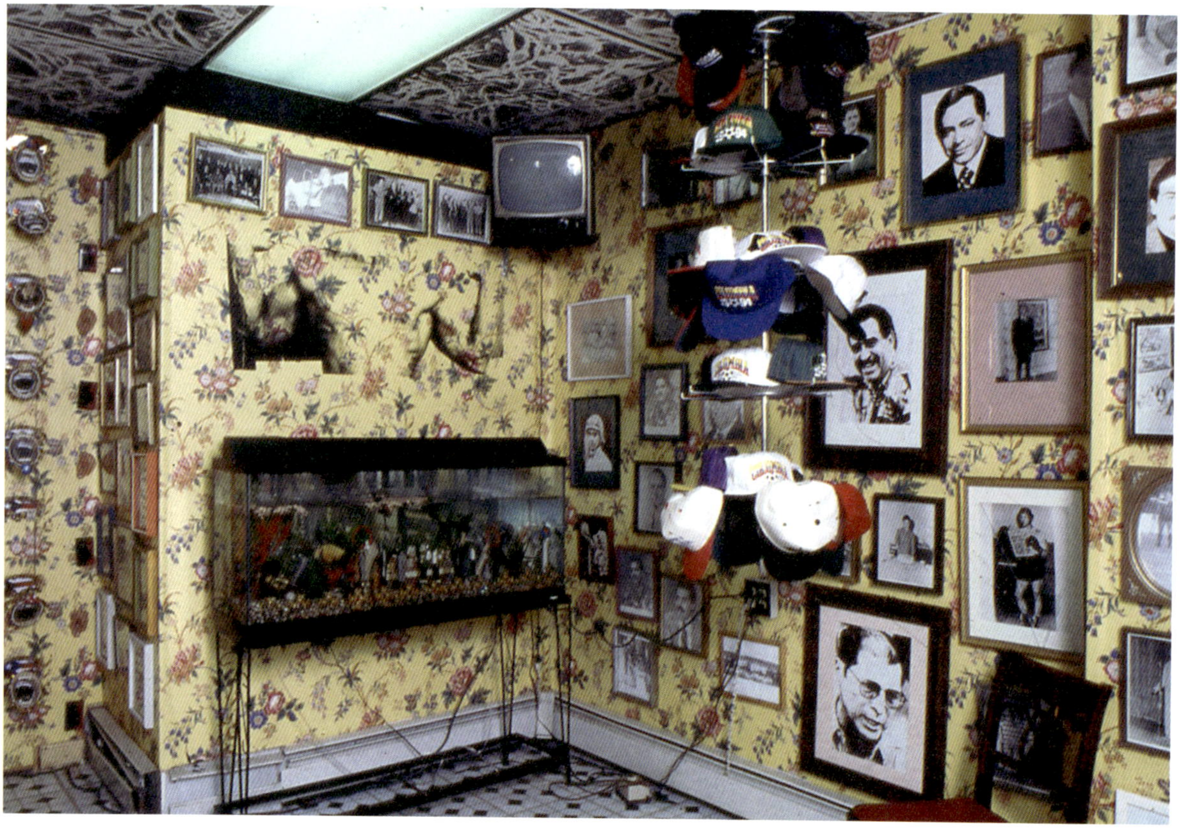

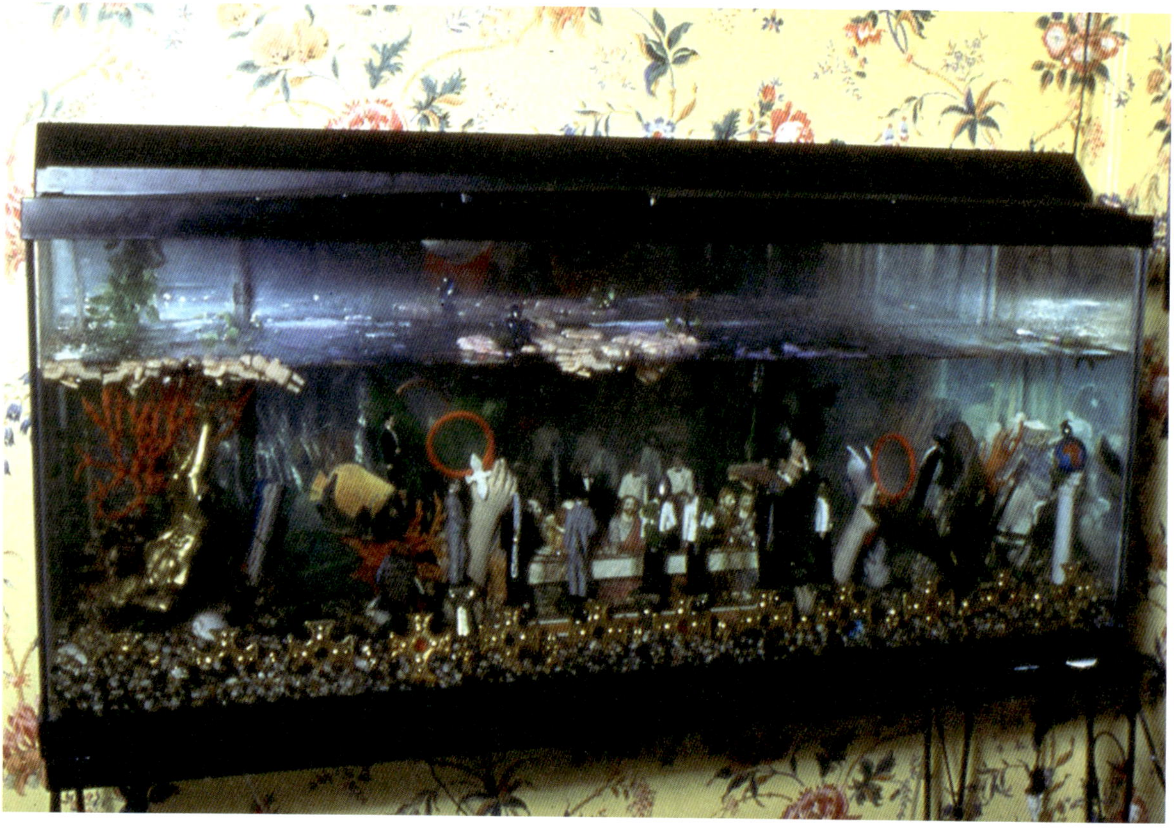

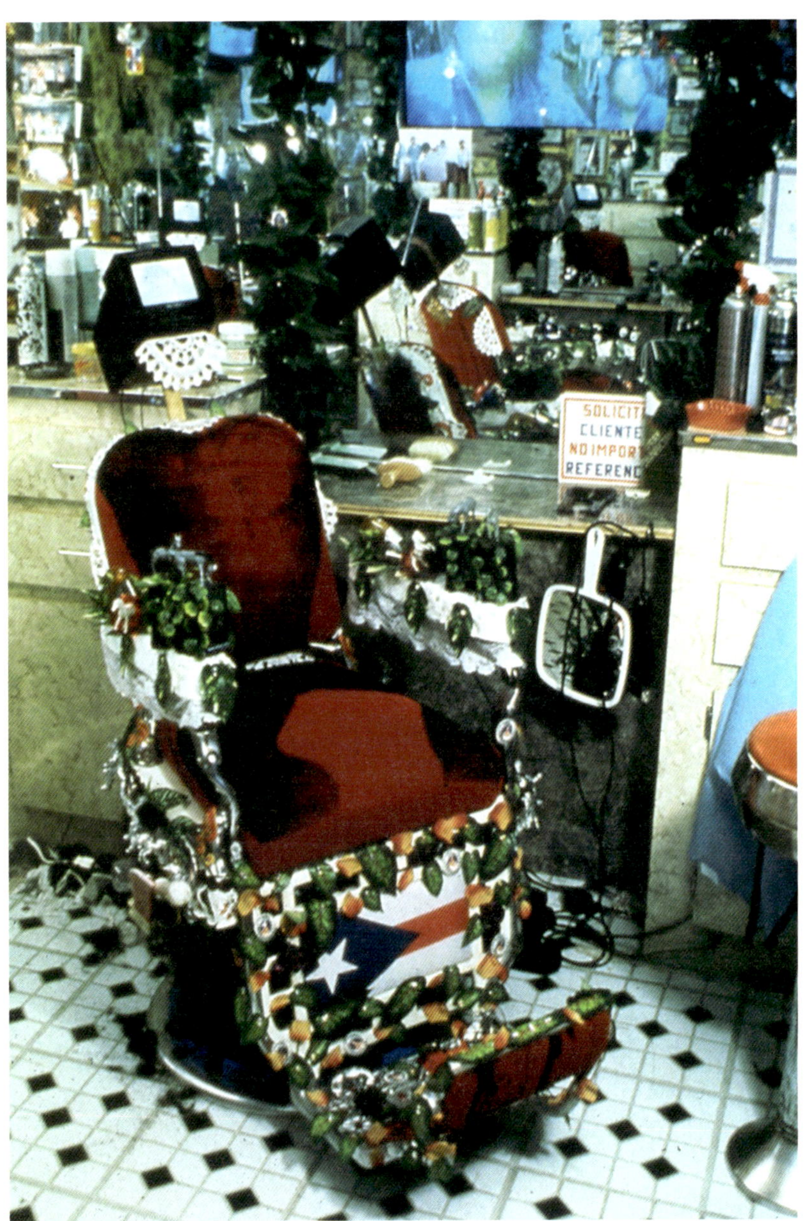
SOLICIT
CLIENTE
NO IMPORT
REFERENC

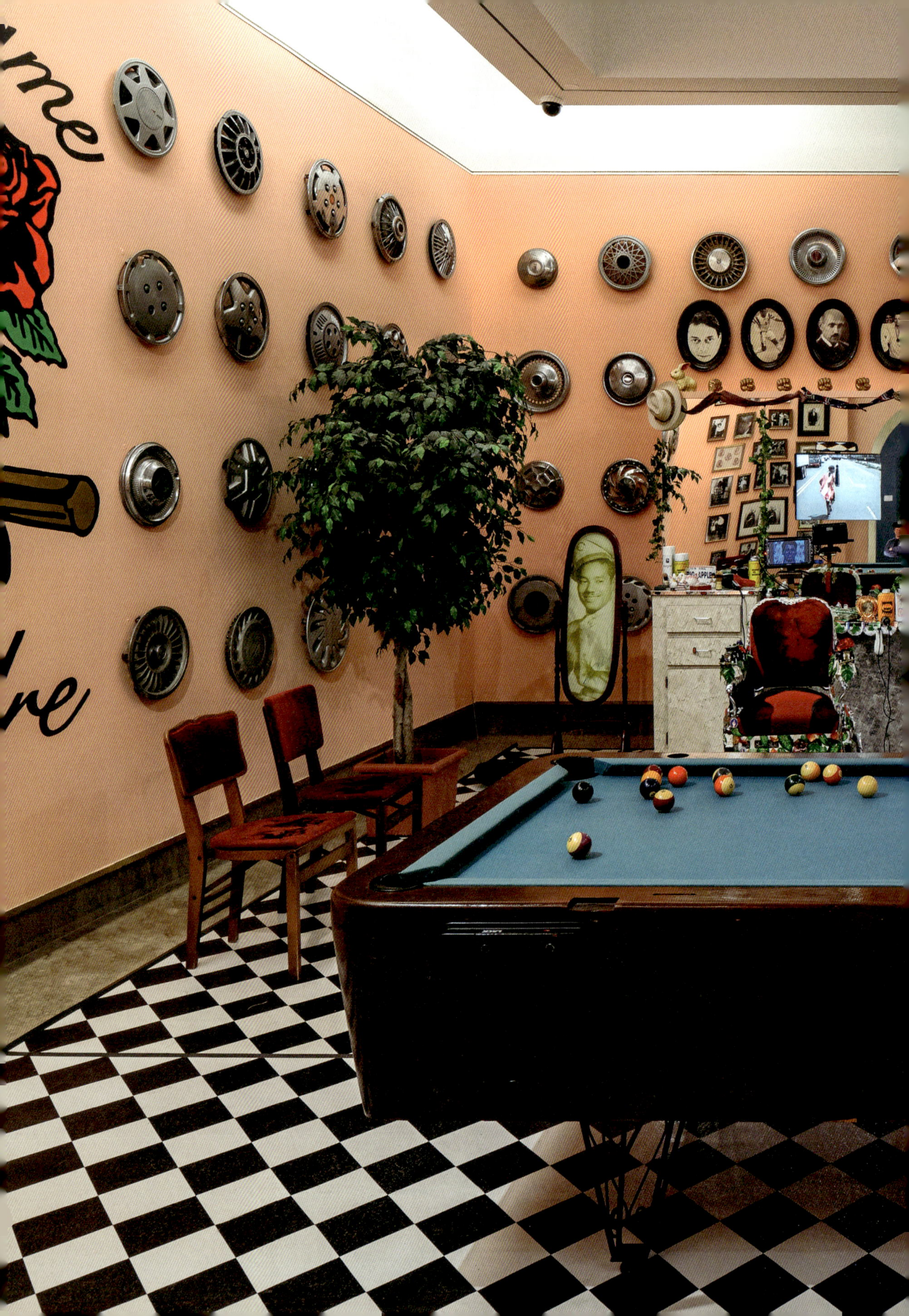

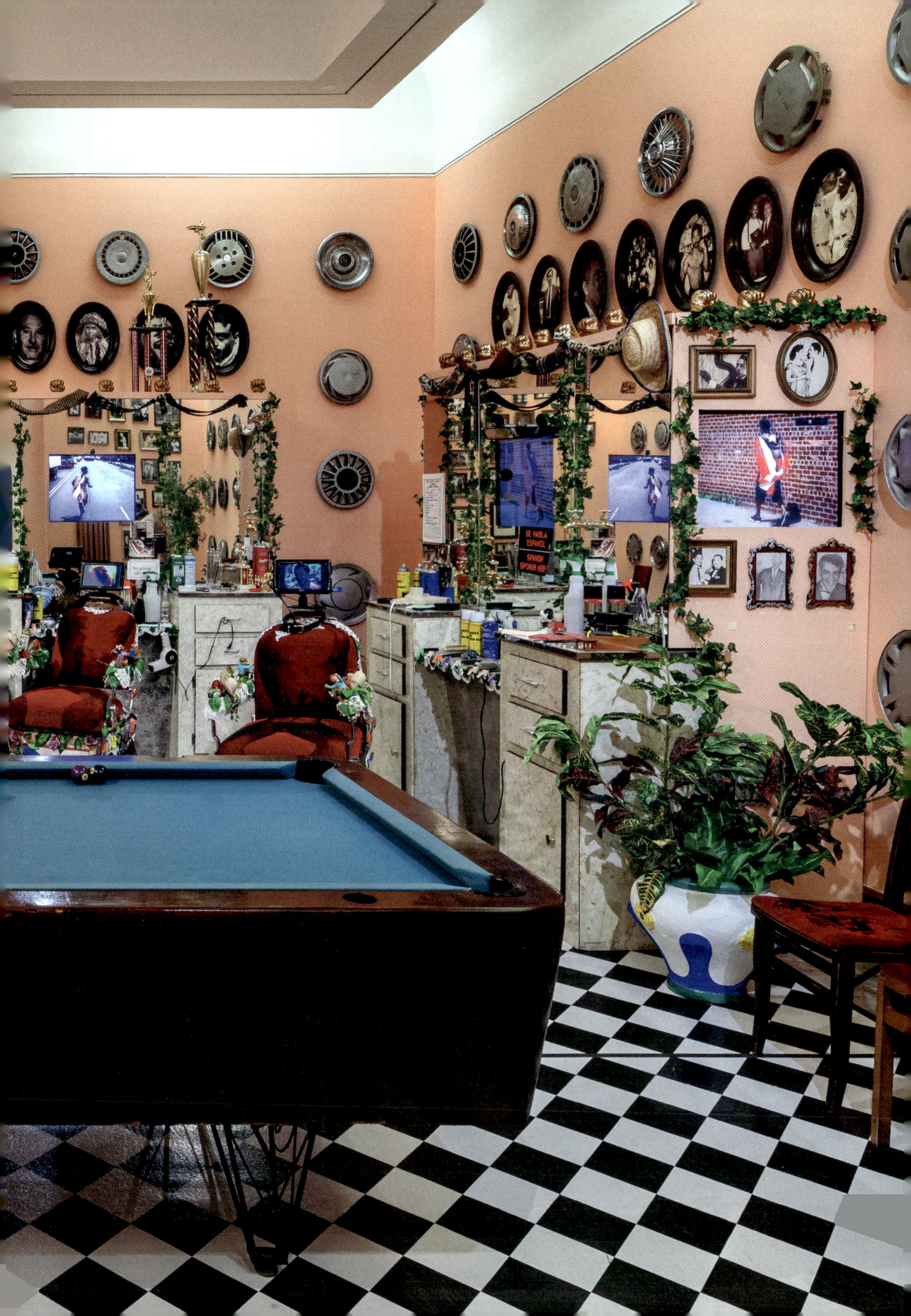
SE HABLA ESPANOL
SPANISH SPOKEN HERE

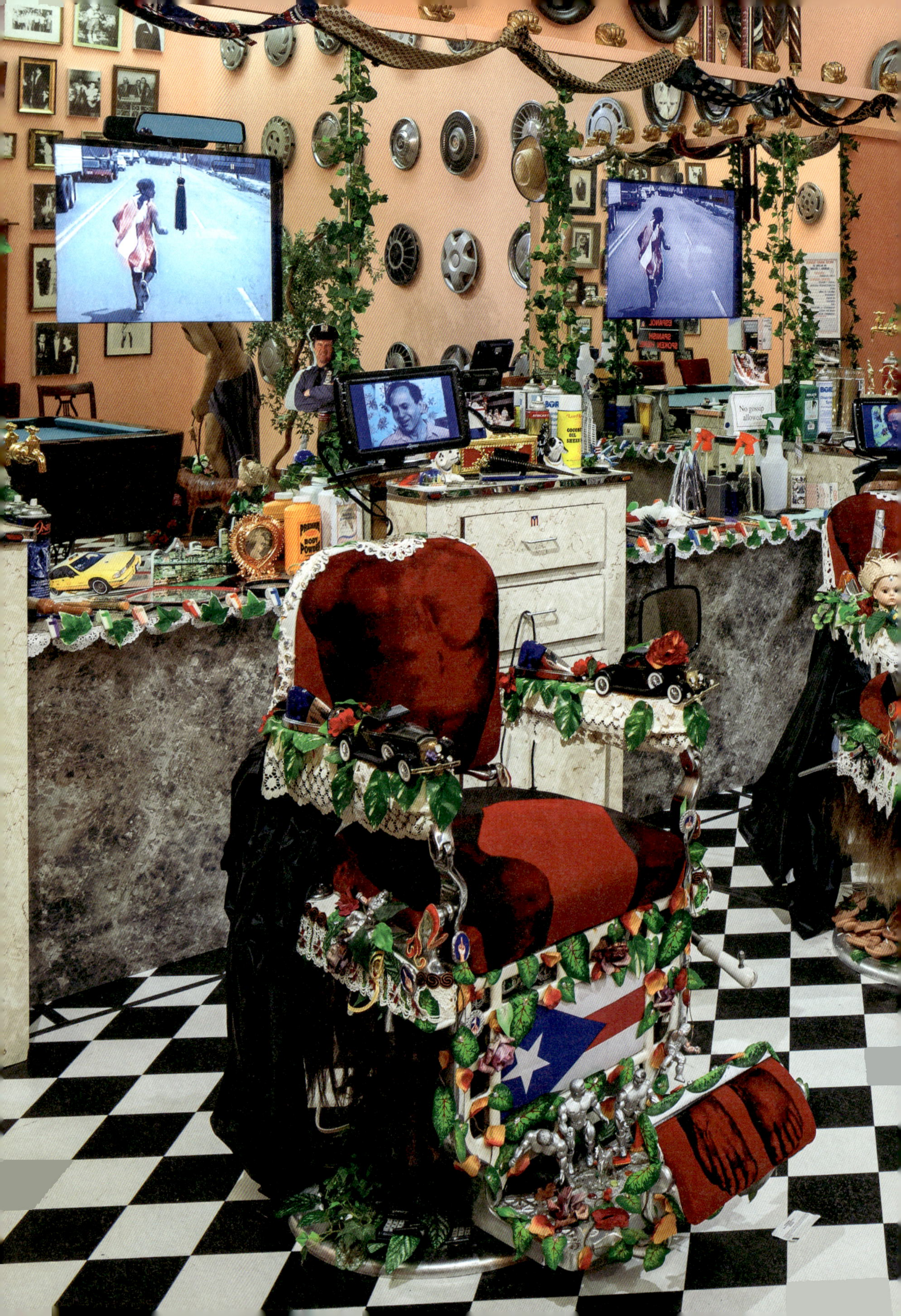
No gossip
allowed

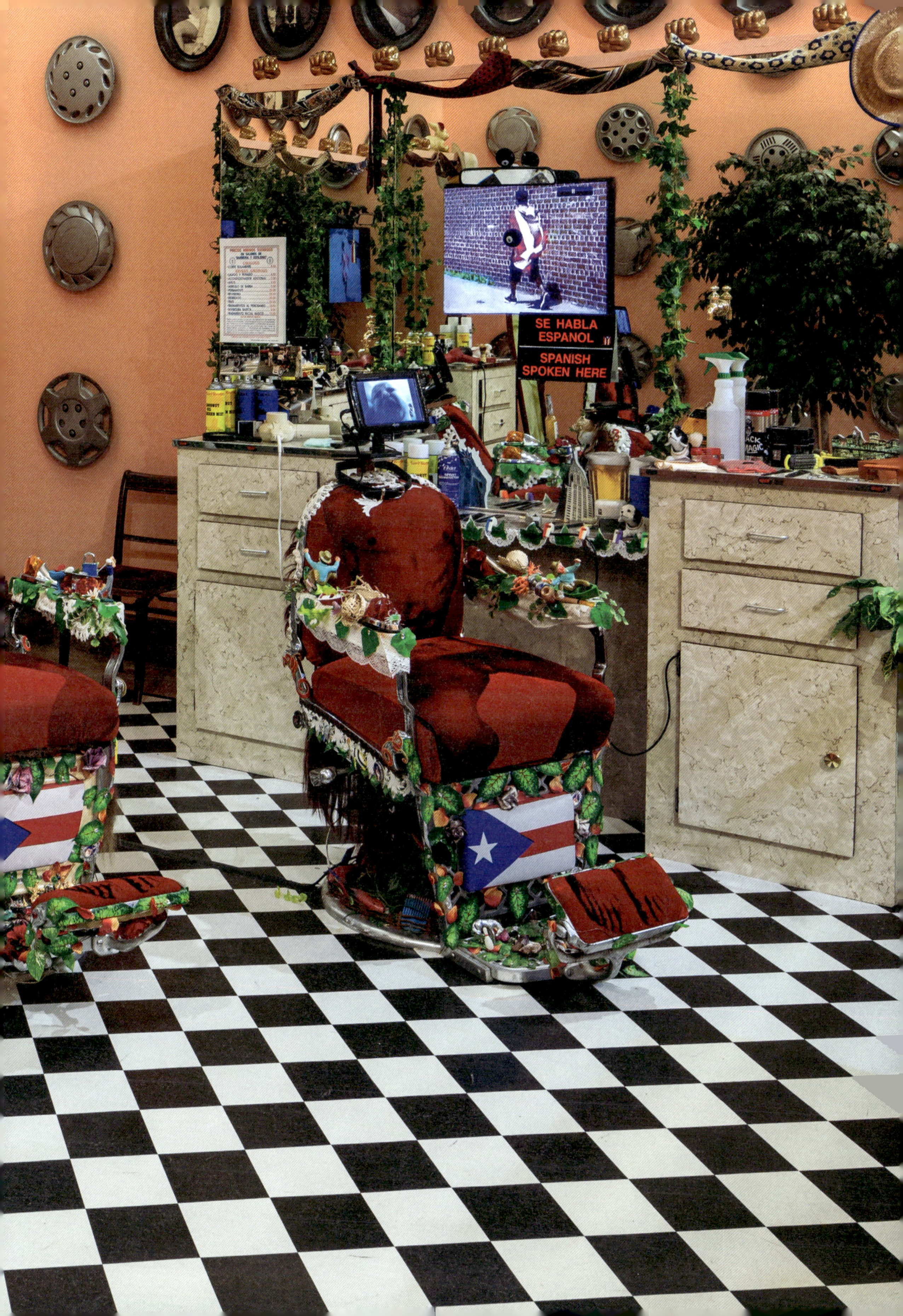
SE HABLA
ESPANOL
SPANISH
SPOKEN HERE

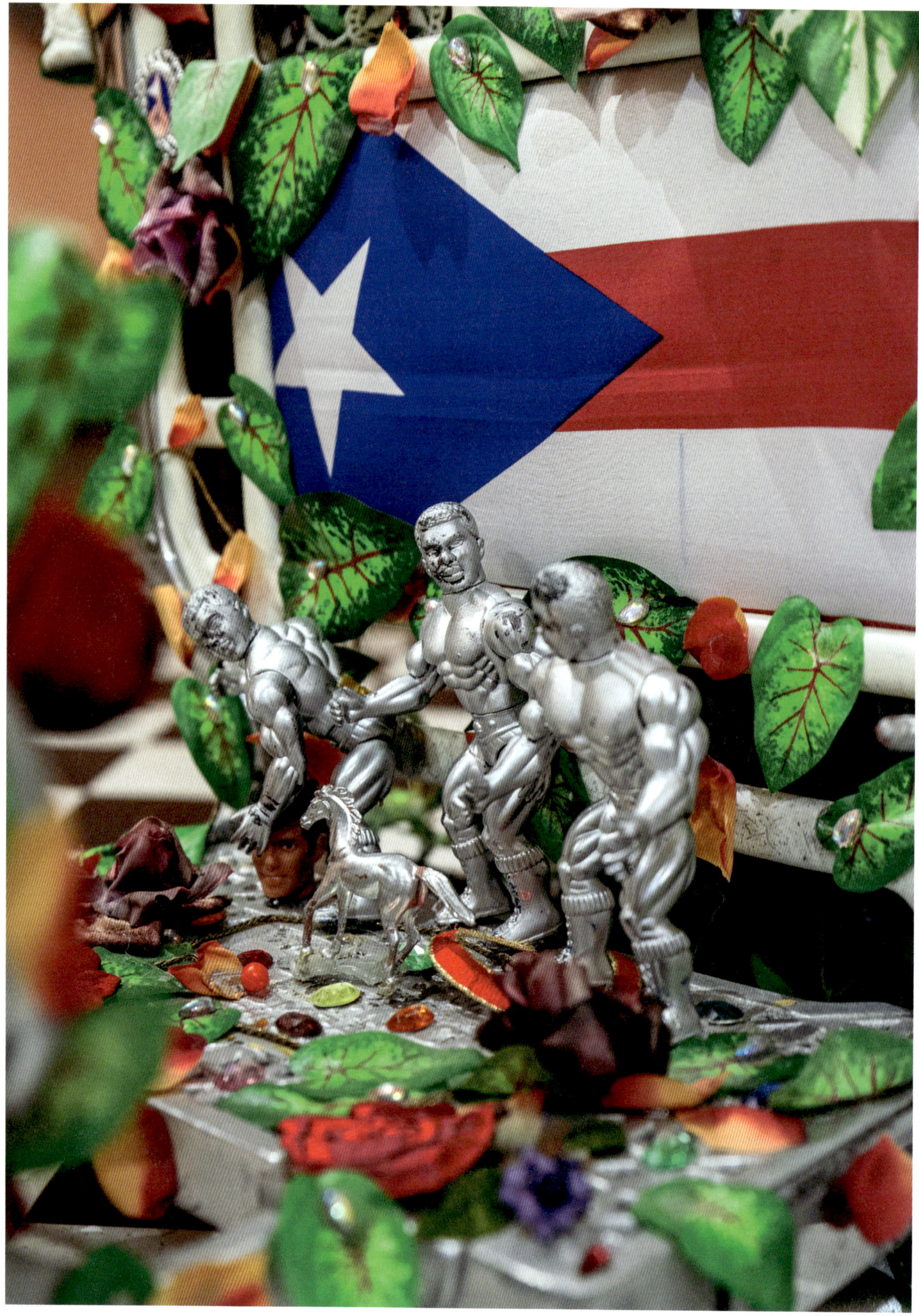

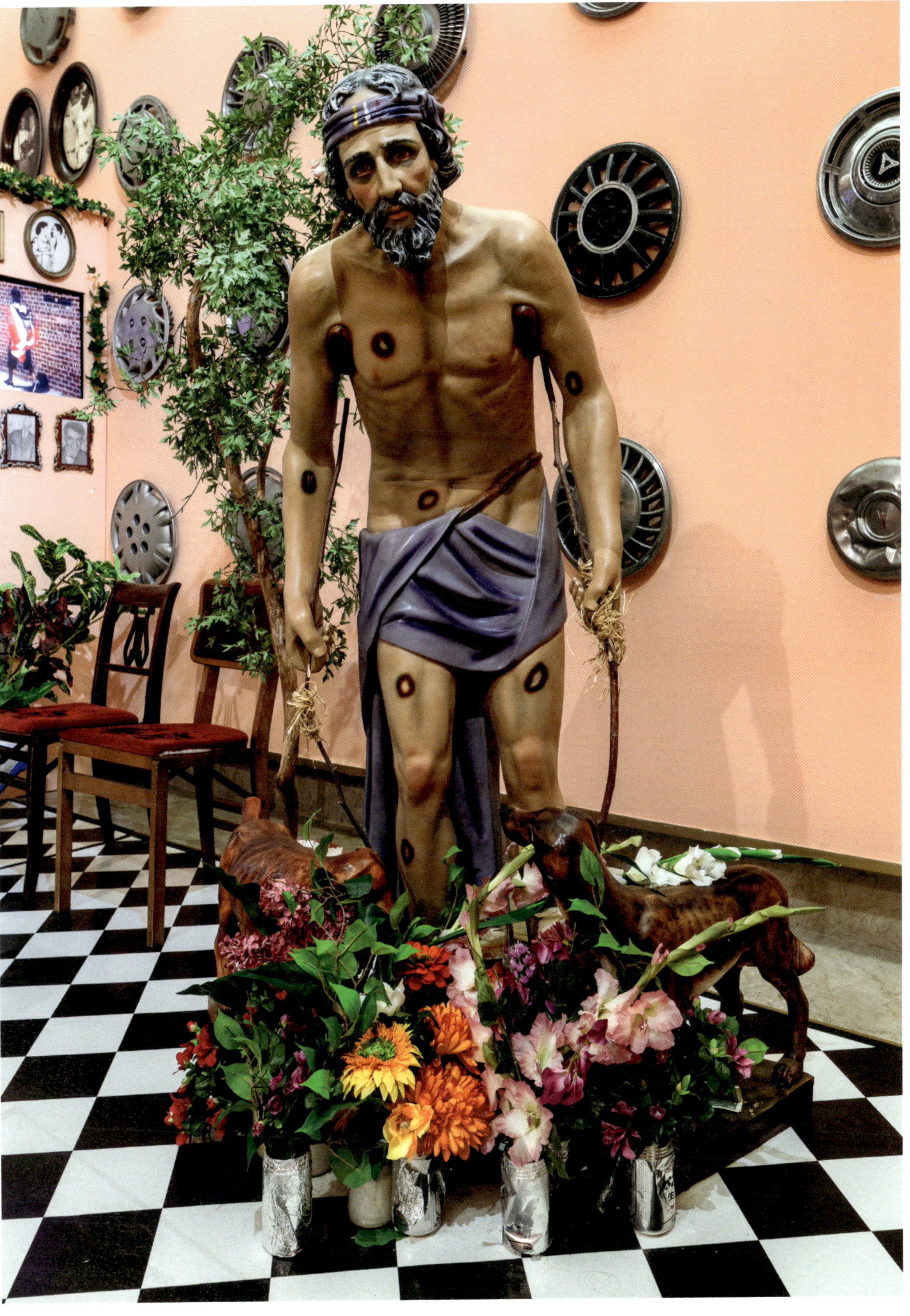

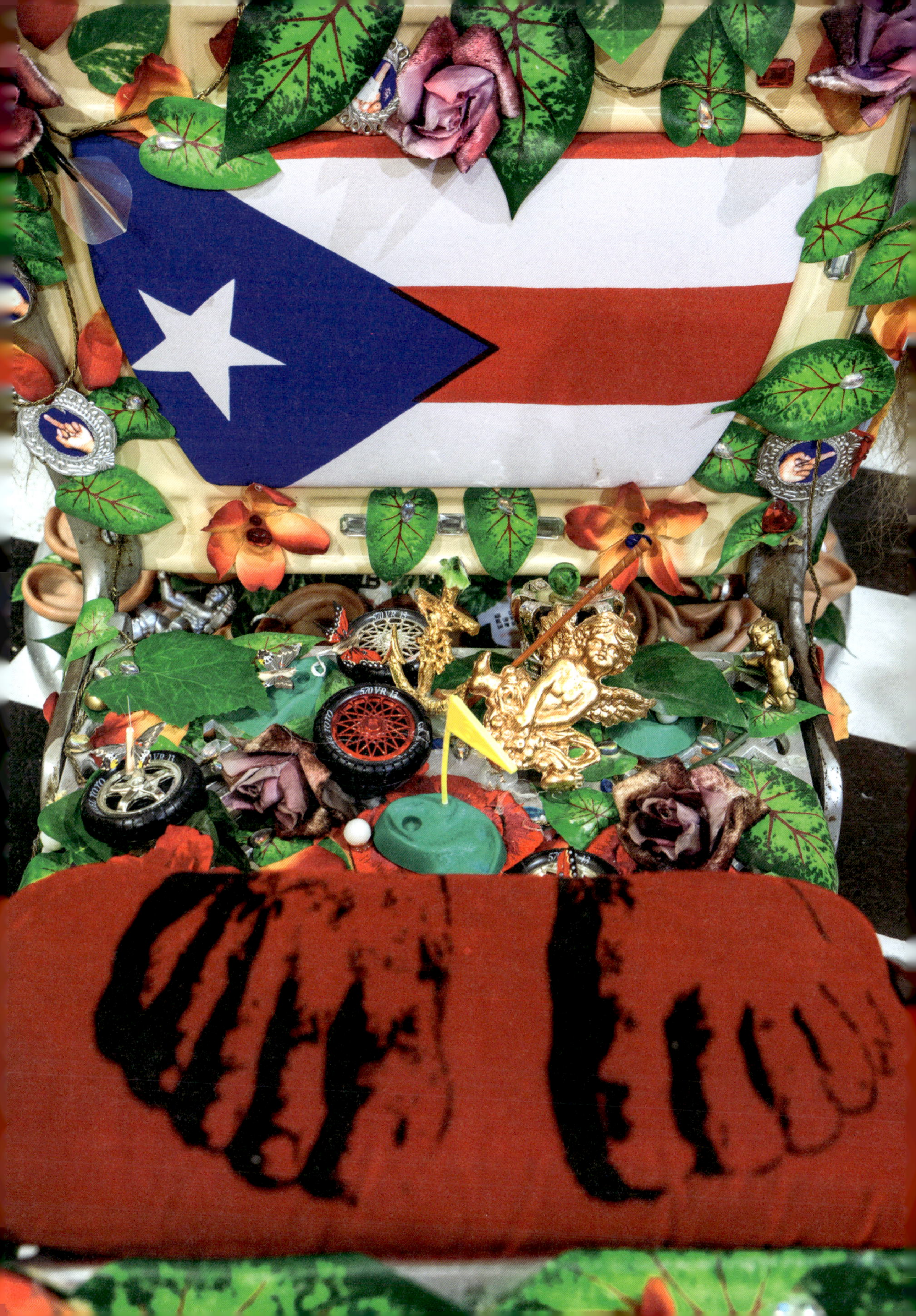

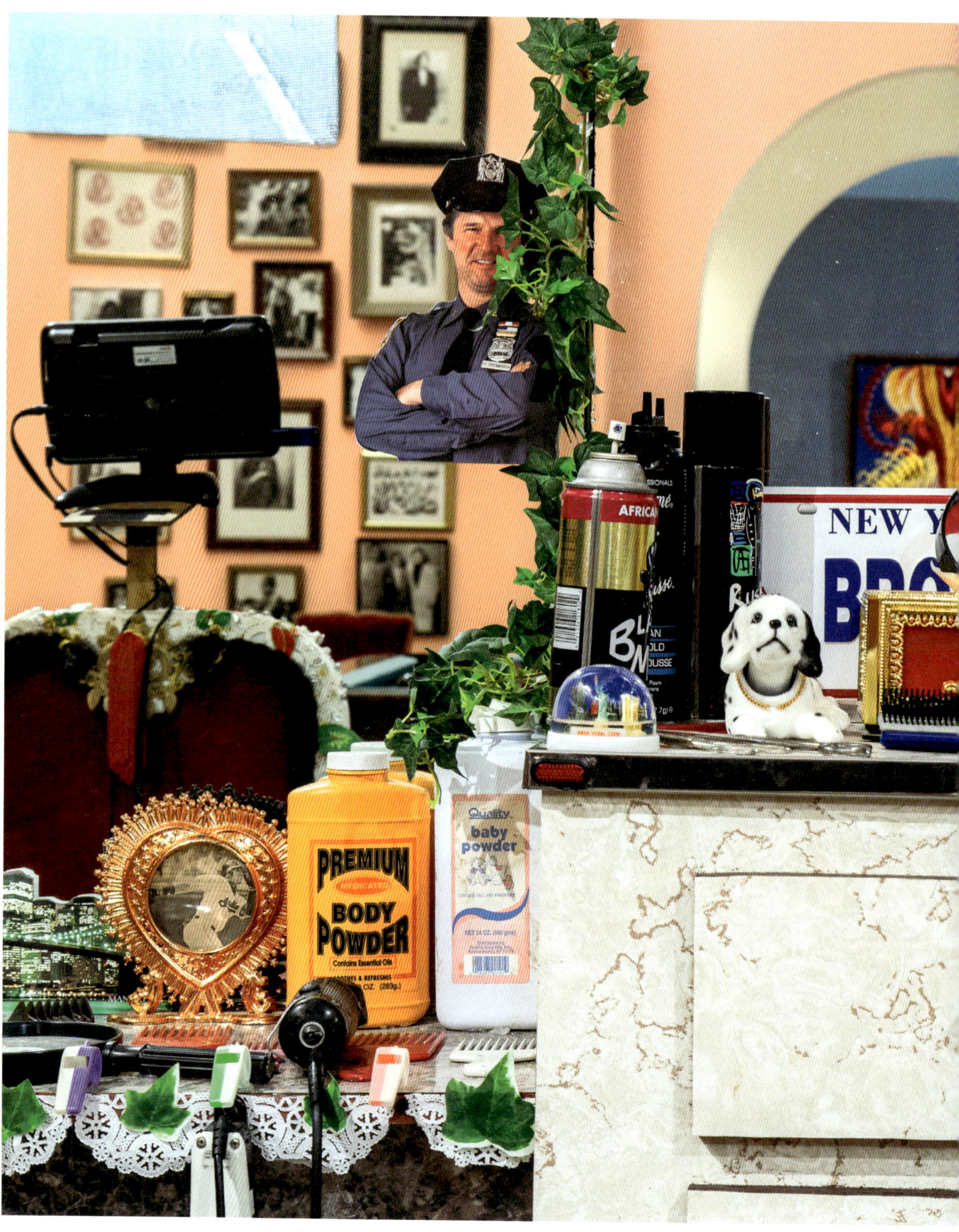
PREMIUM
BODY
POWDER
Contains Essential Oils
Quality
baby
powder

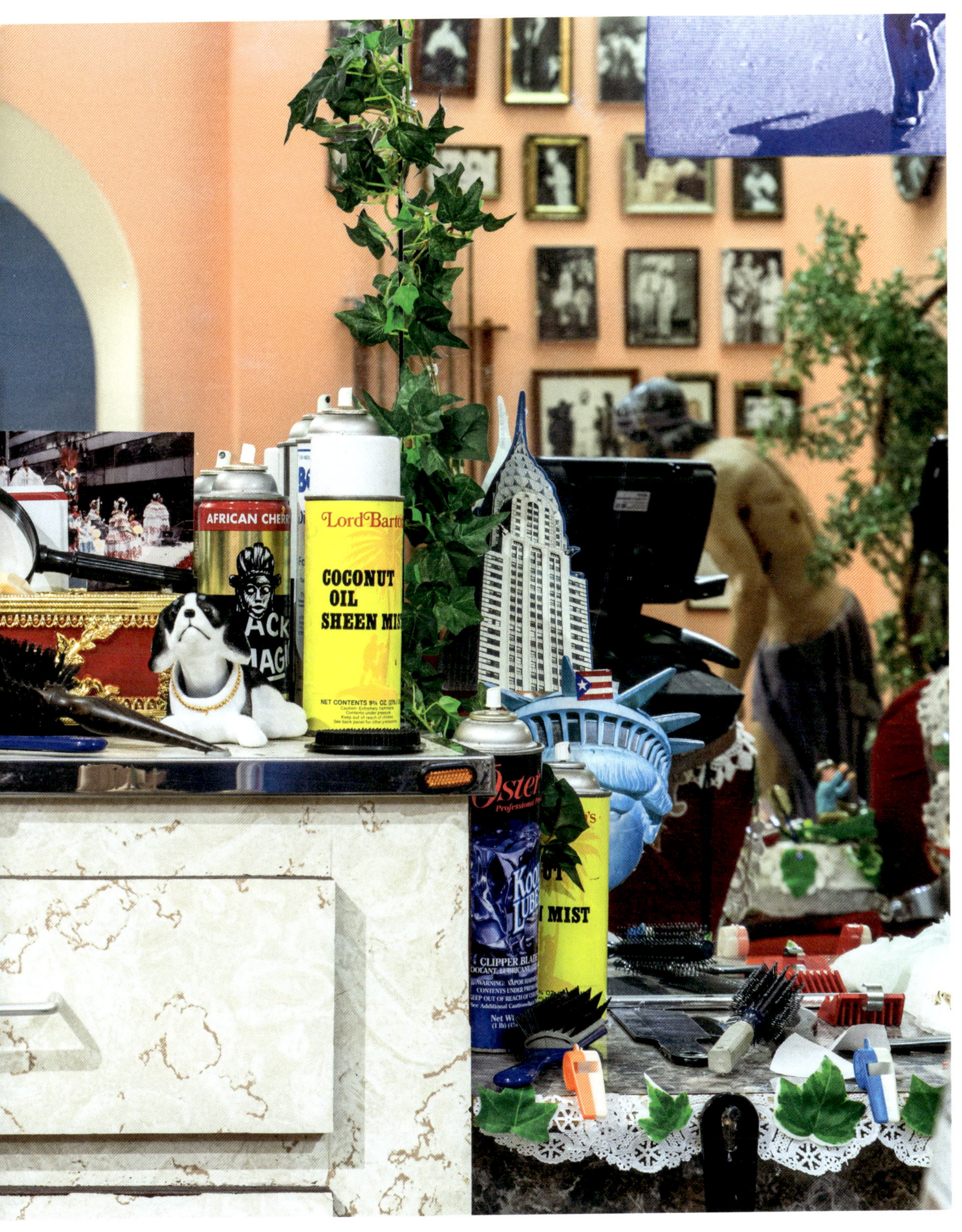

AFRICAN CHERR
Lord Barto
COCONUT
OIL
SHEEN MIS
MIST
CLIPPER BLAD

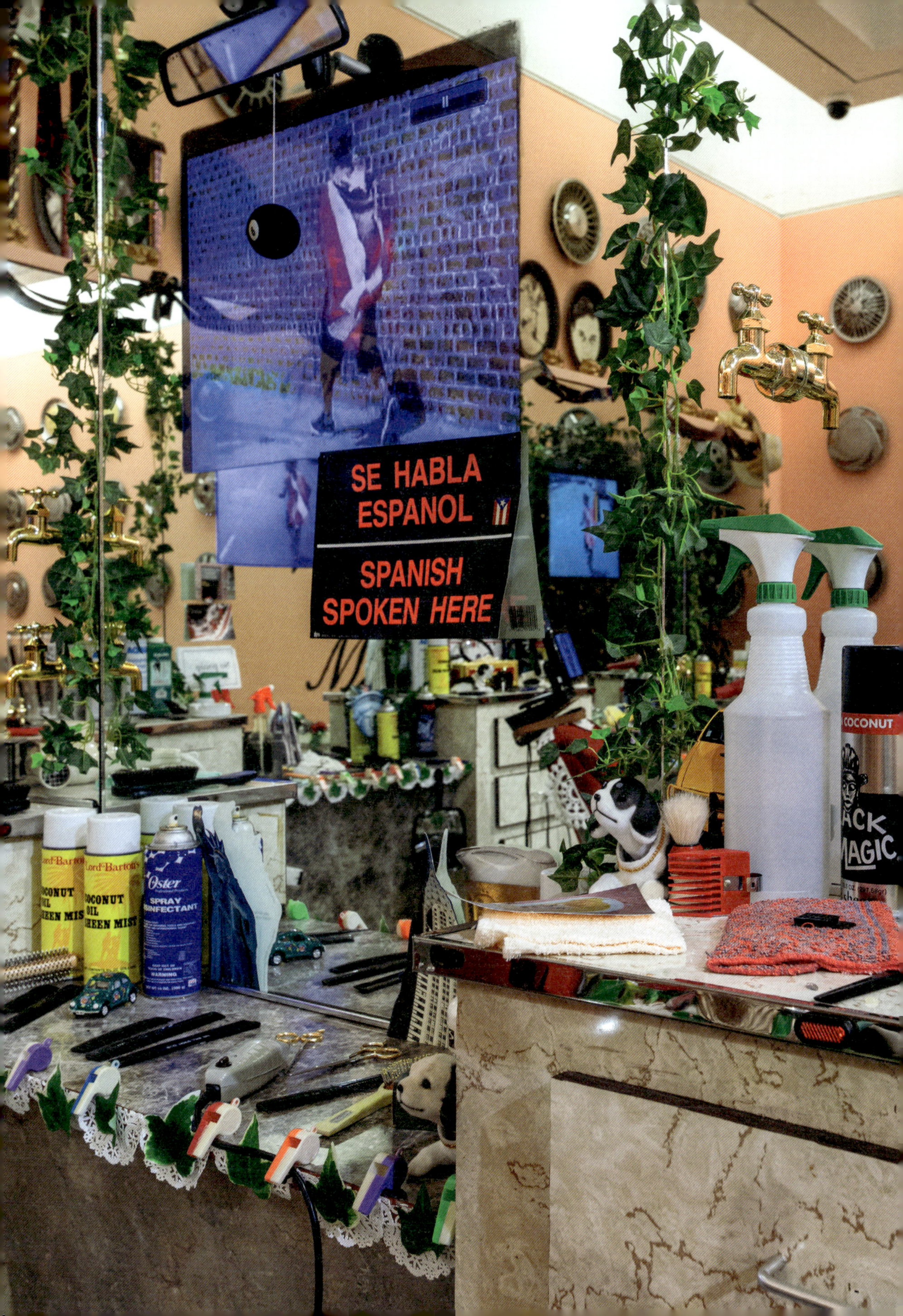
SE HABLA
ESPANOL
SPANISH
SPOKEN HERE

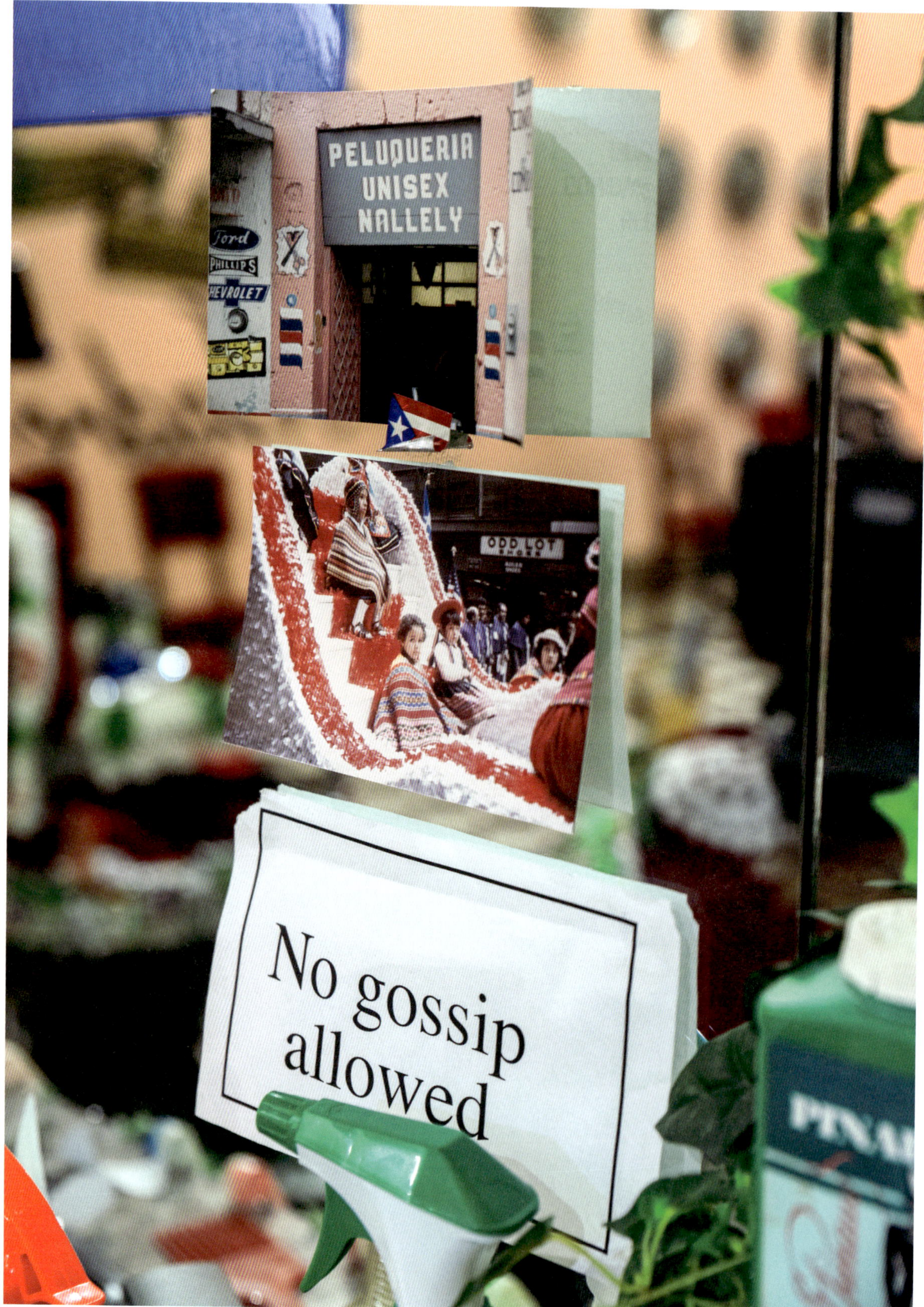
PELUQUERIA
UNISEX
NALLELY
Ford
PHILLIPS
ODD LOT
No gossip
allowed

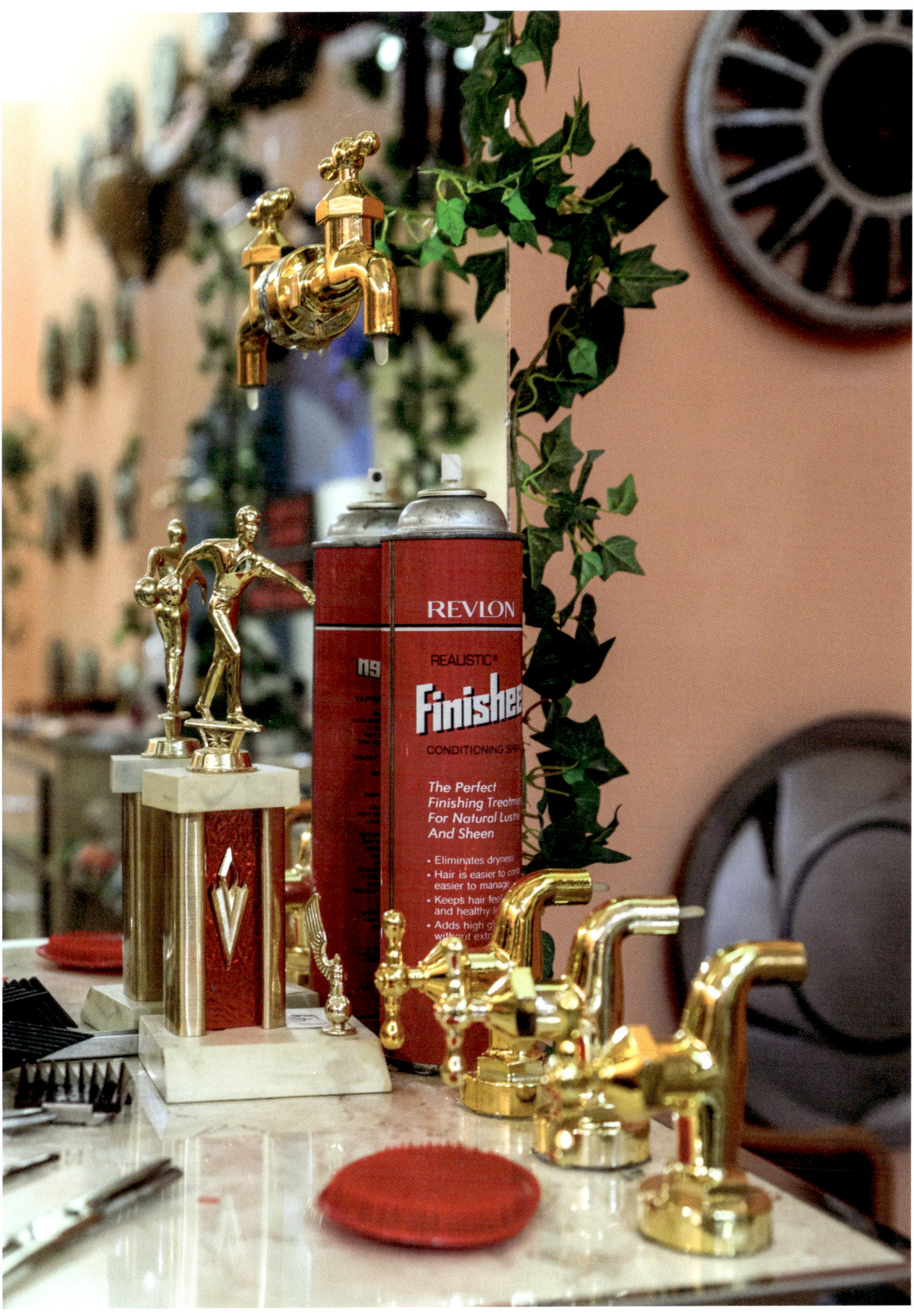
REVLON
REALISTIC®
The Perfect
And Sheen
• Eliminates dryness

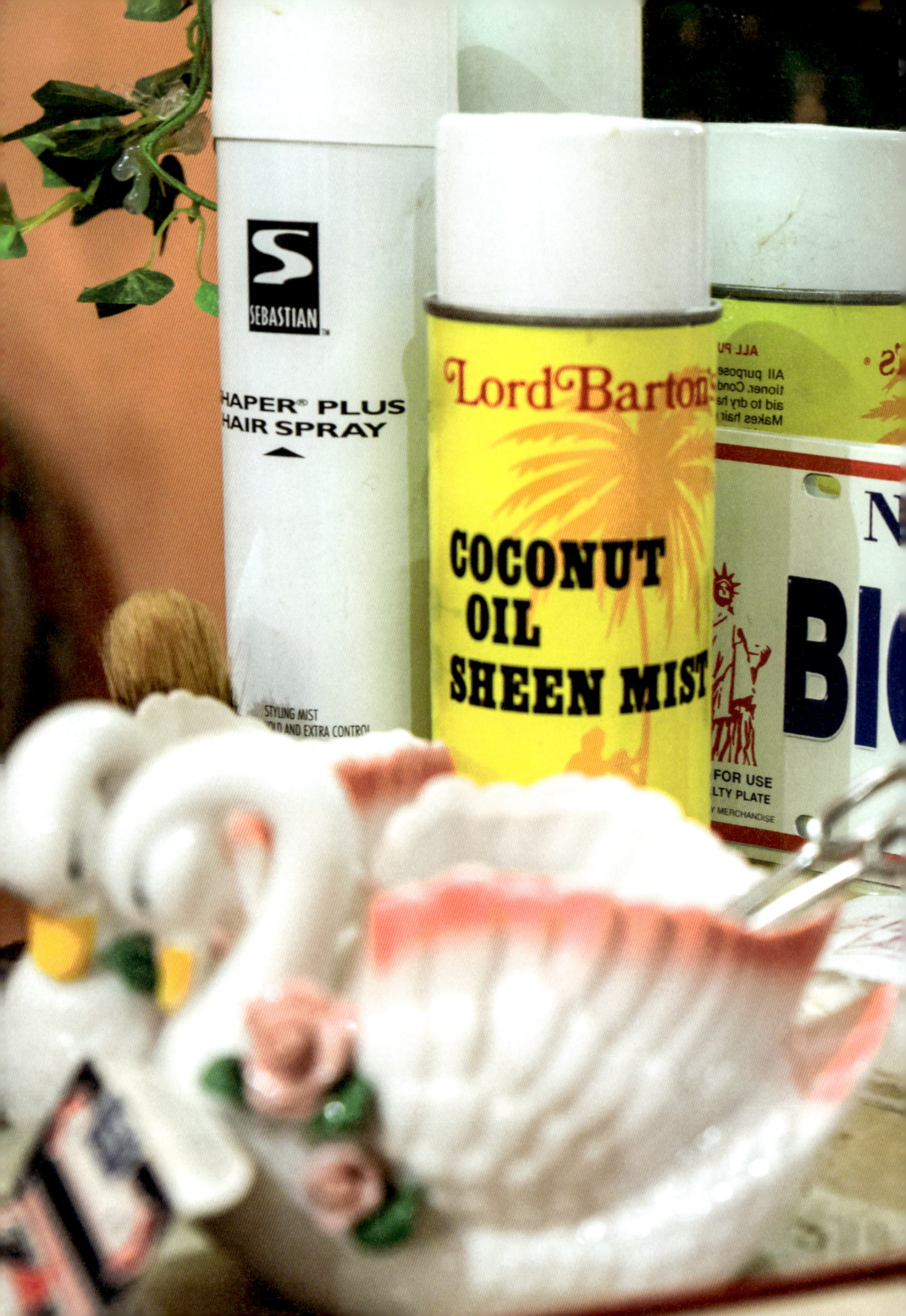
SEBASTIAN
HAPER® PLUS
HAIR SPRAY
STYLING MIST
Lord Barton's
COCONUT
OIL
SHEEN MIST
FOR USE
LTY PLATE

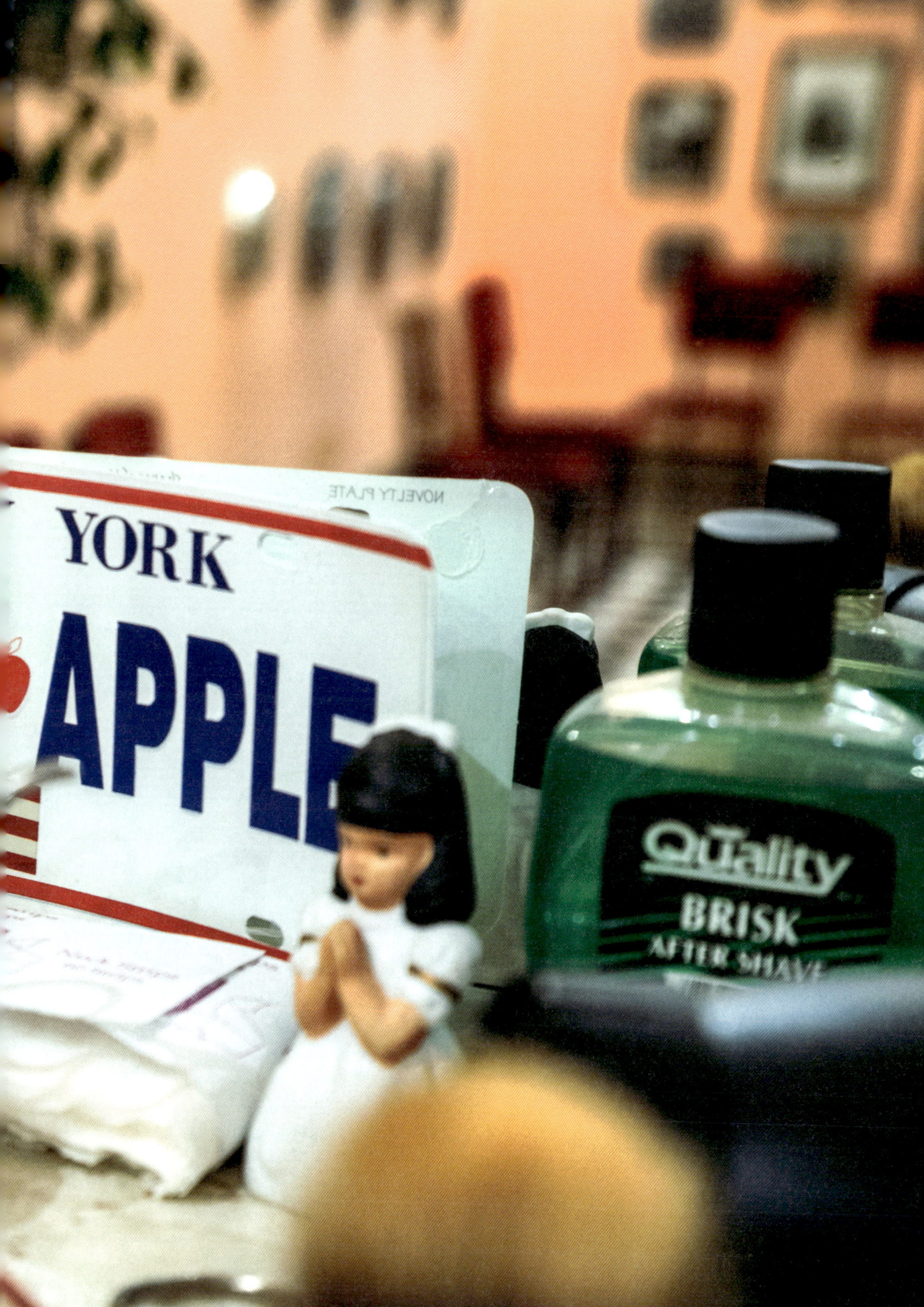

YORK
APPLE
NOVELTY PLATE
Quality
BRISK
AFTER SHAVE

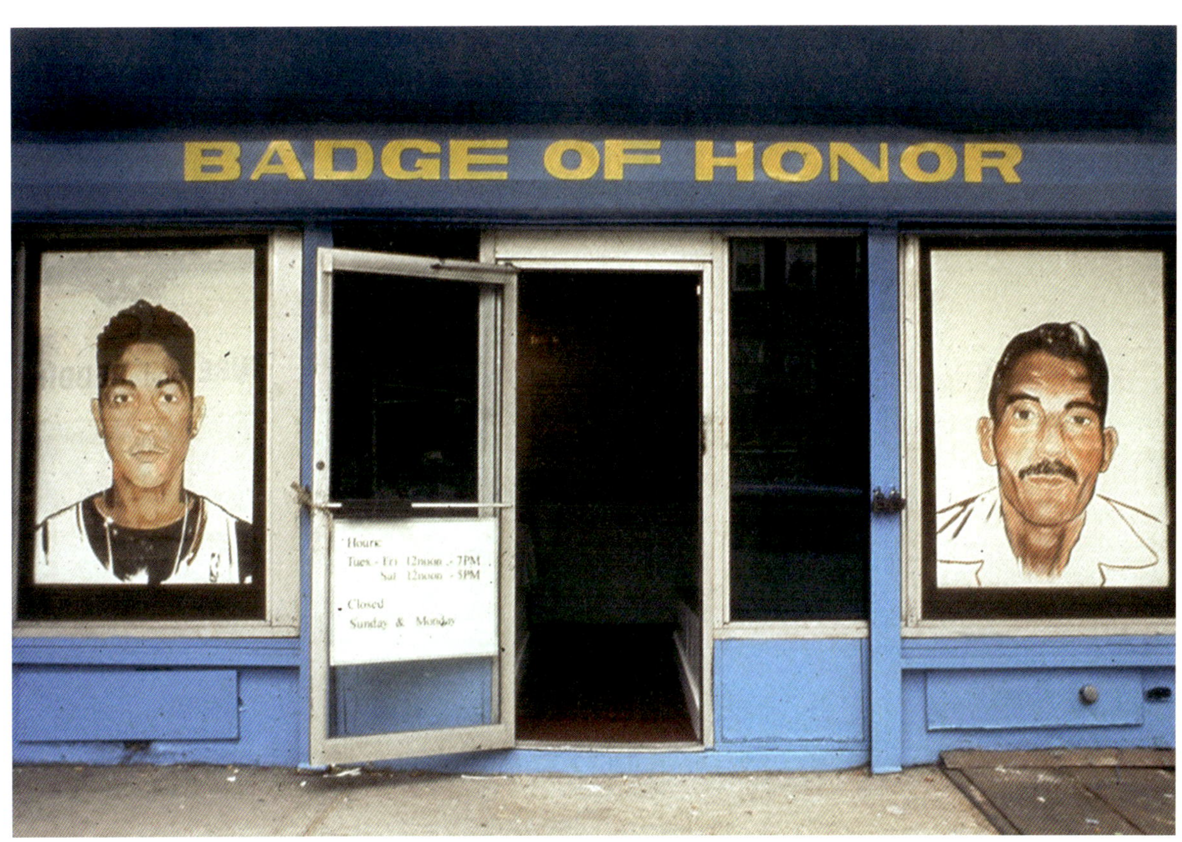
BADGE OF HONOR
Hours
Closed
Sunday & Monday

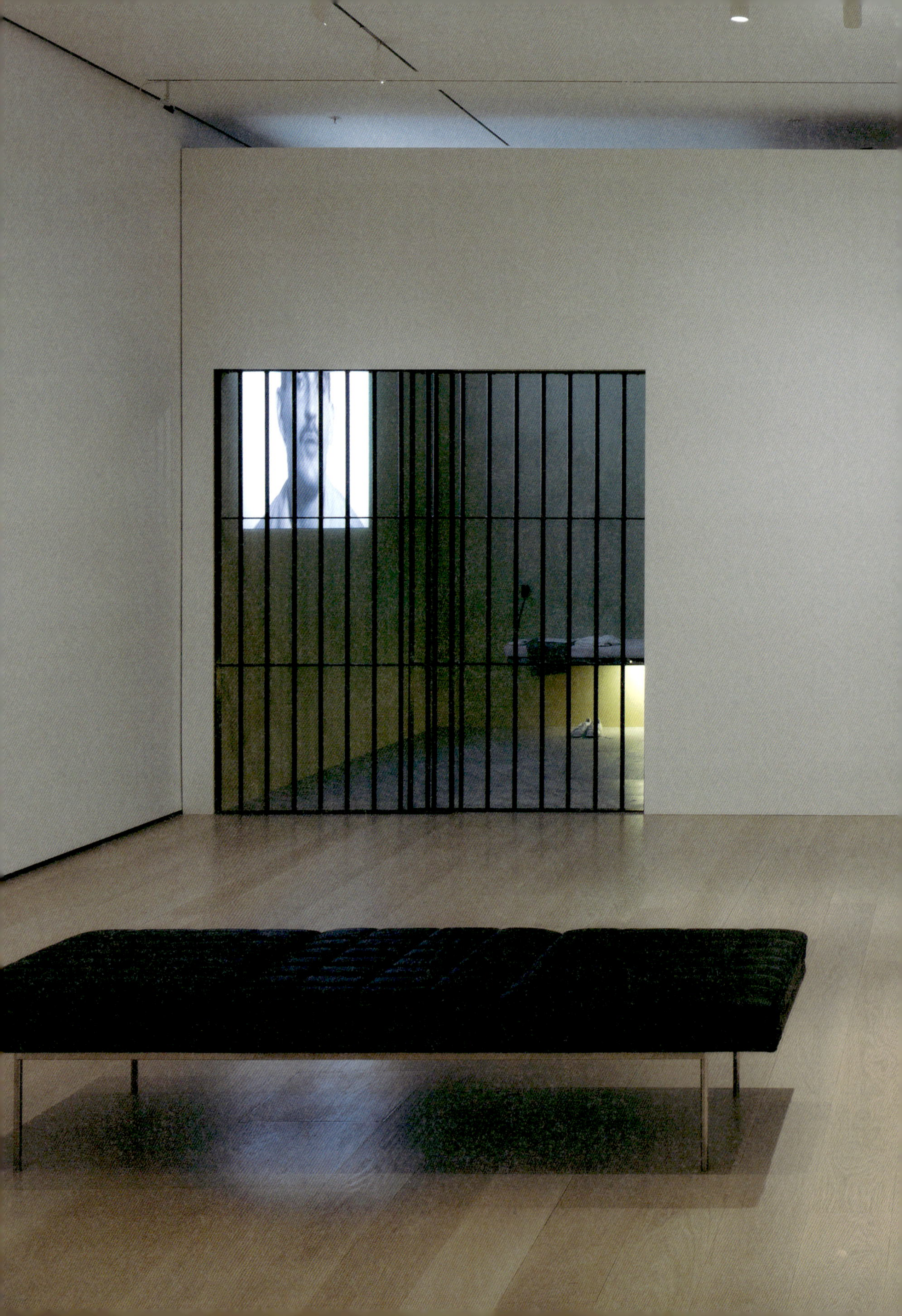

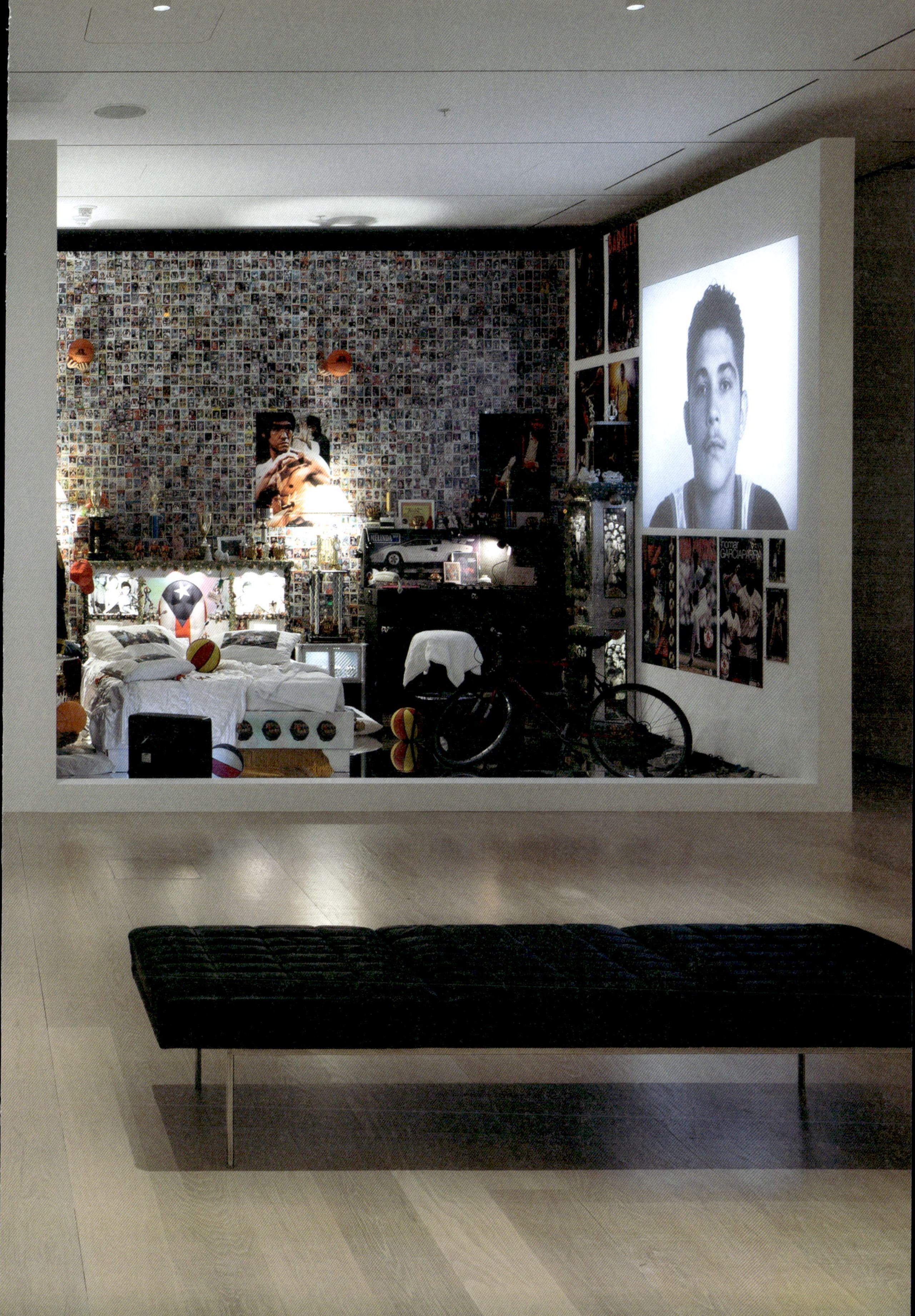
nomar
GARCIAPARRA

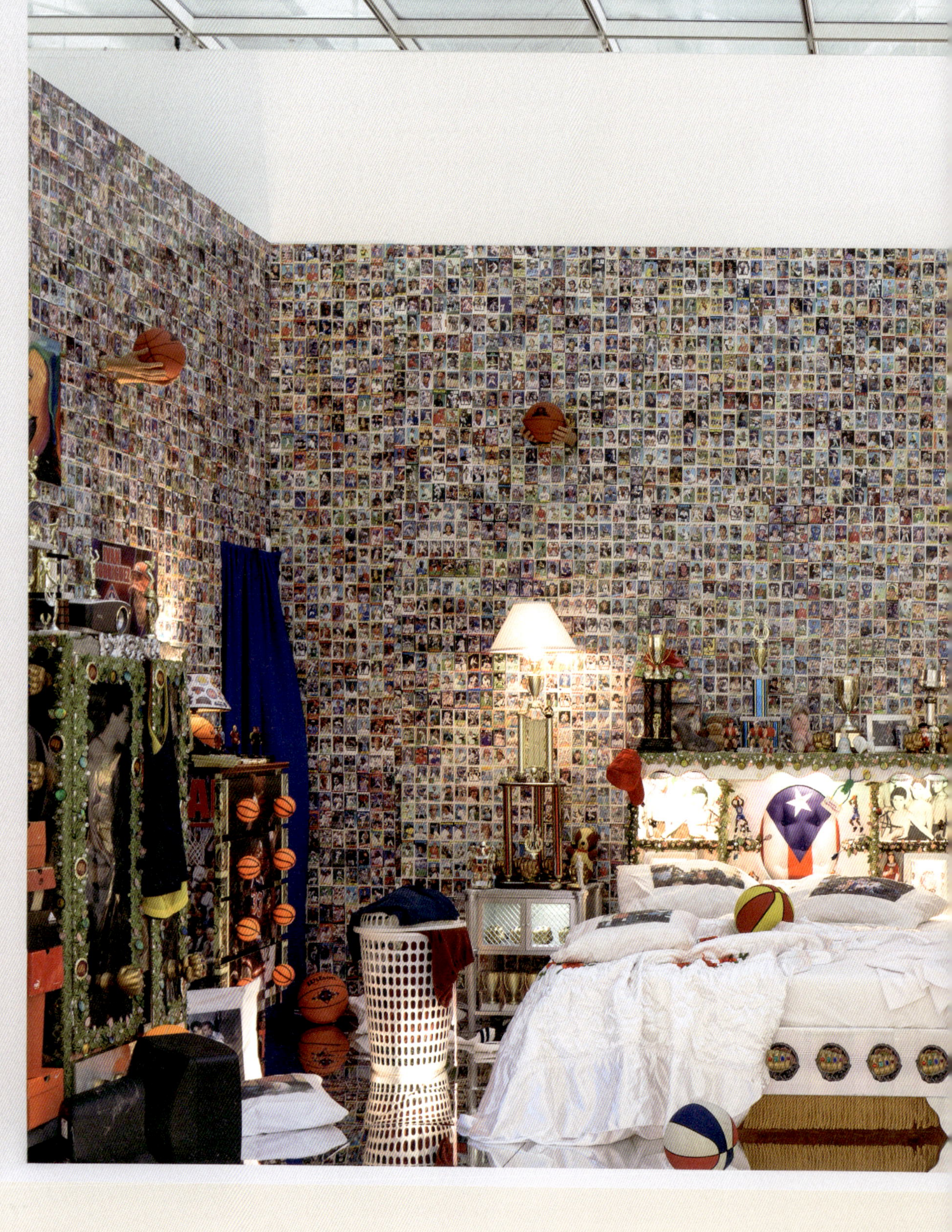

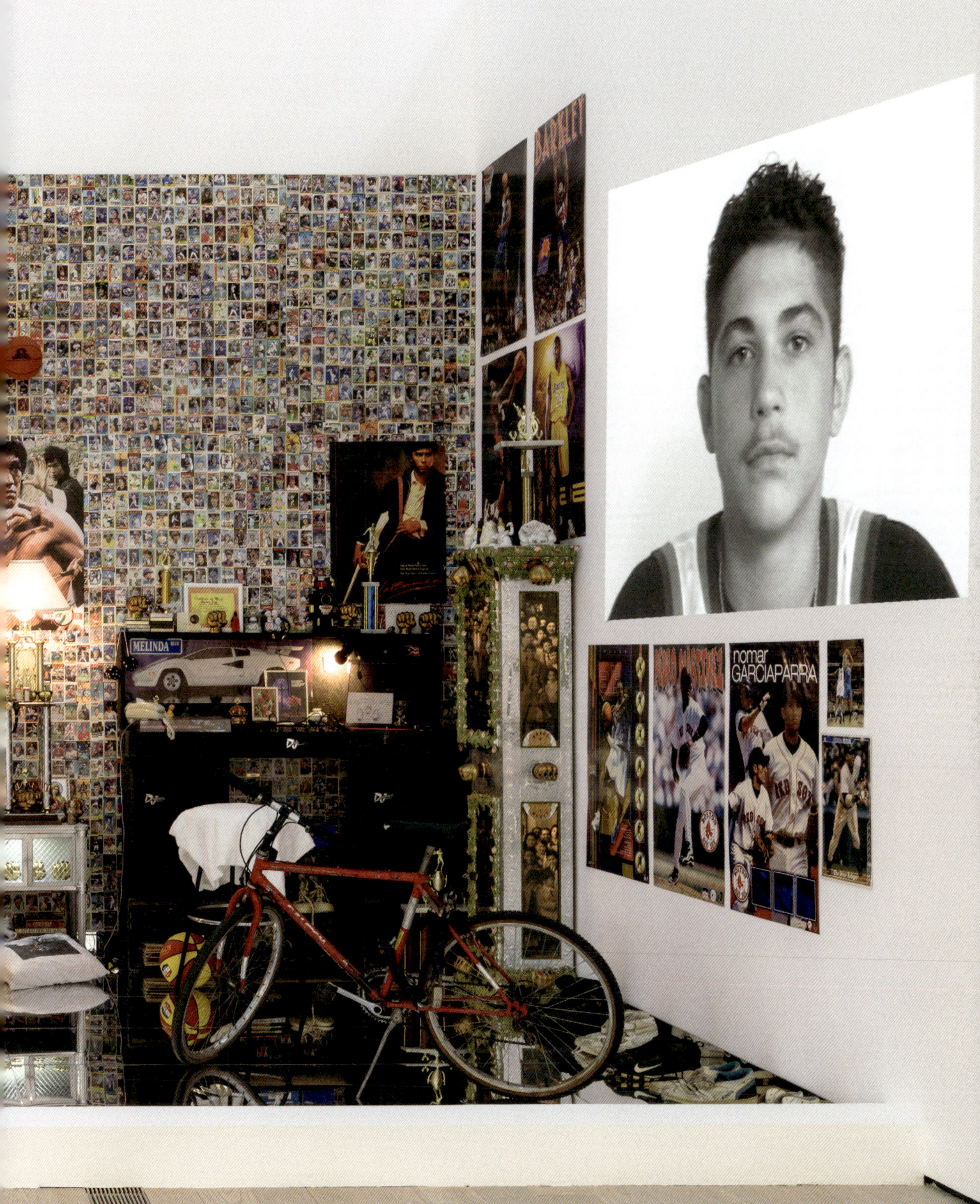
BARKLEY
MELINDA
nomar
GARCIAPARRA

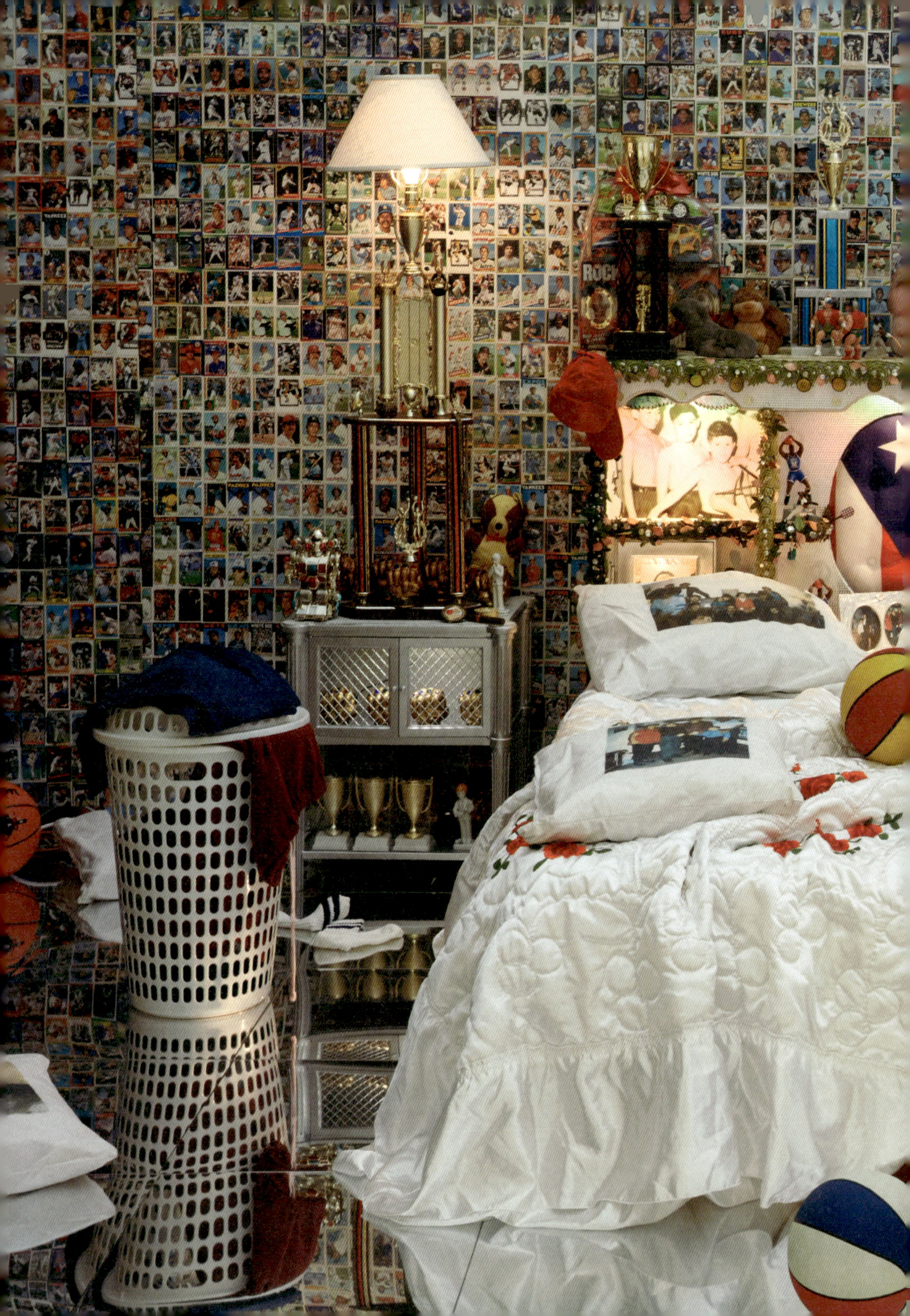

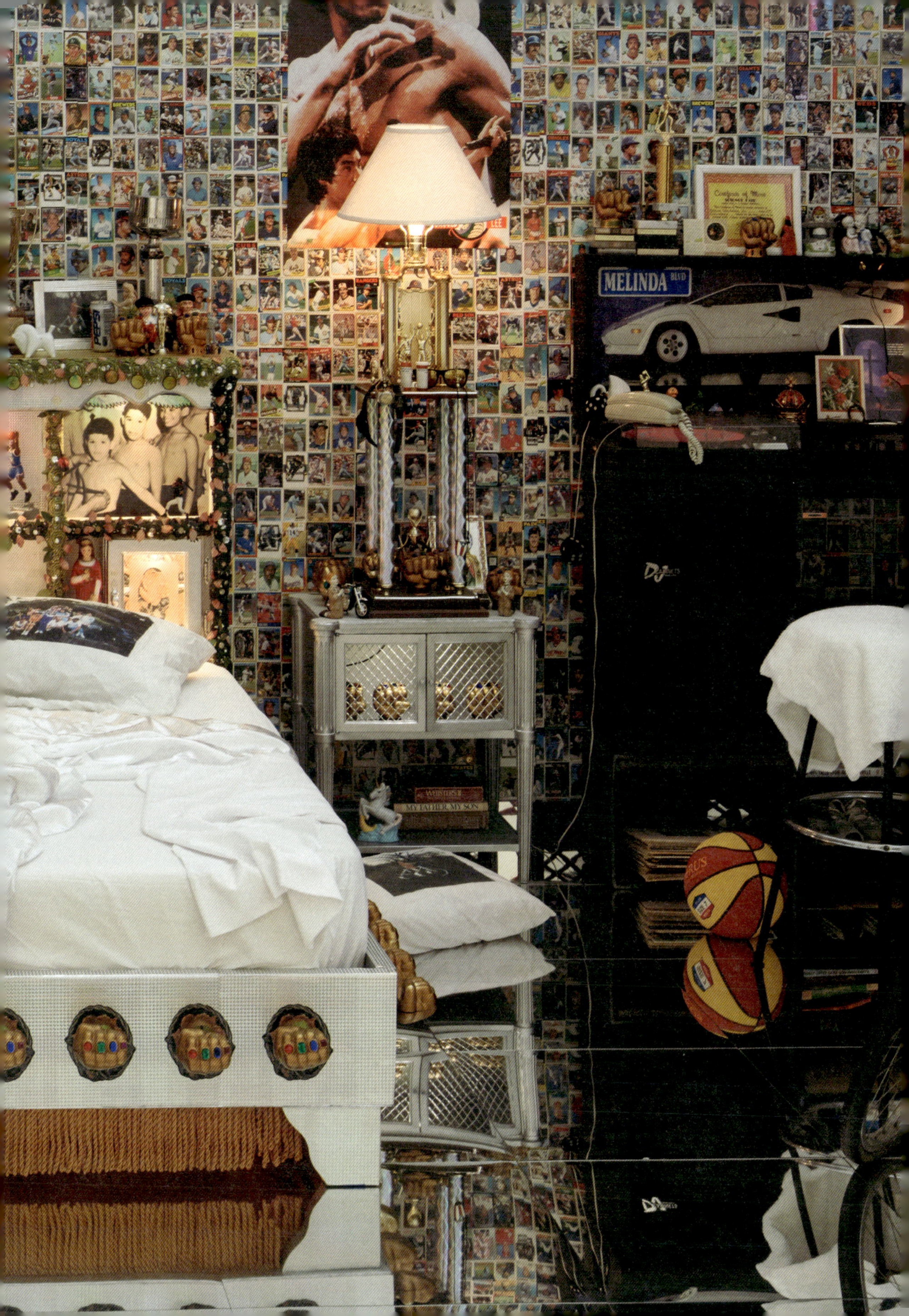
MELINDA
MY FATHER, MY SON

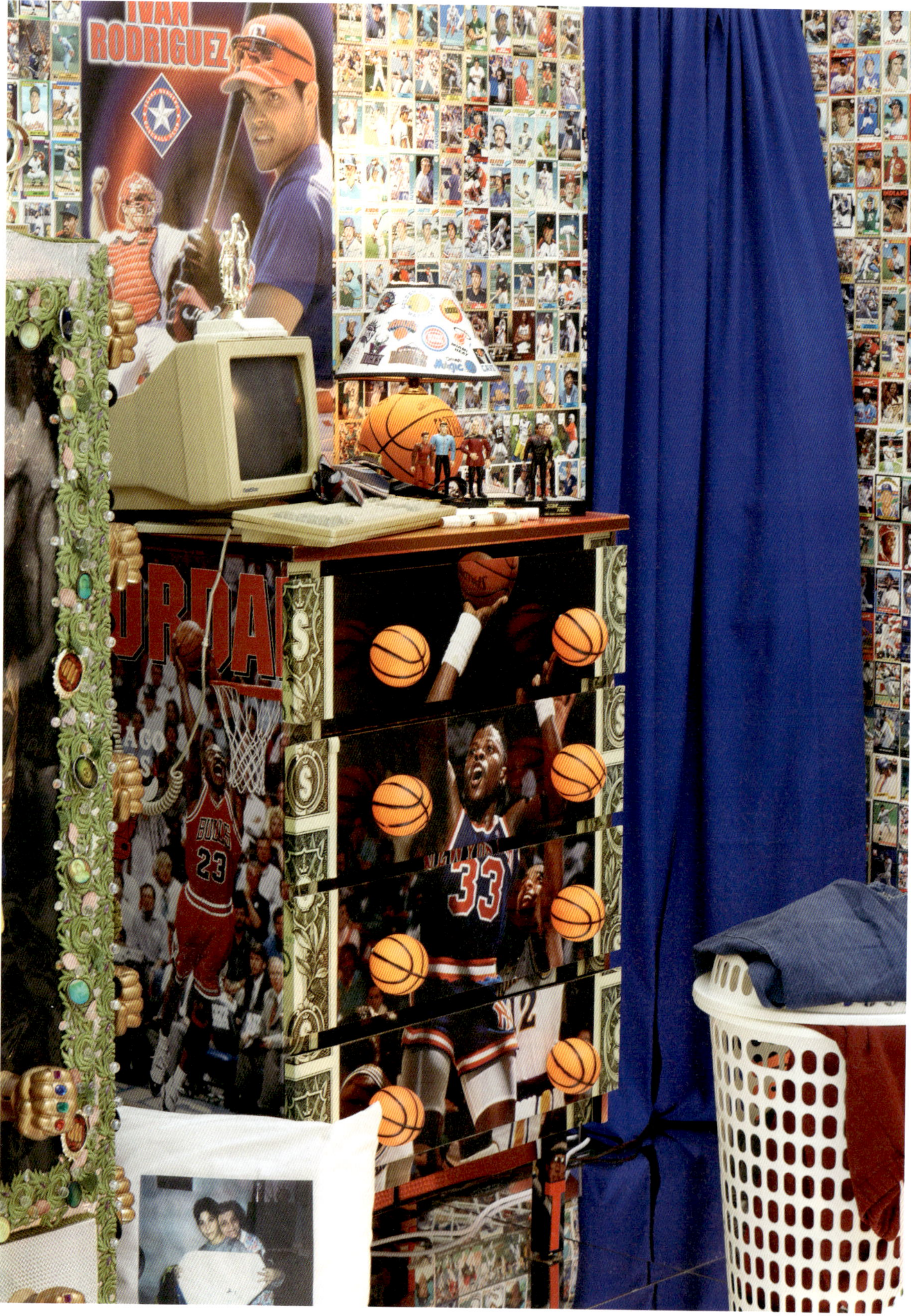
RODRIGUEZ
23
33

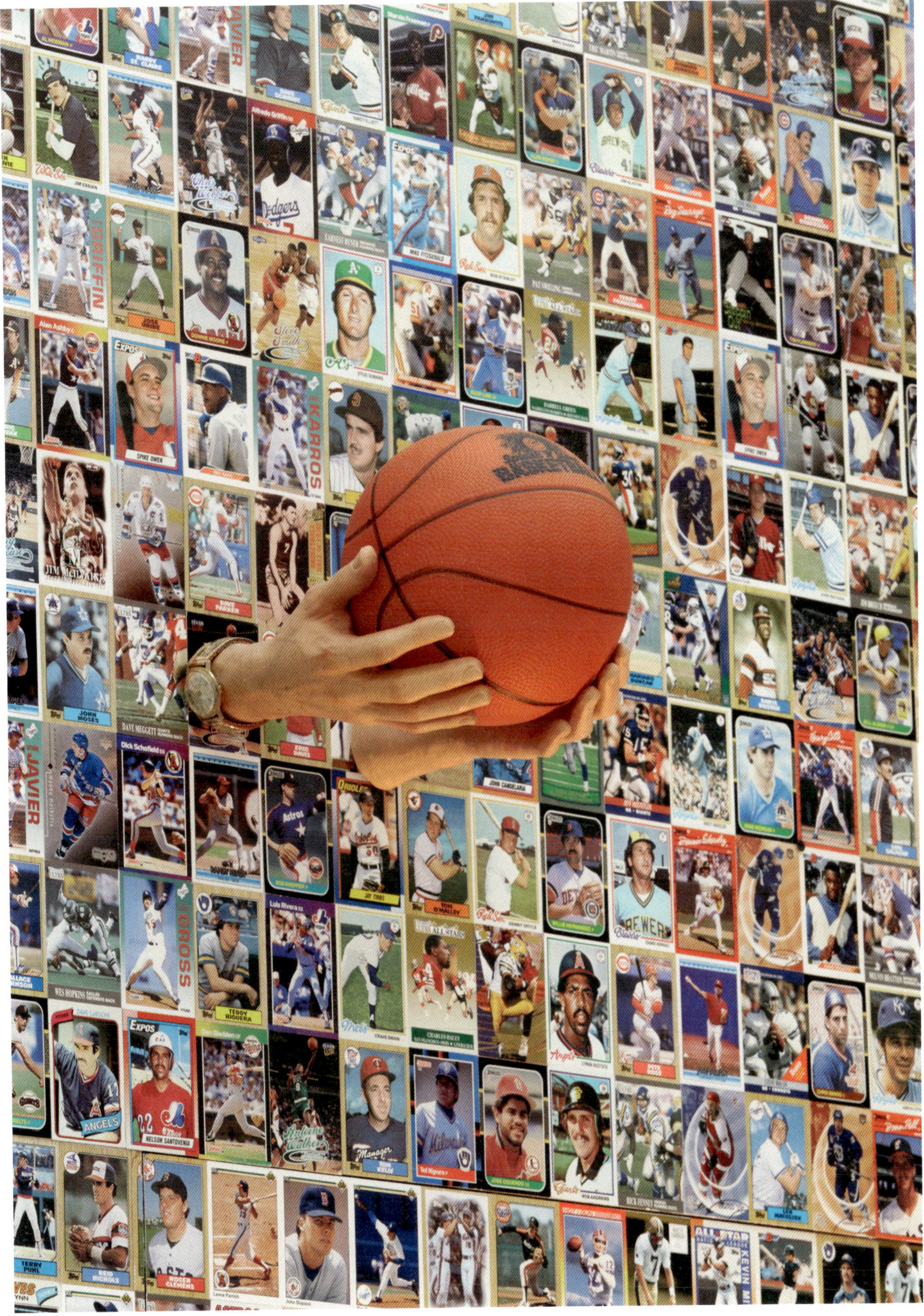
GRIFFIN
Alan Ashby
EXPOS
SPIKE OWEN
KARROS
Dodgers
JOHN MOSES
DAVE MEGGETT
JAVIER
Dick Schofield
Astros
JAY TIBBS
Luis Rivera
GROSS
TEDDY HIGUERA
WES HOPKINS
CHARLES HALEY
ANGELS
NELSON SANTOVENIA
ROGER CLEMENS
TERRY PUHL
KEVIN MI

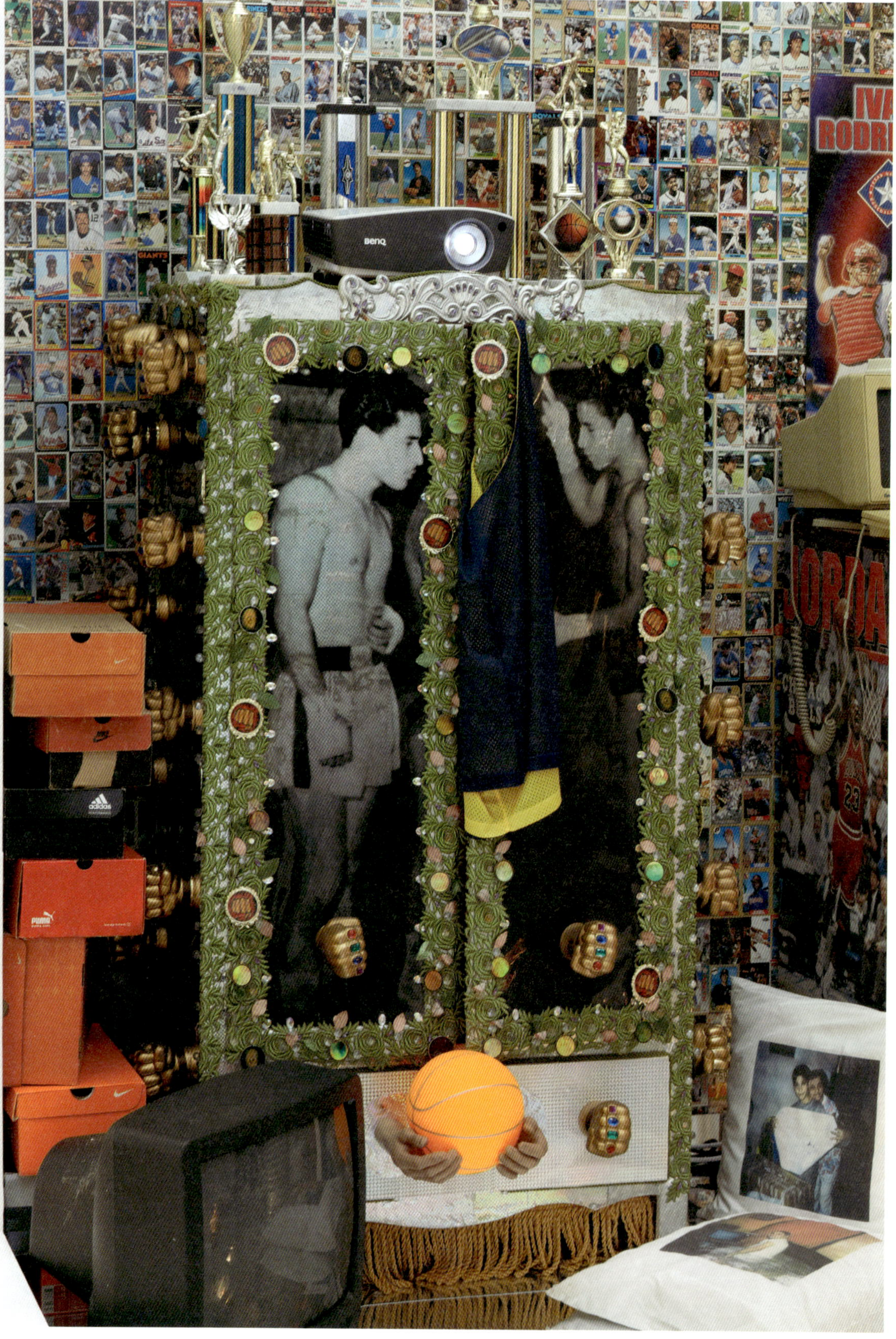
BenQ
adidas

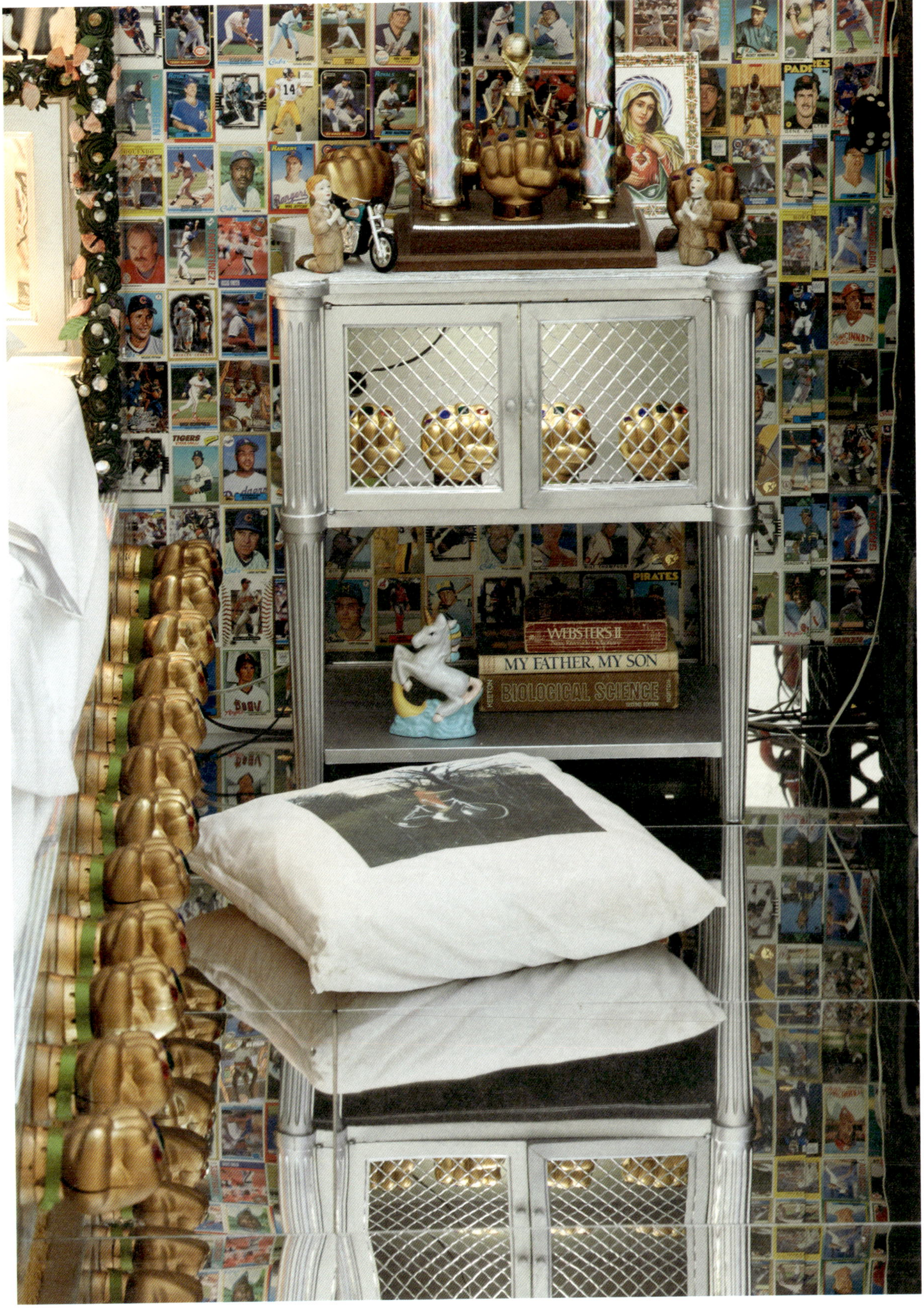
PADRES
TIGERS
PIRATES
WEBSTER'S II
MY FATHER, MY SON
BIOLOGICAL SCIENCE

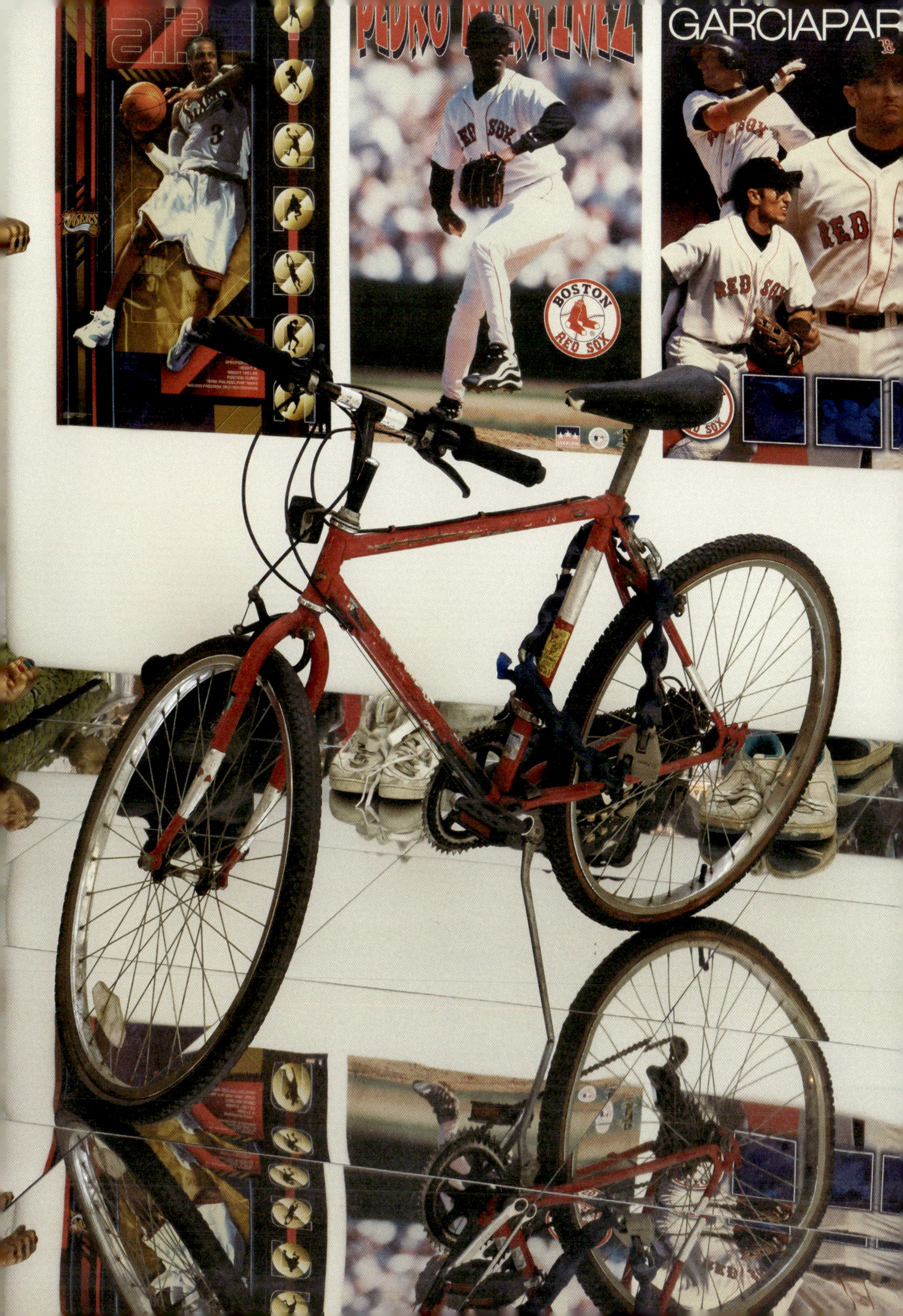
PEDRO
GARCIAPAR
BOSTON
RED SOX

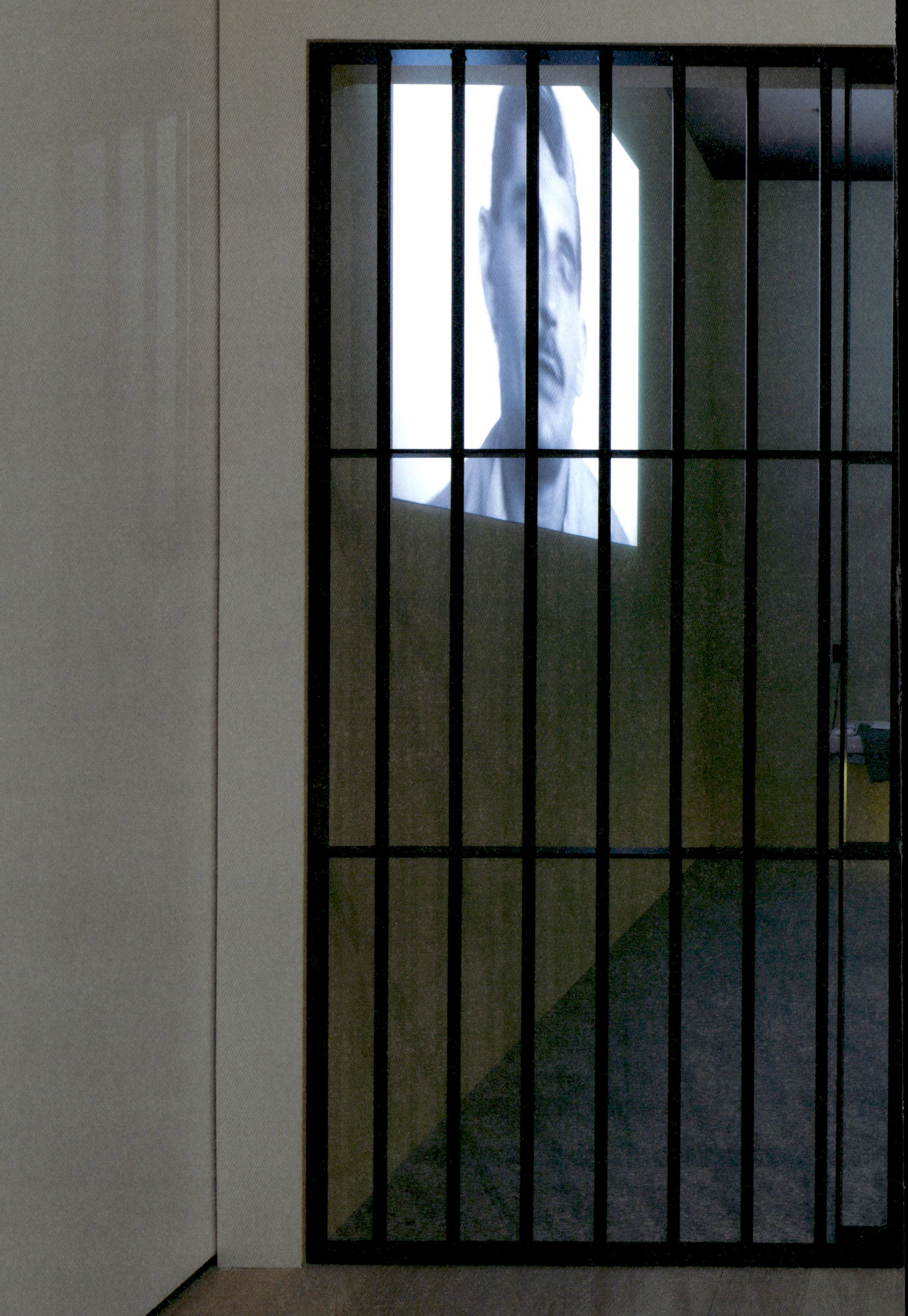

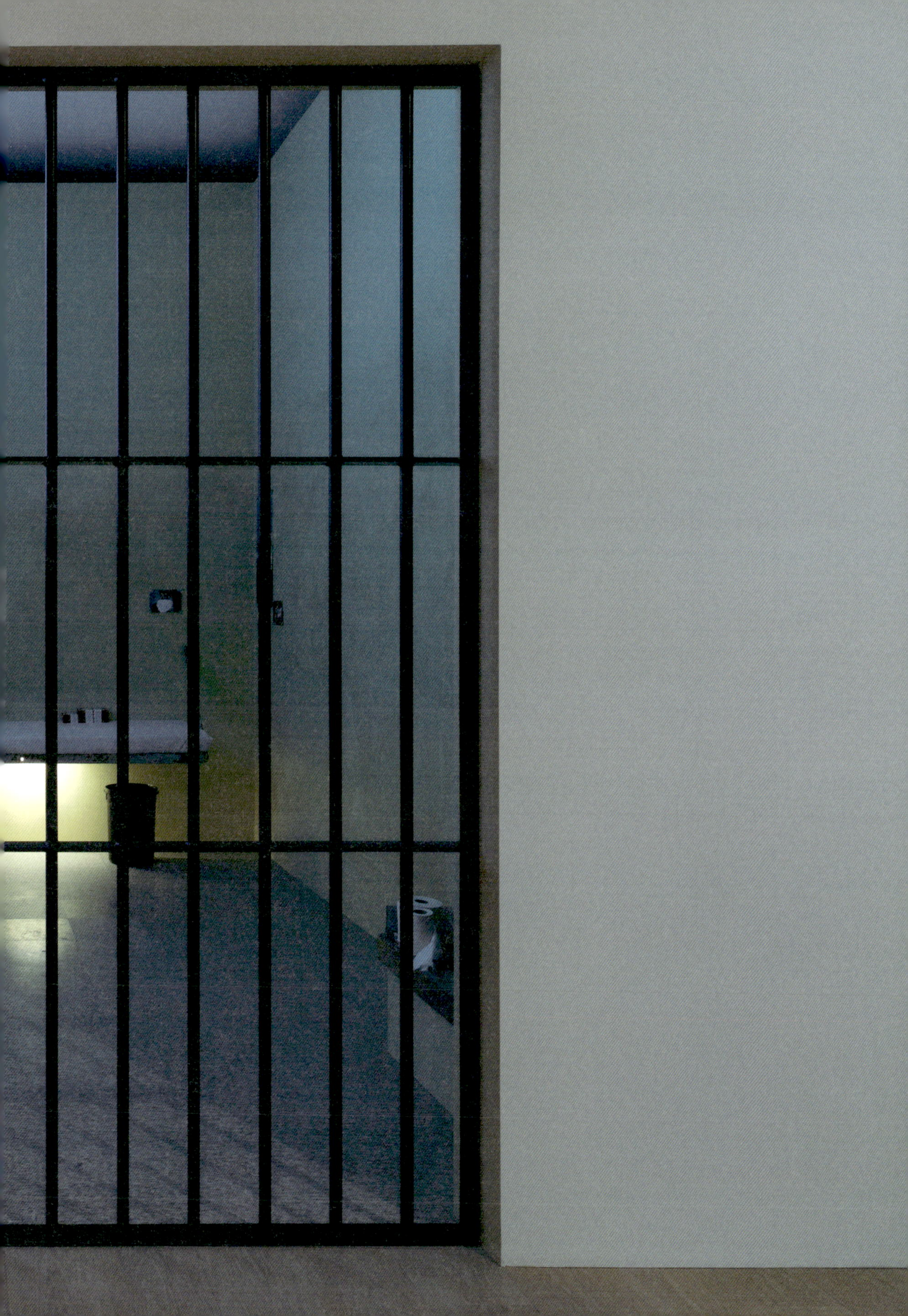

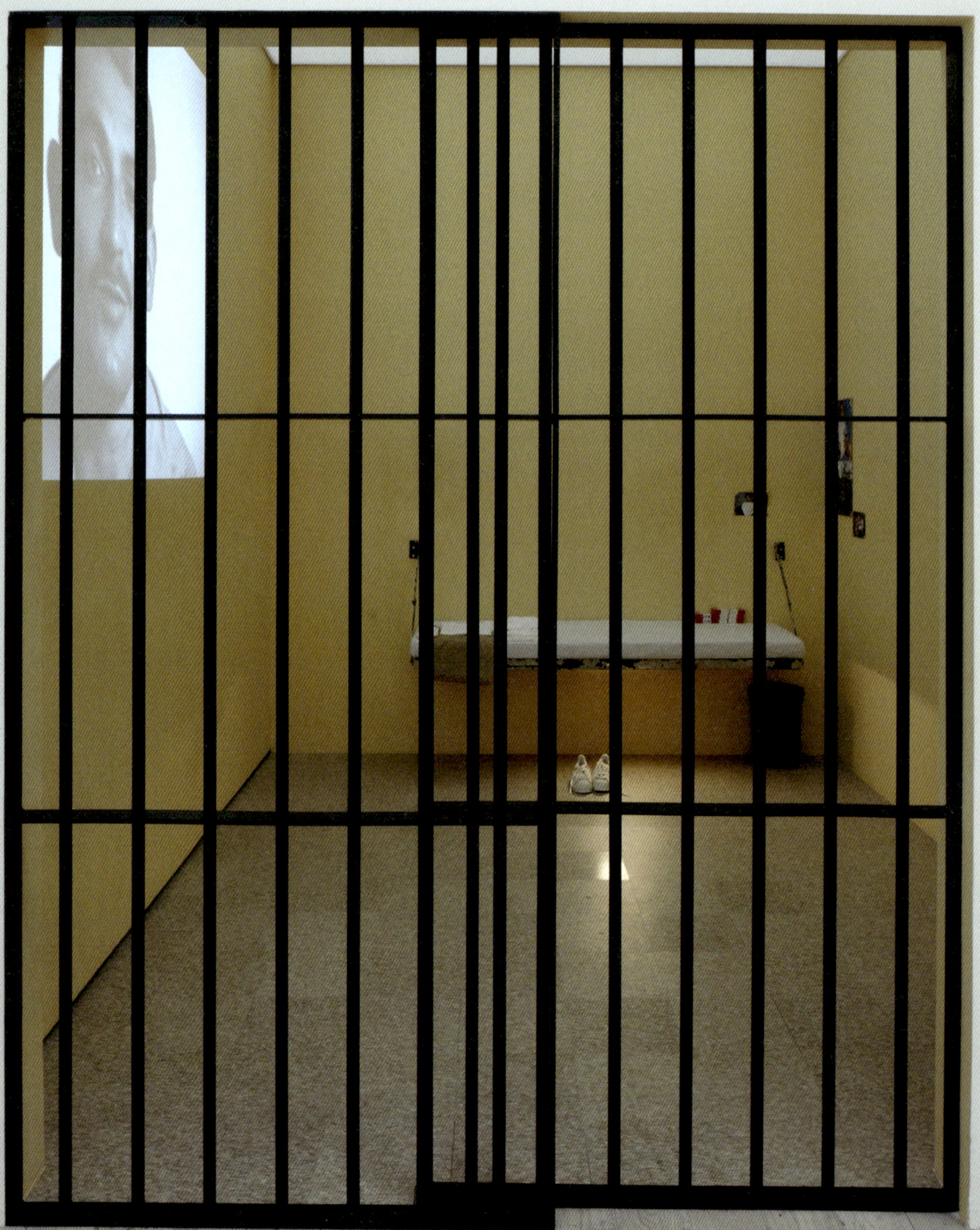

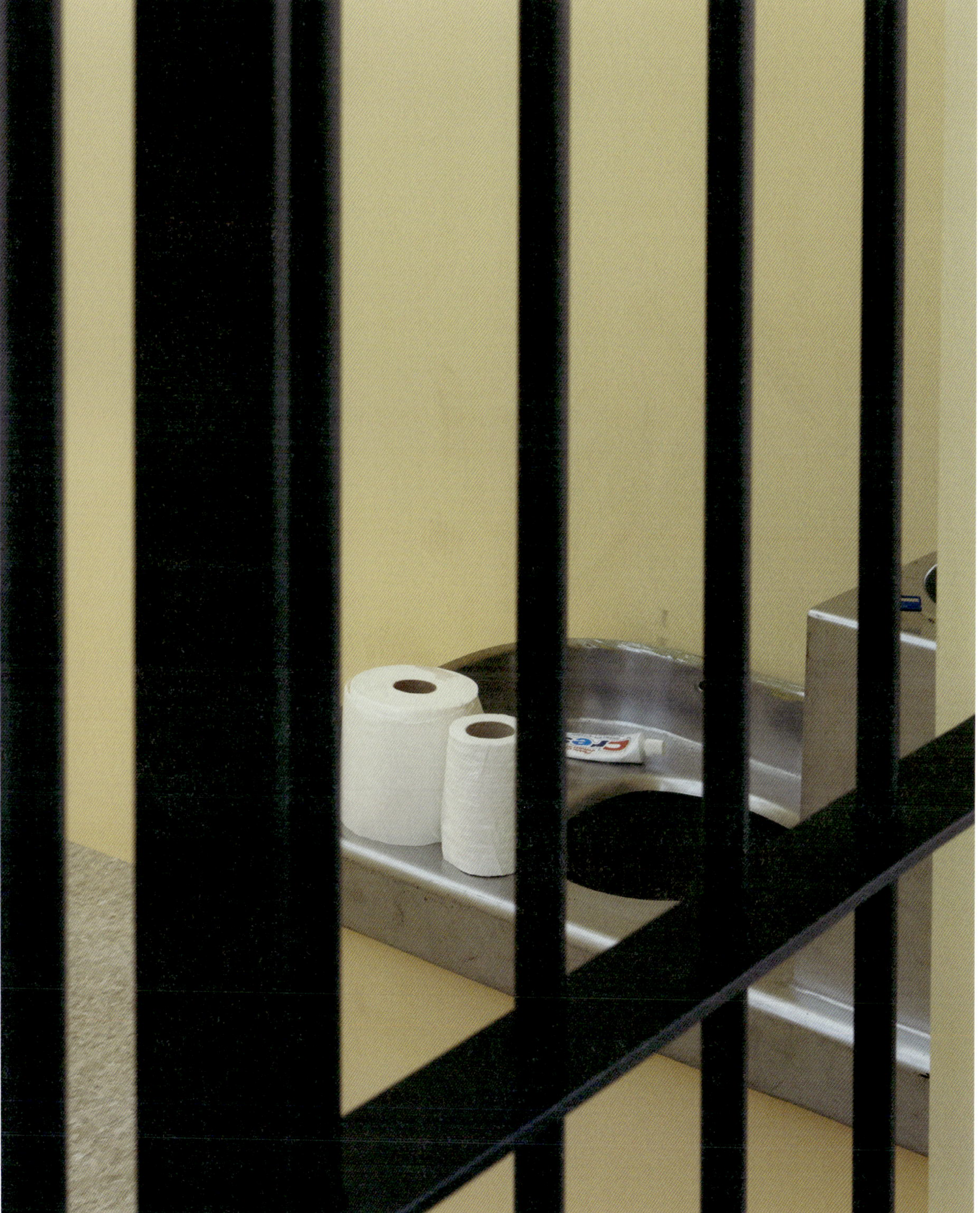

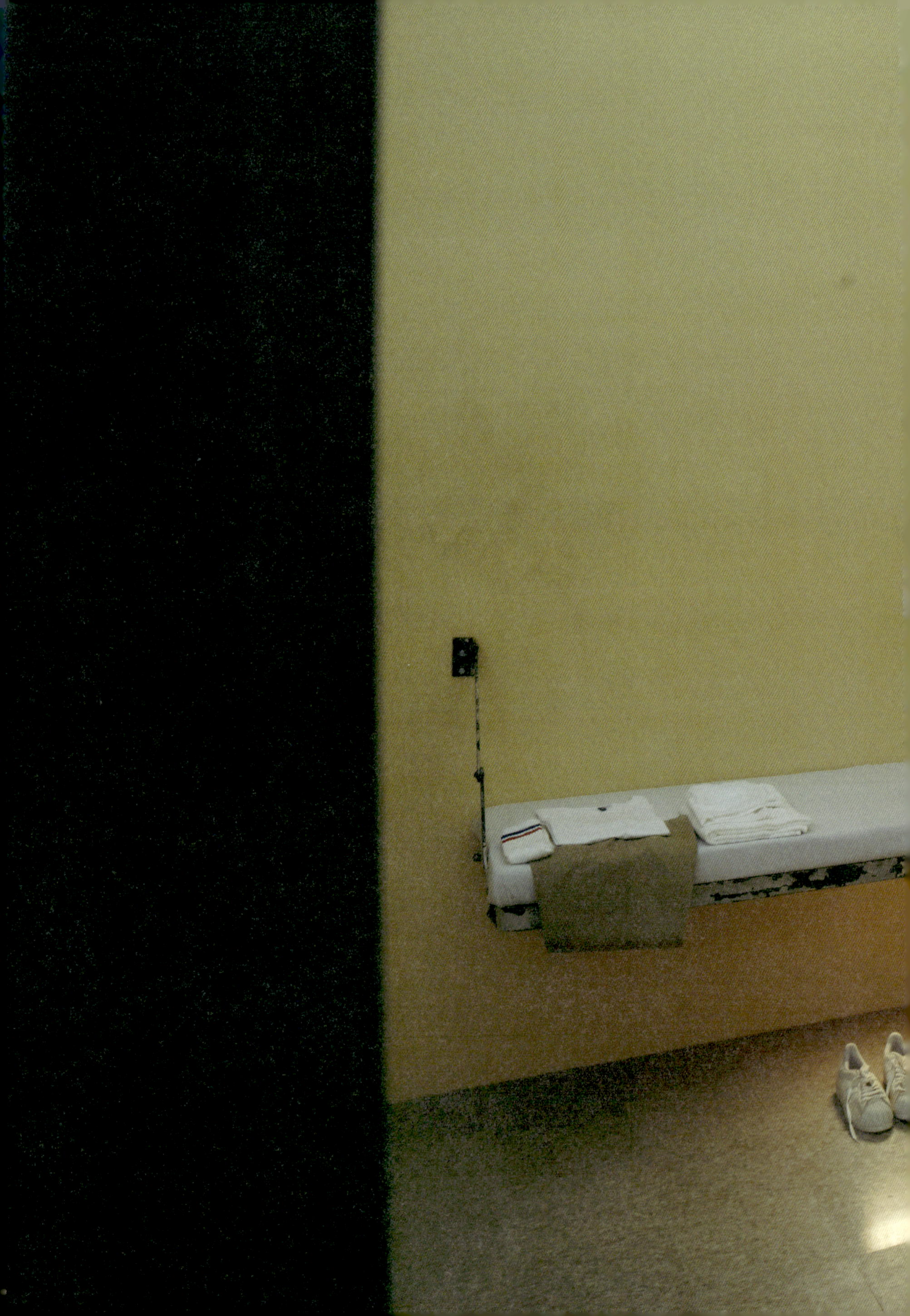

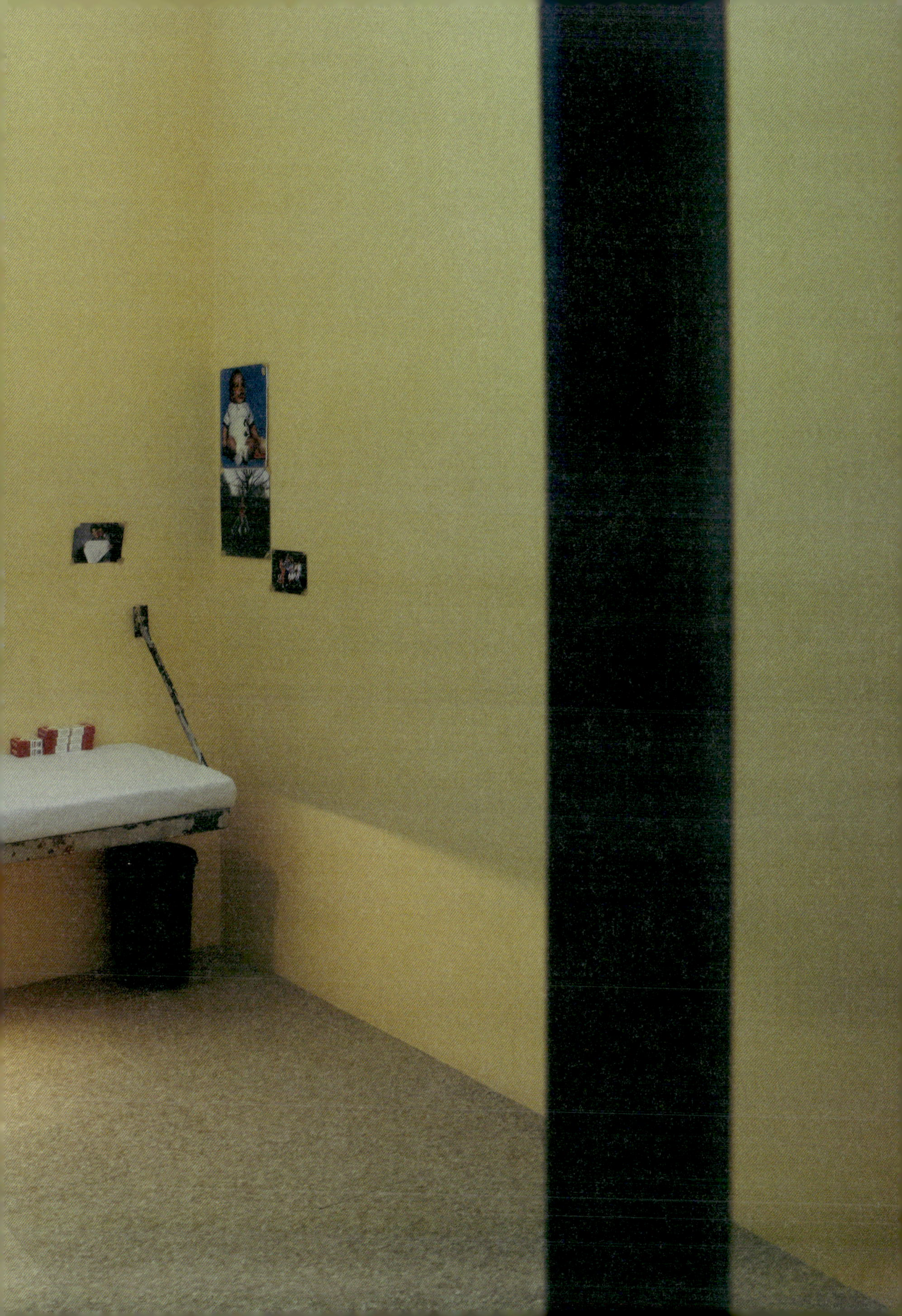

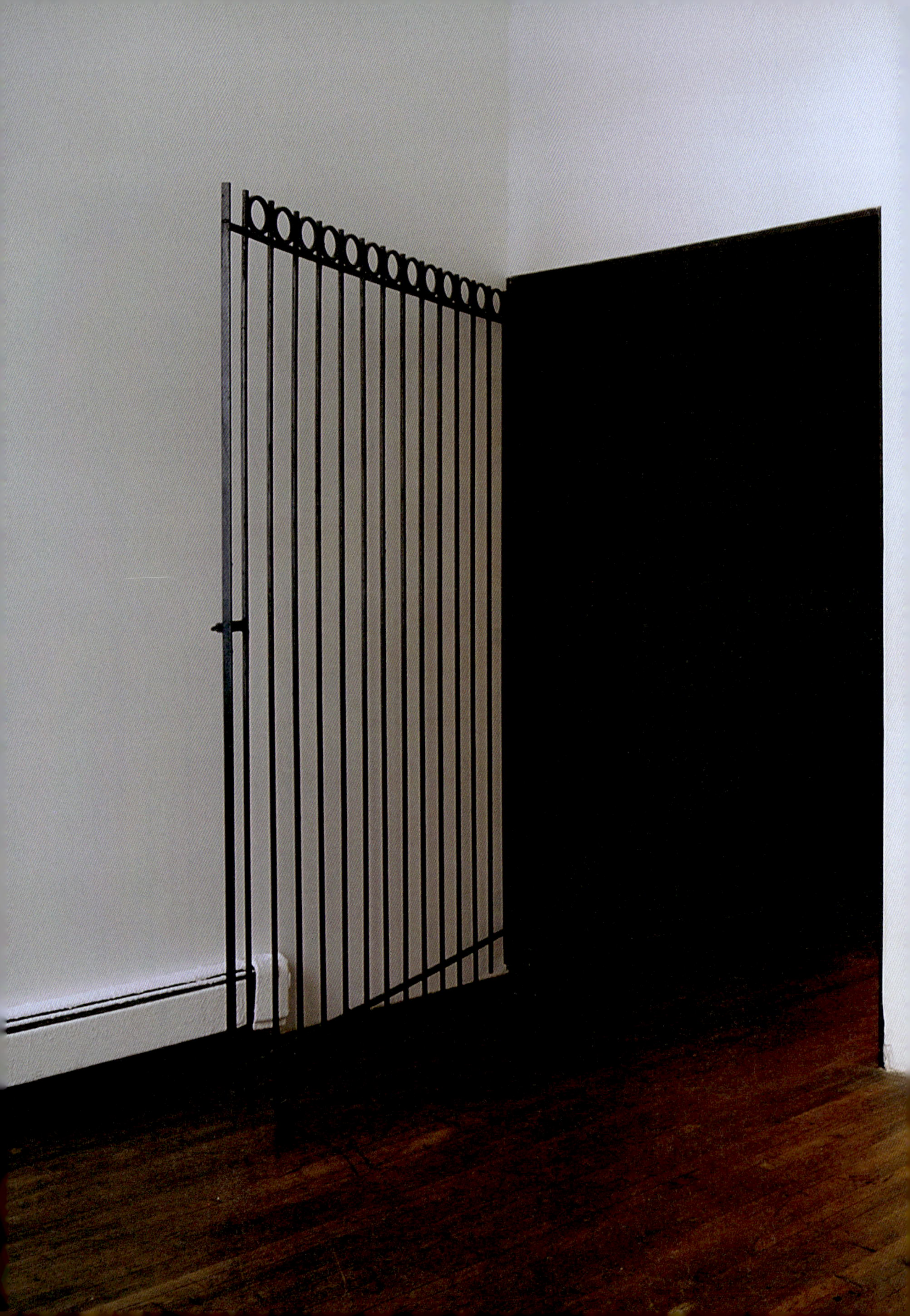

PEPÓN OSORIO

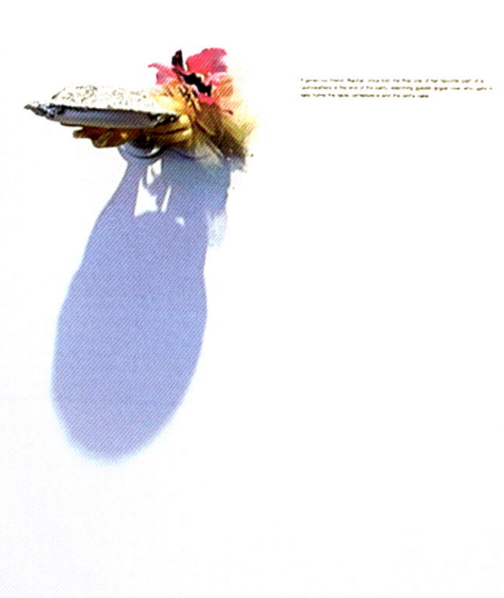

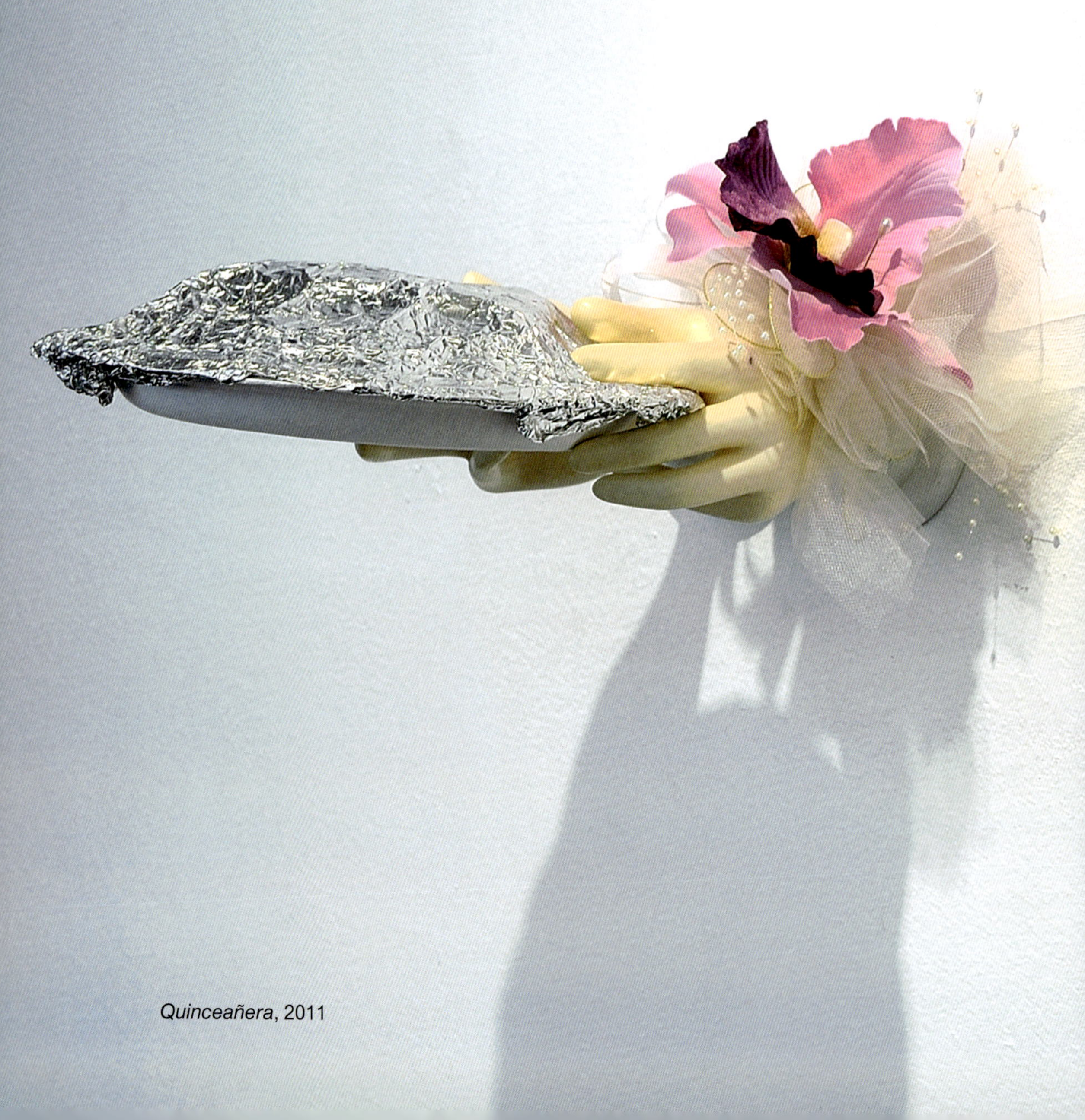

Quinceañera, 2011

A generous friend, Rachel, once told me that one of her favorite part of a Quinceañera is the end of the party, watching guests argue over who gets to take home the table centerpiece and the extra cake.

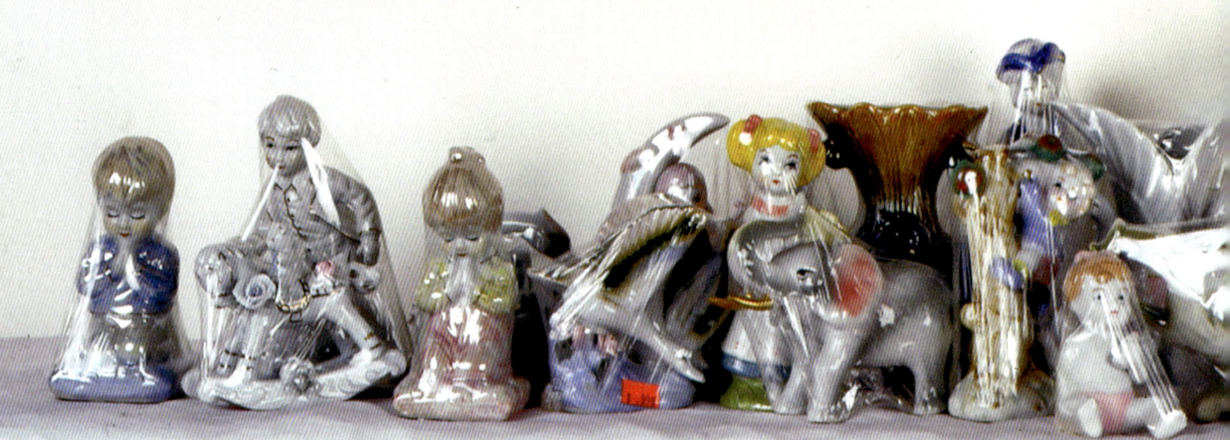

State of Preservation, 1996

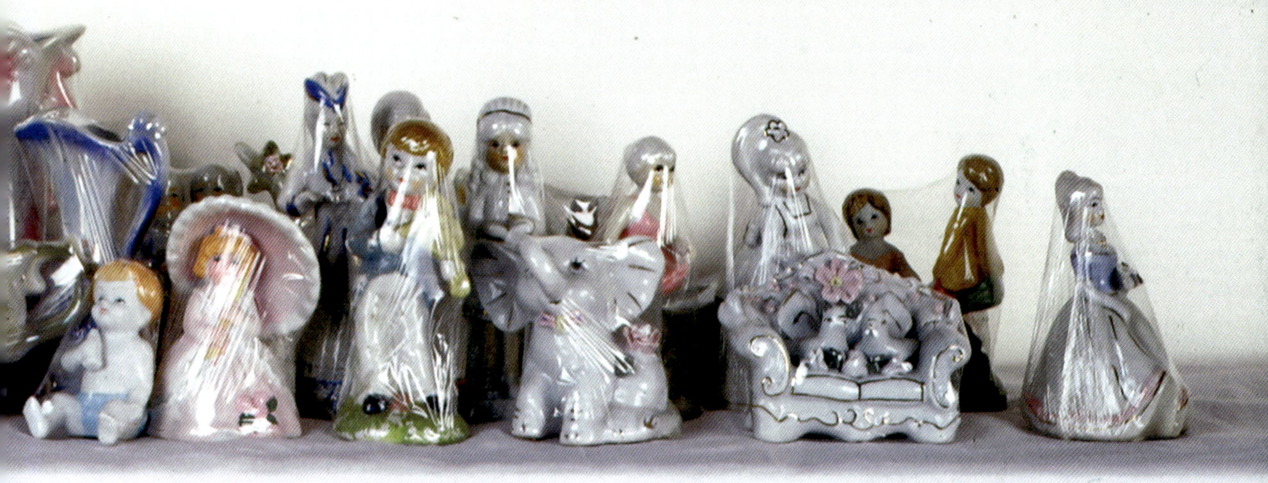

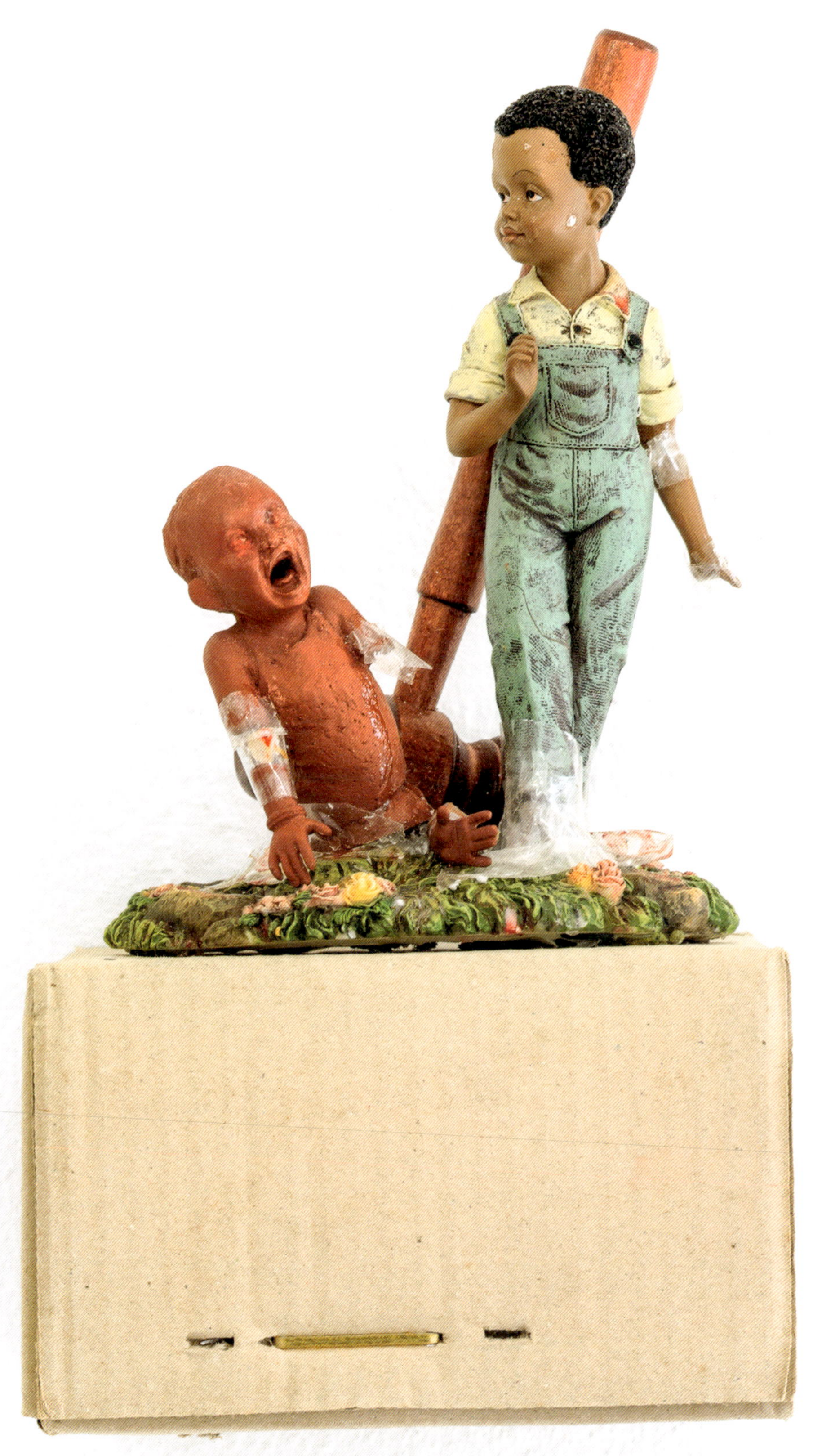

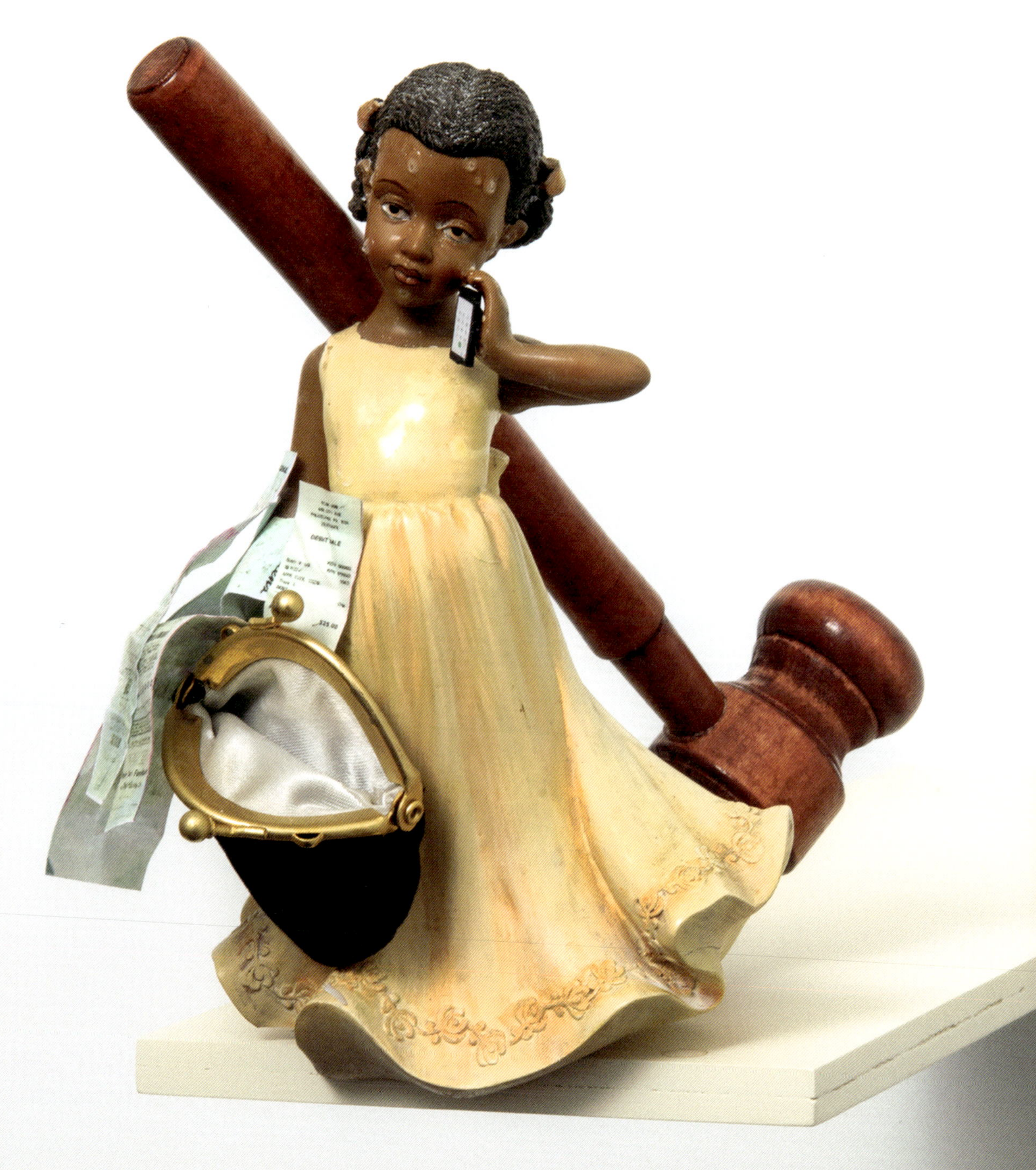

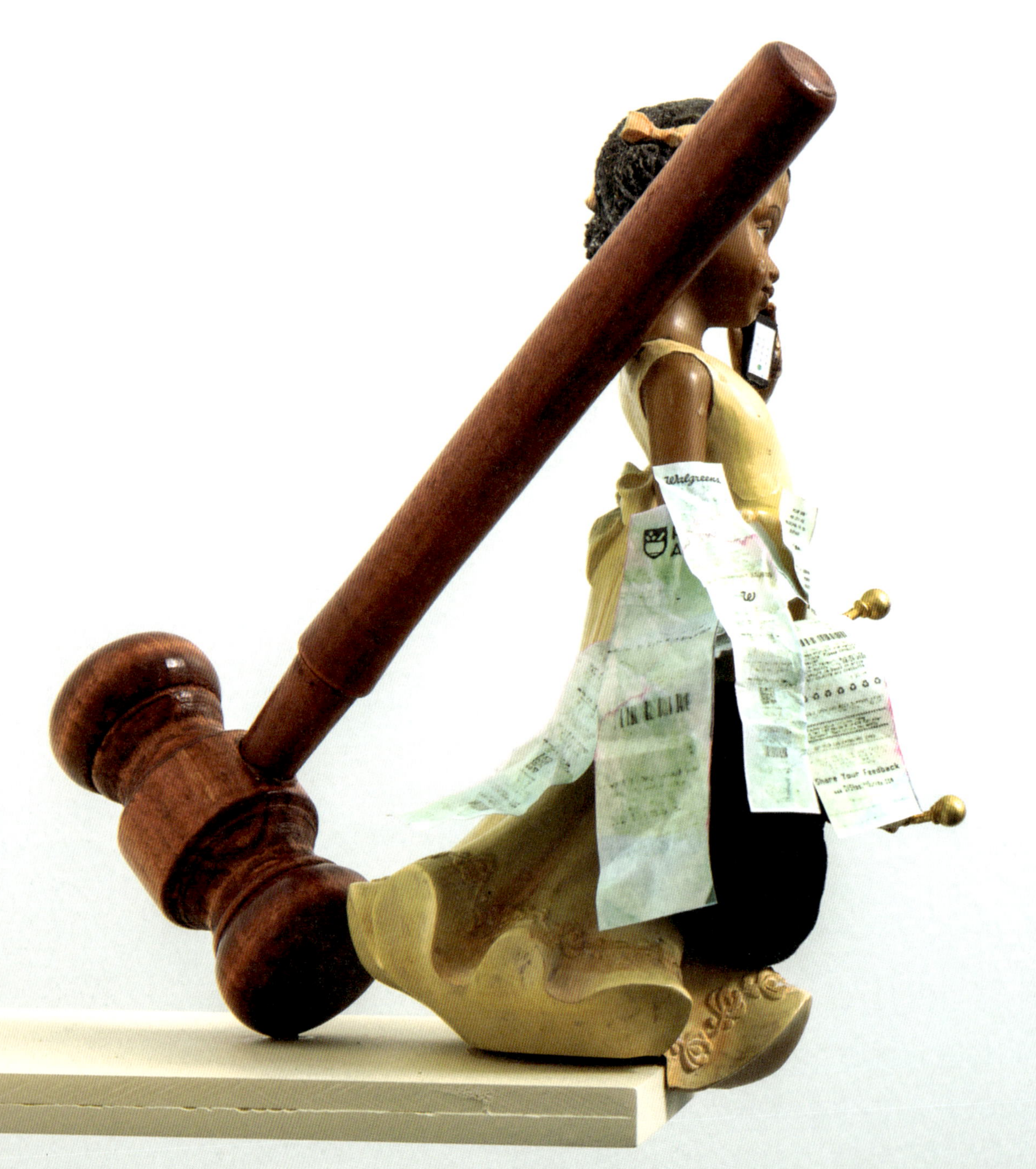
Walgreens
Share Your Feedback

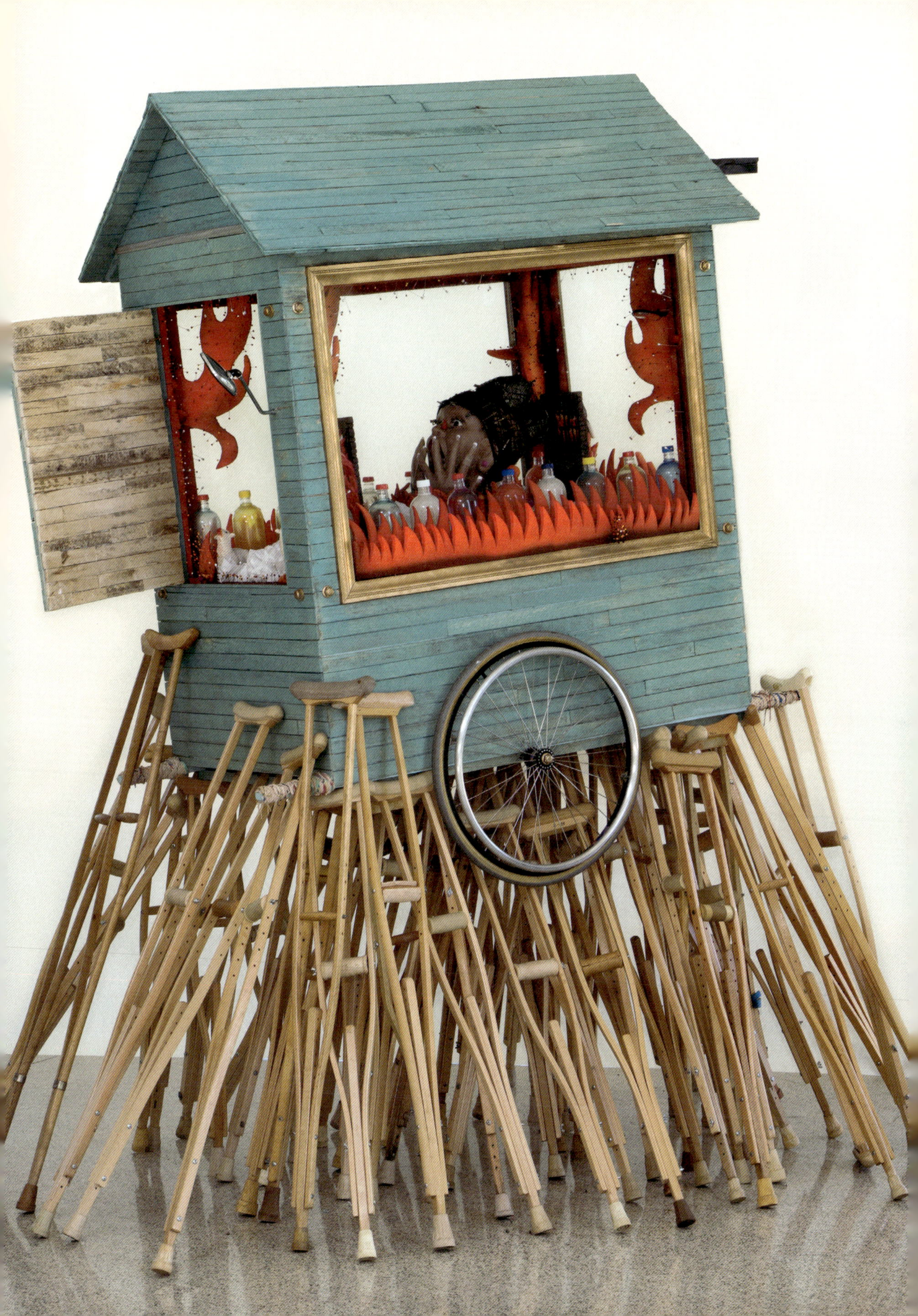

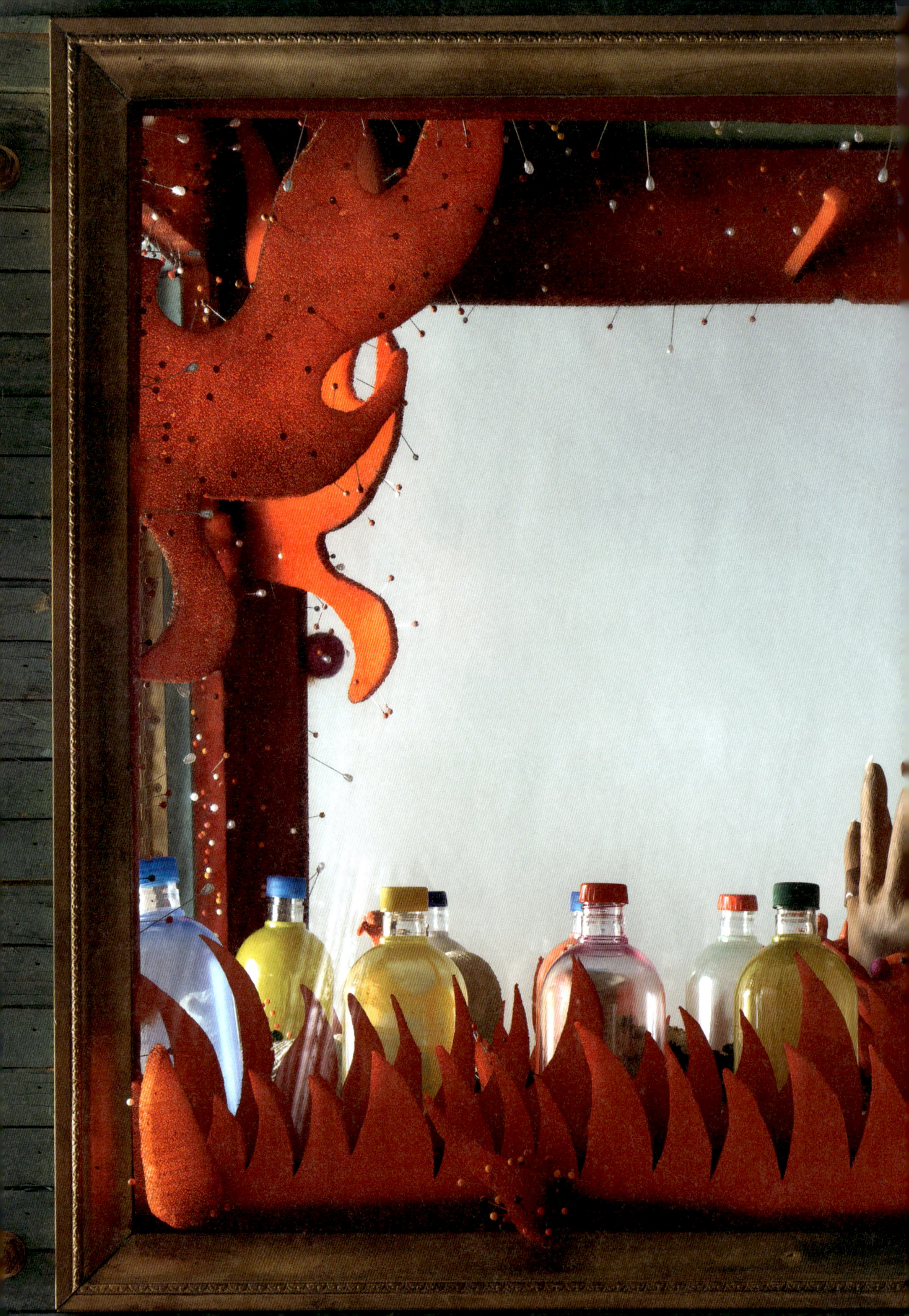

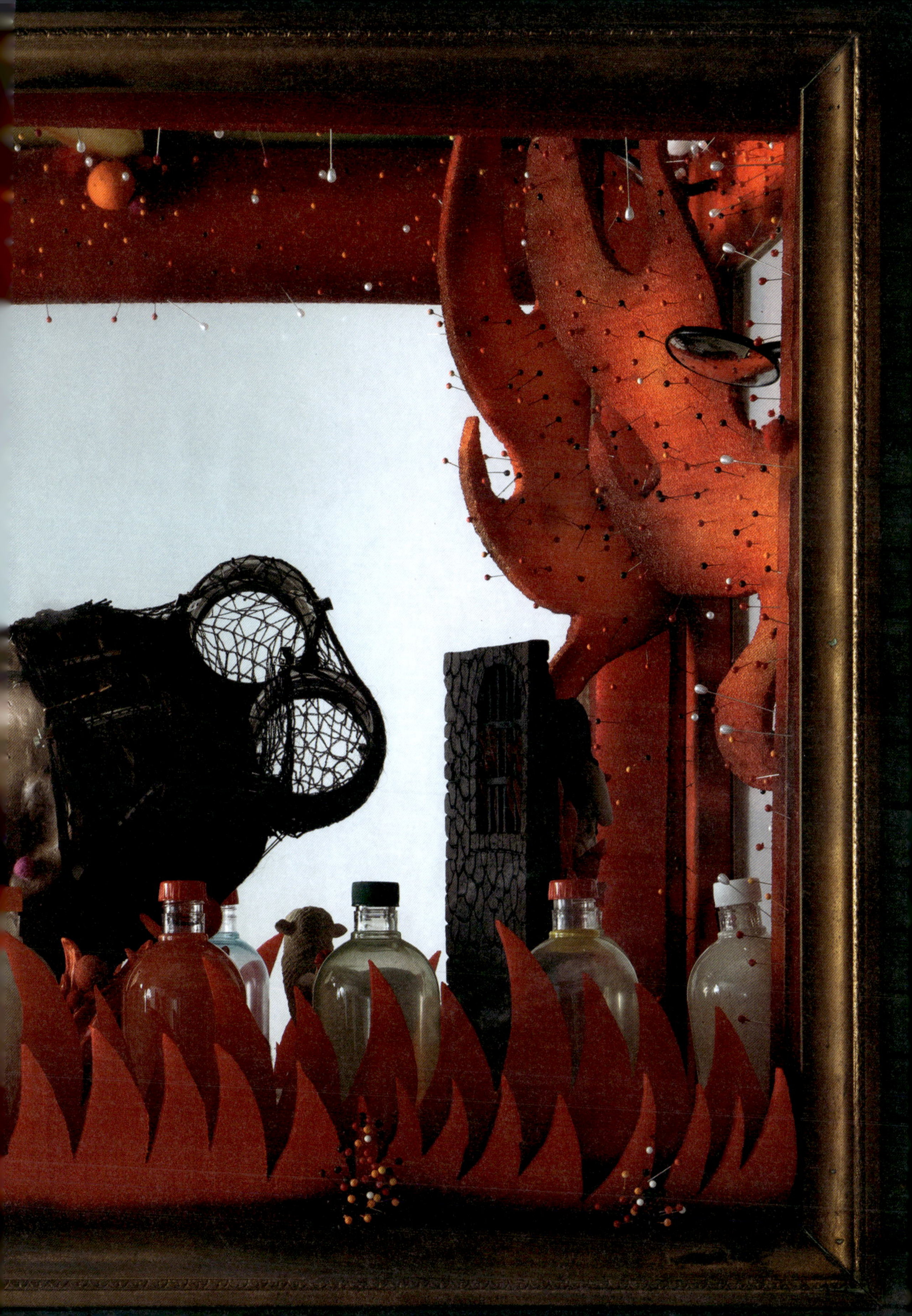

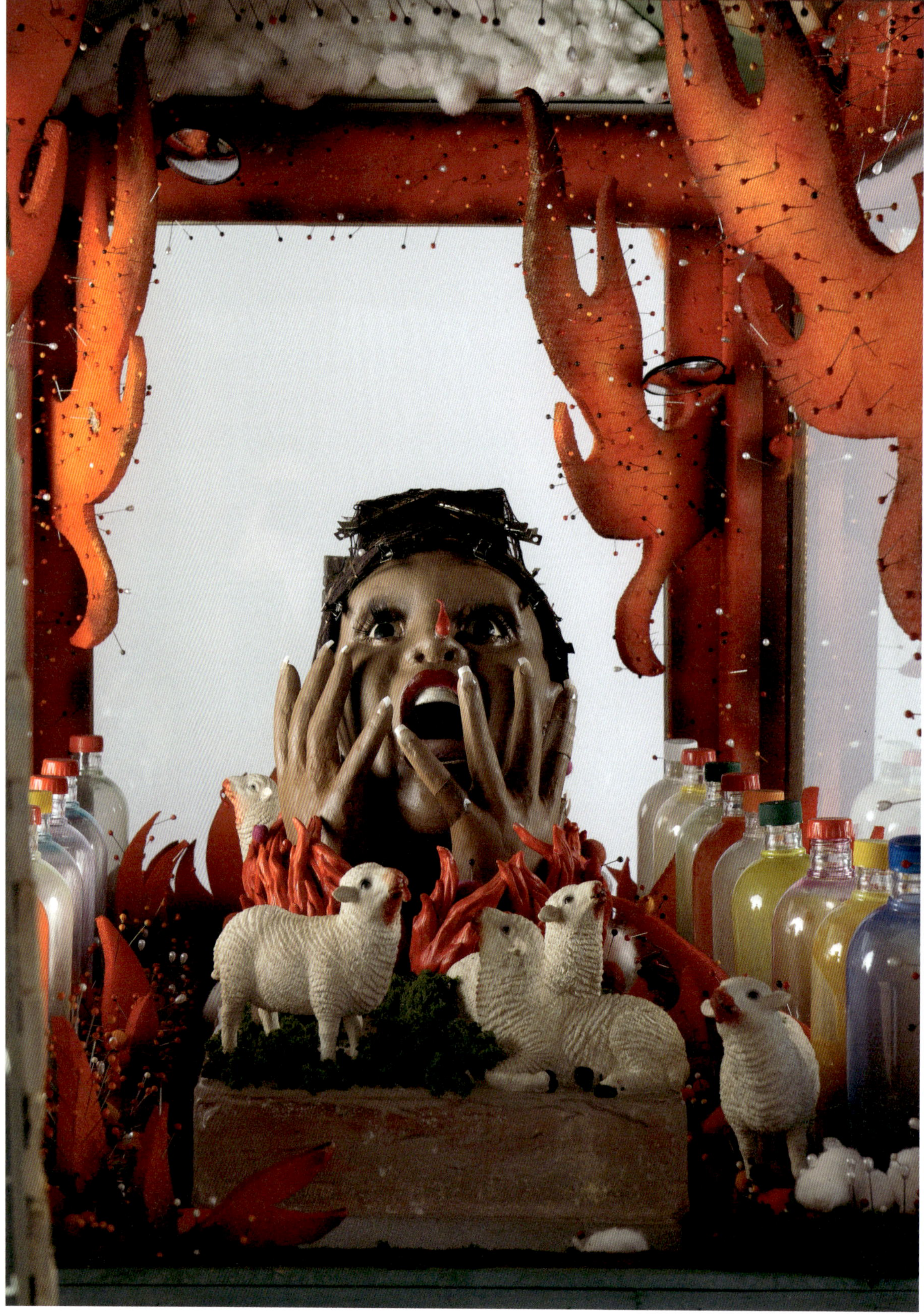

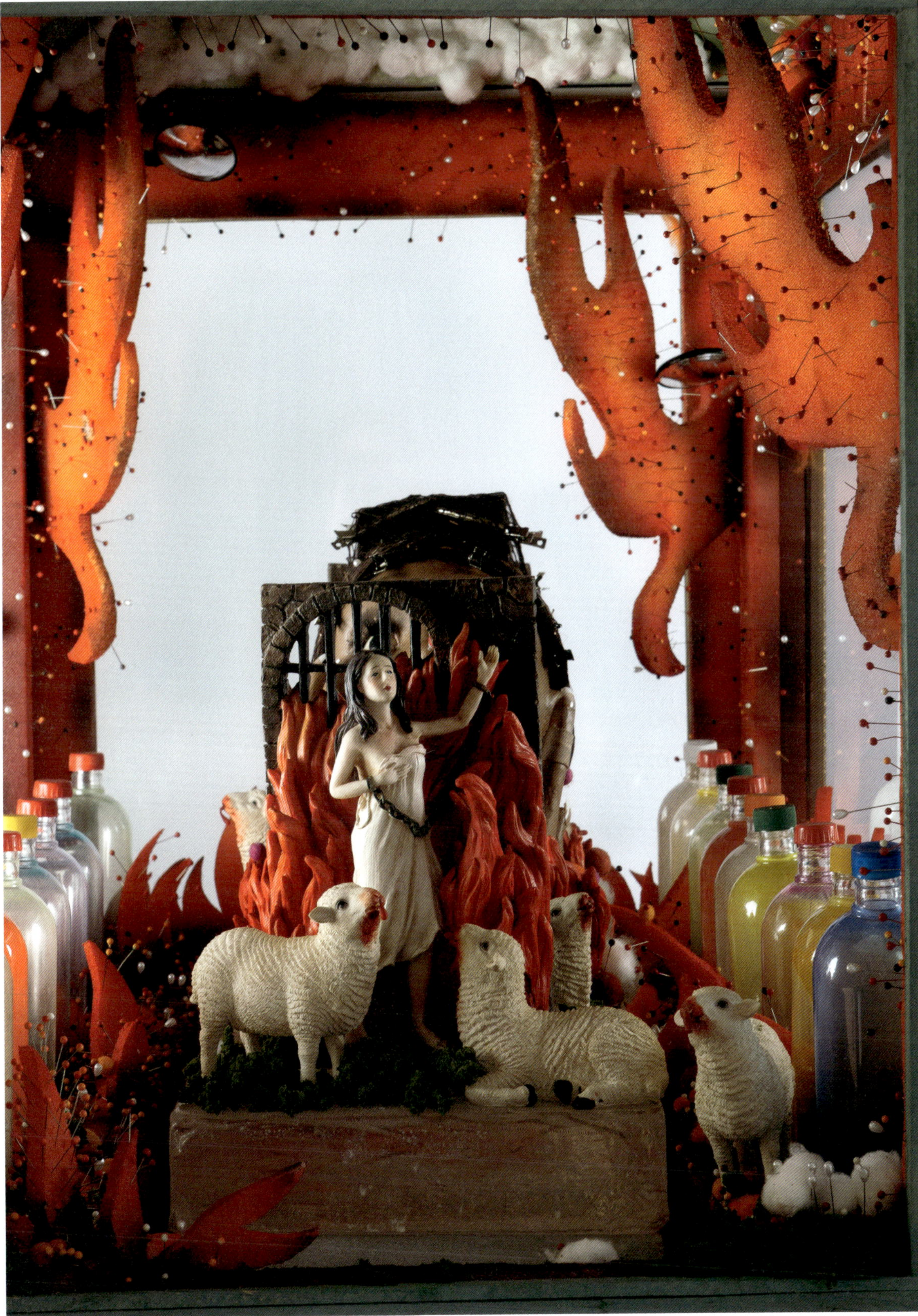

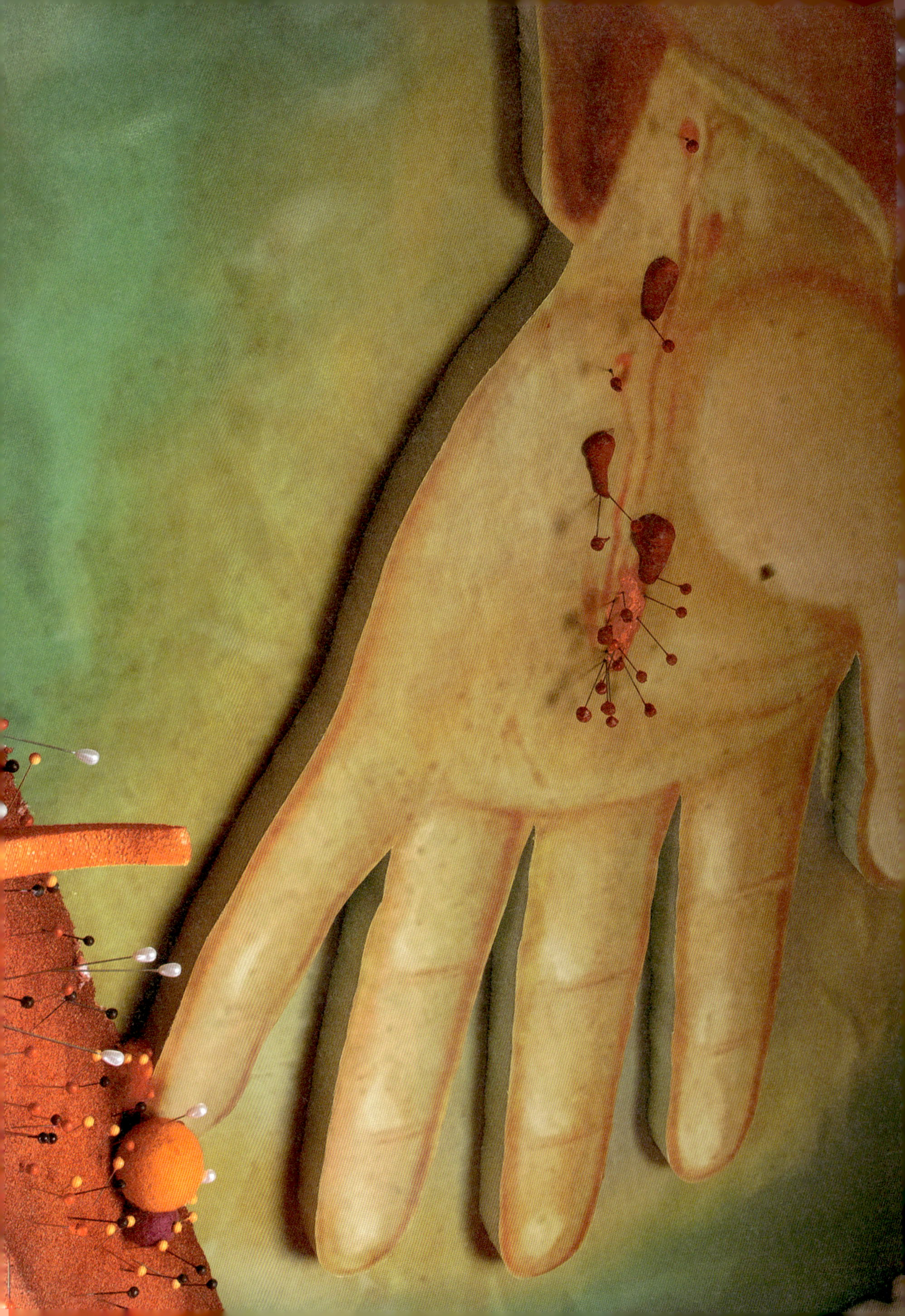

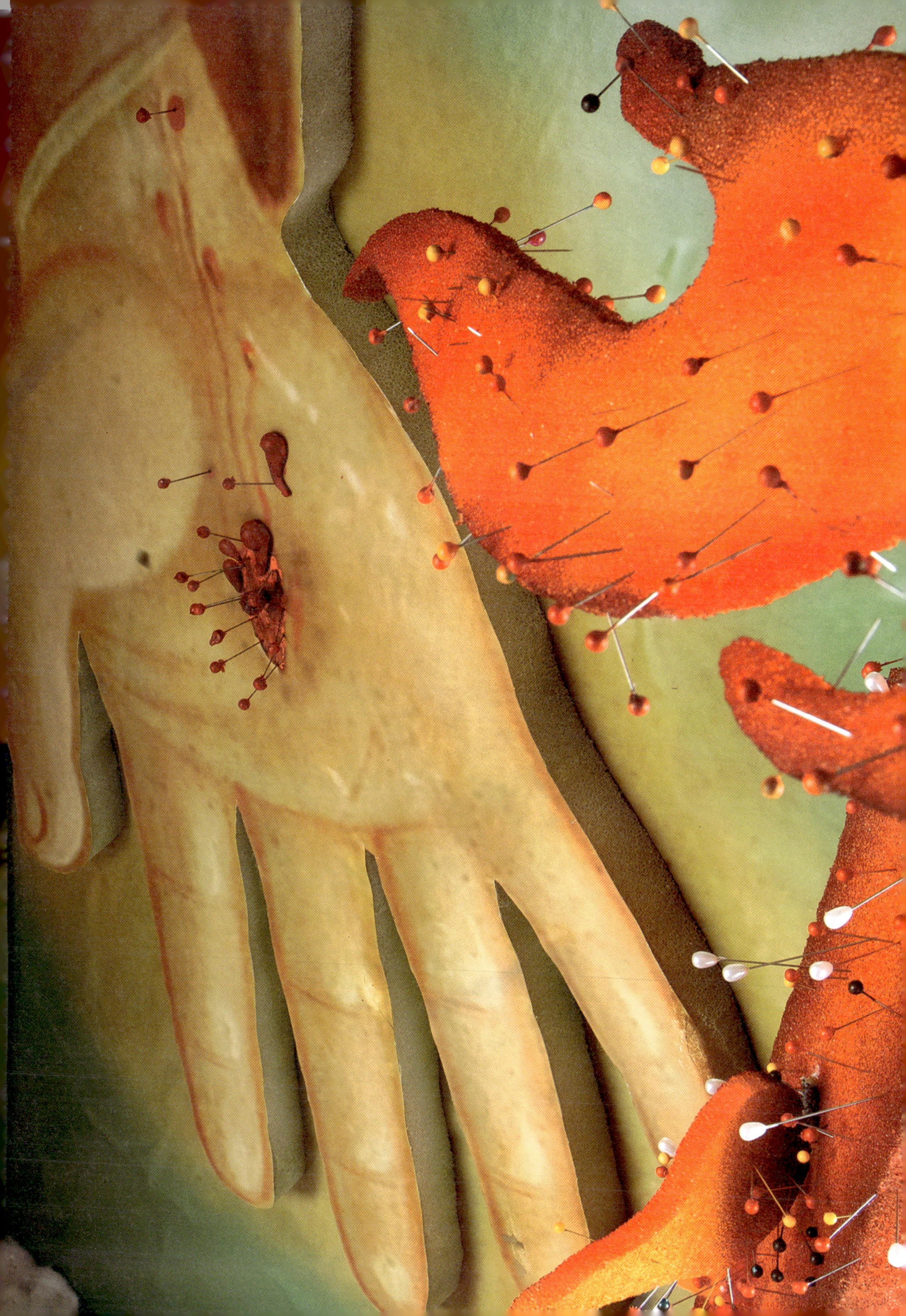

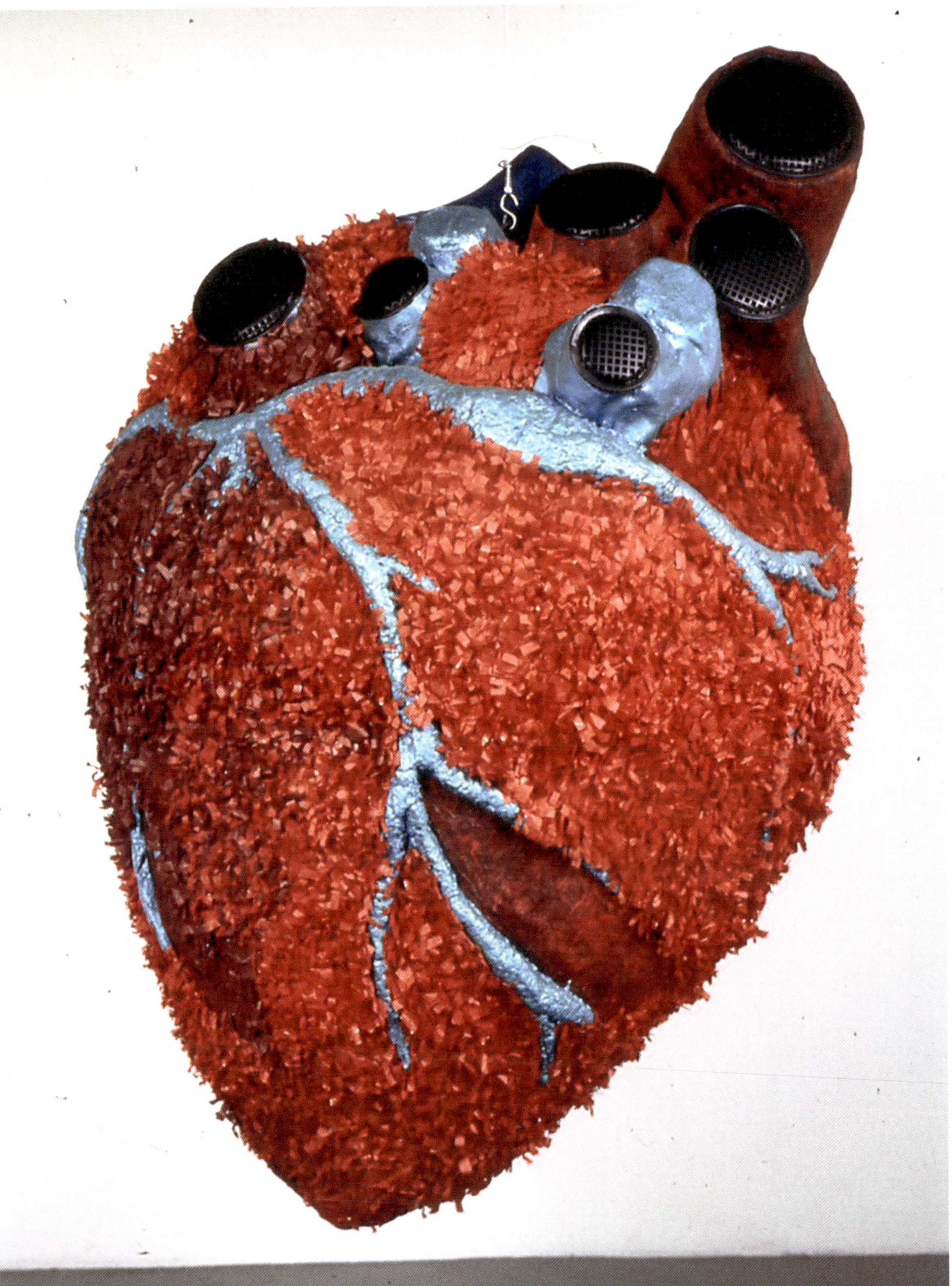

Purifier, 2011

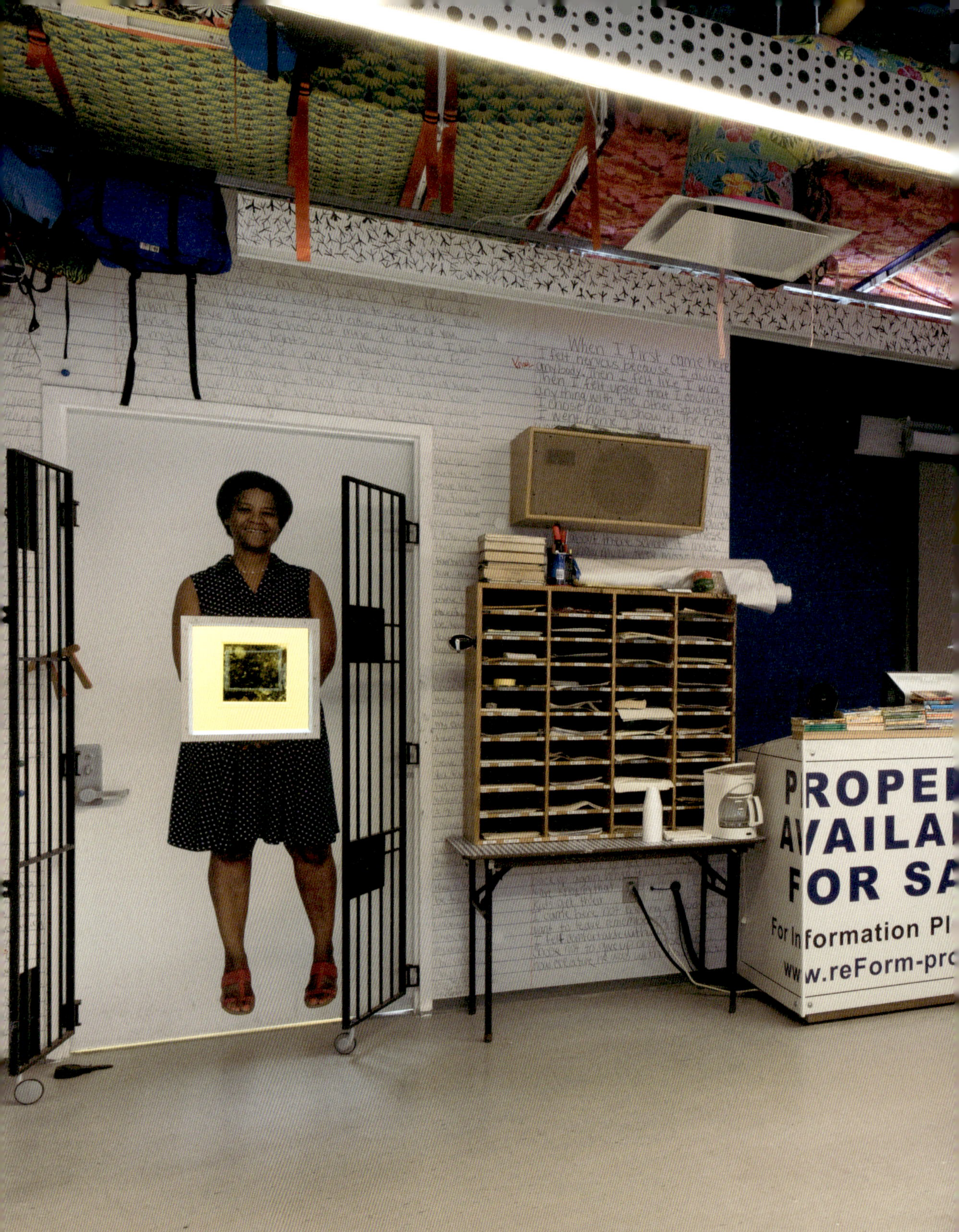

reForm, 2014–17

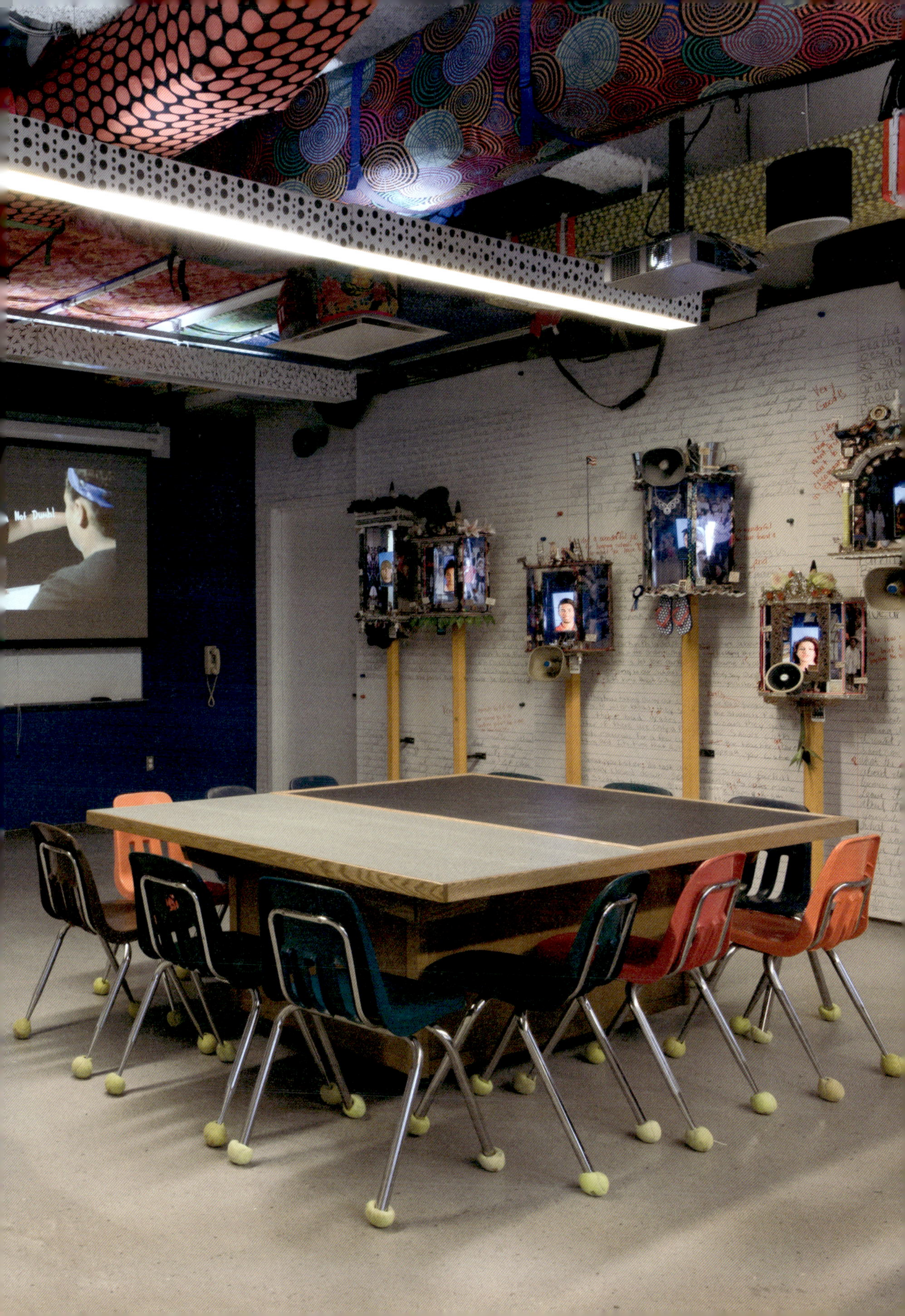
Not Dumb!

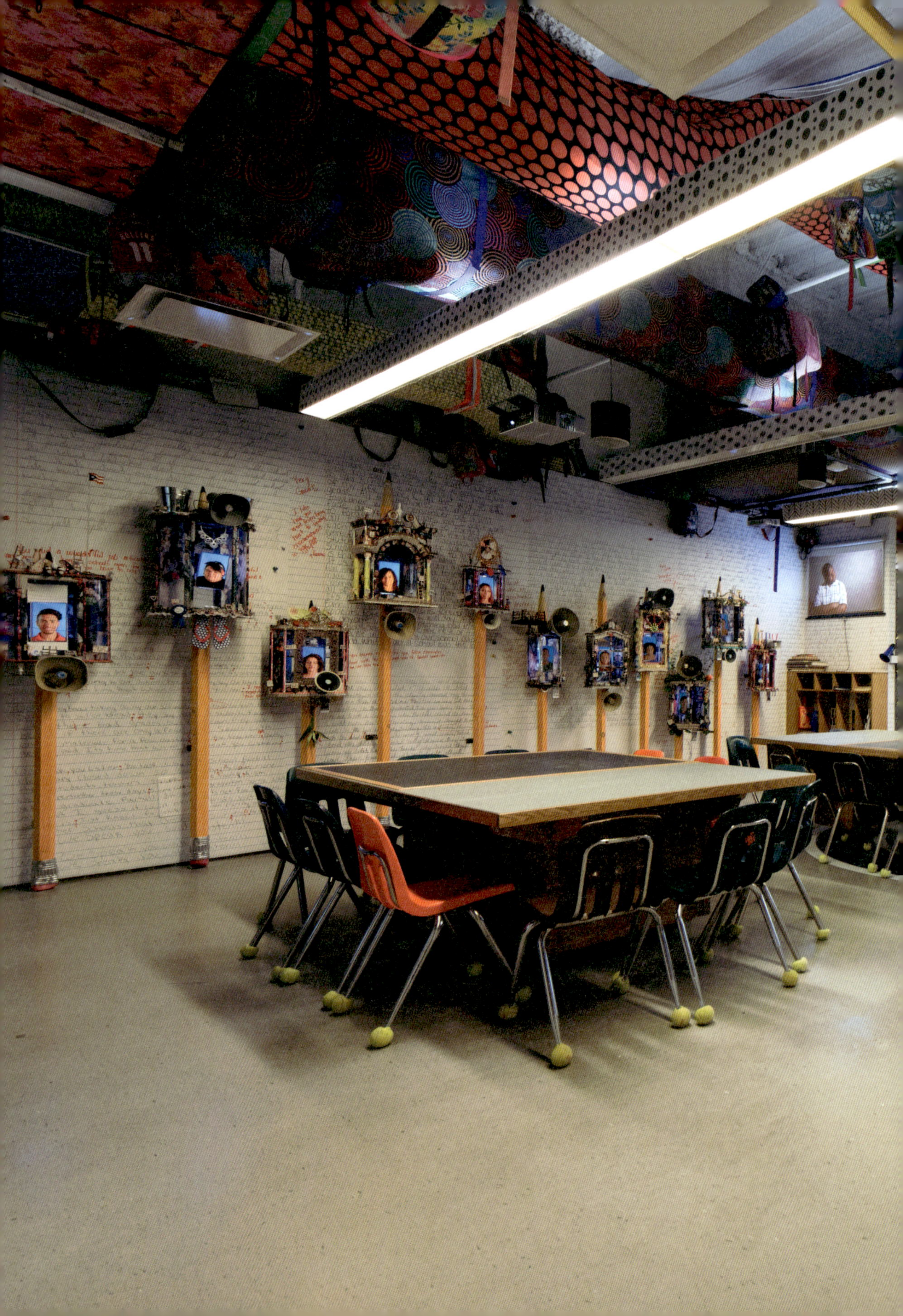

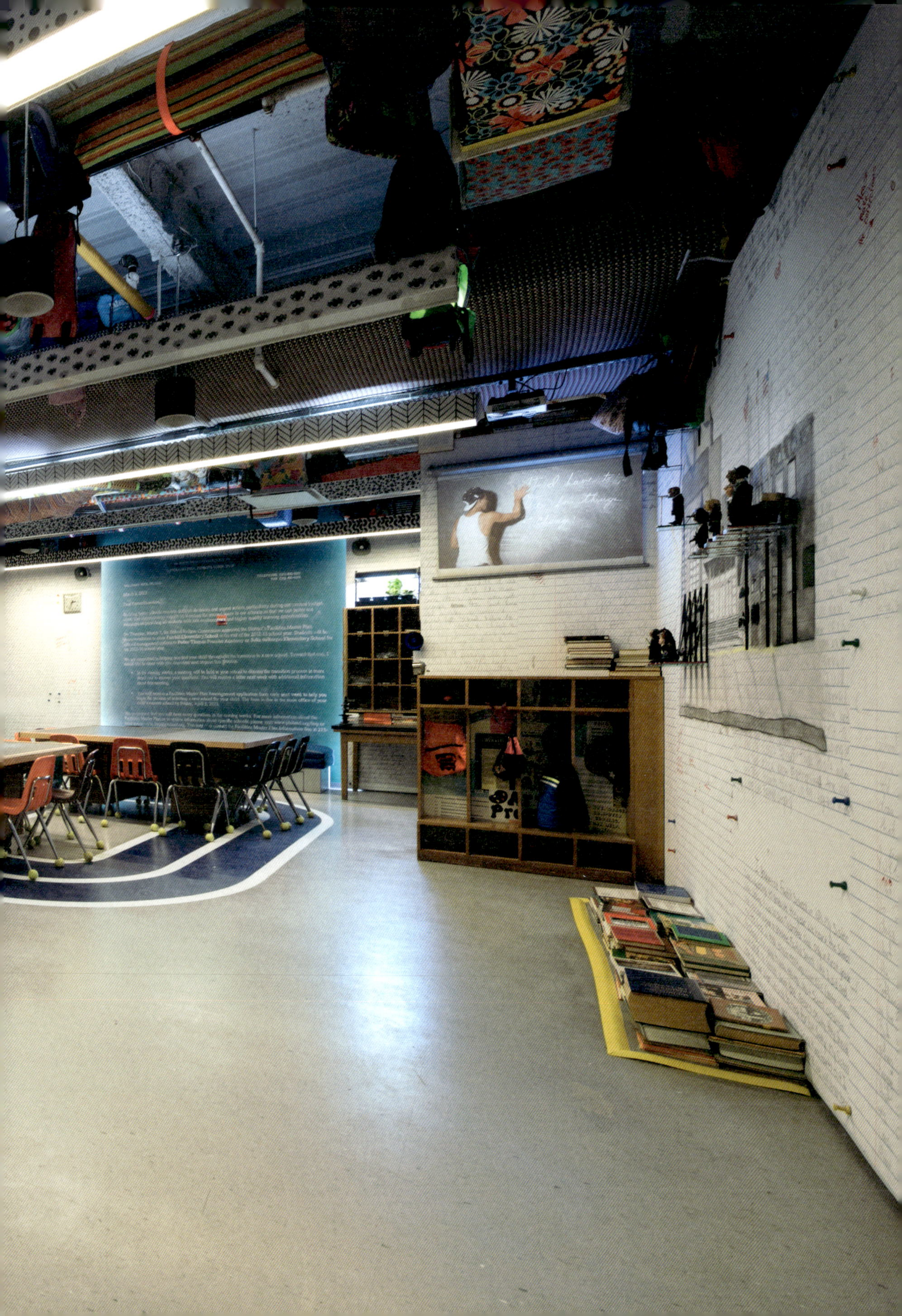

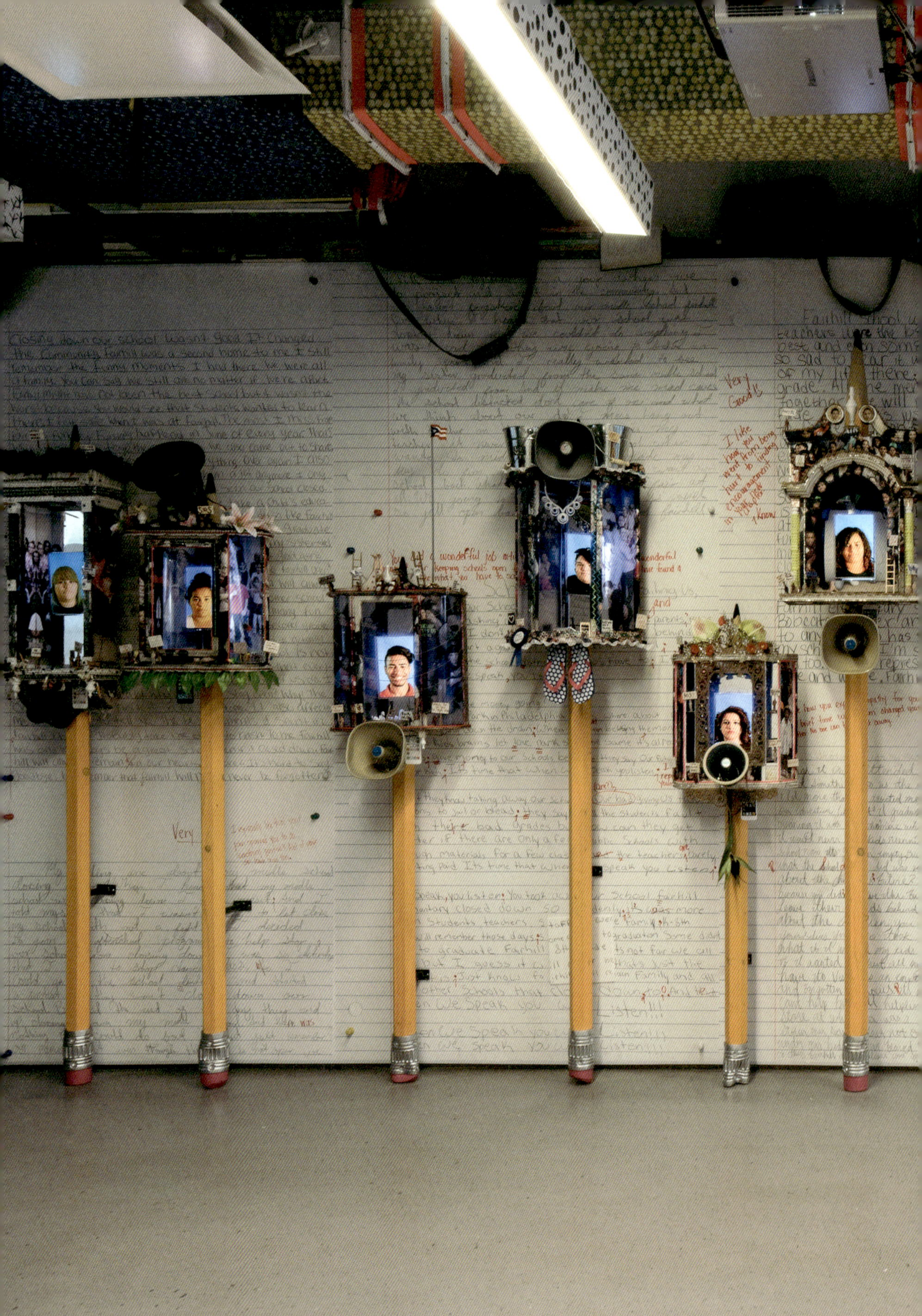

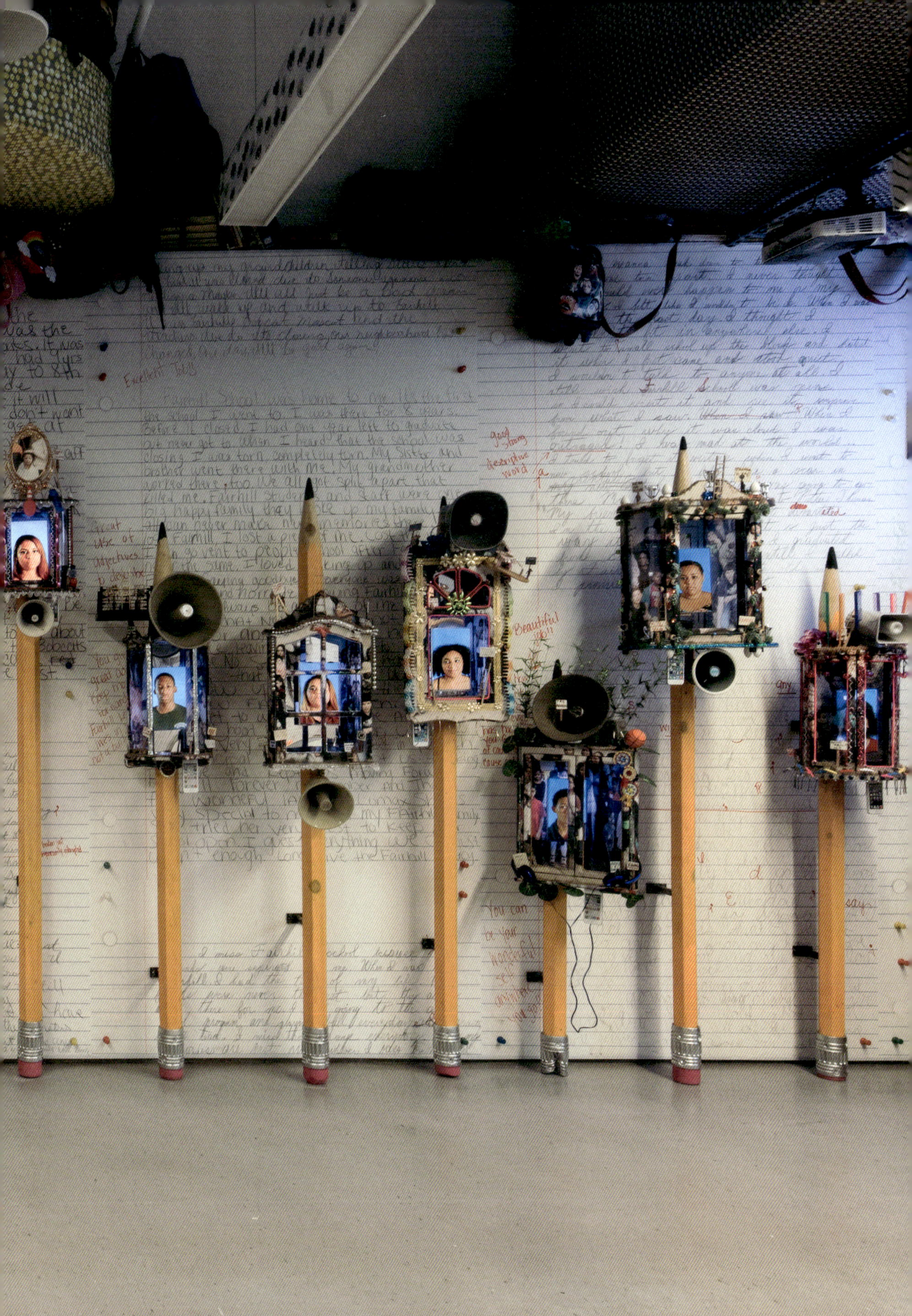

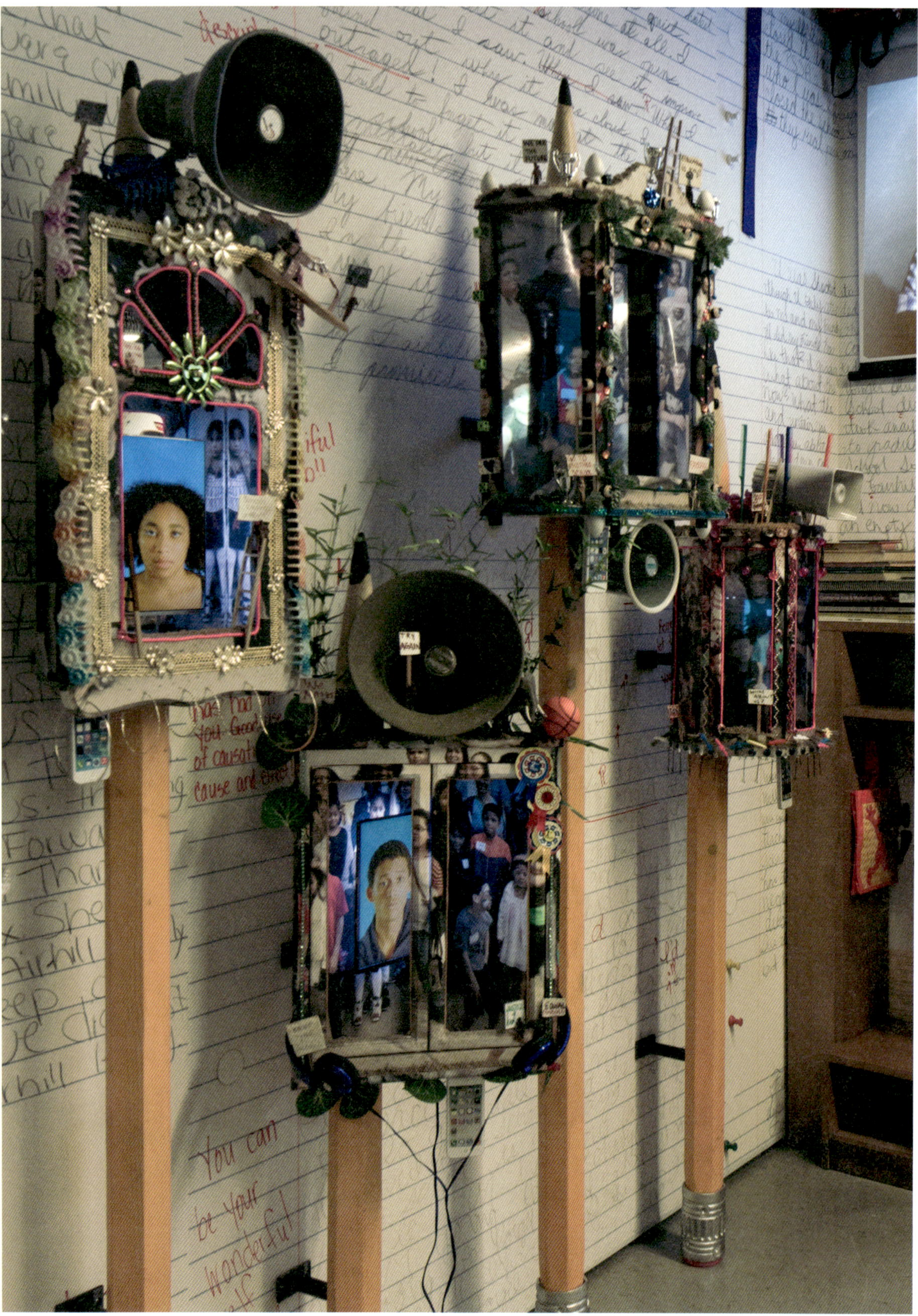

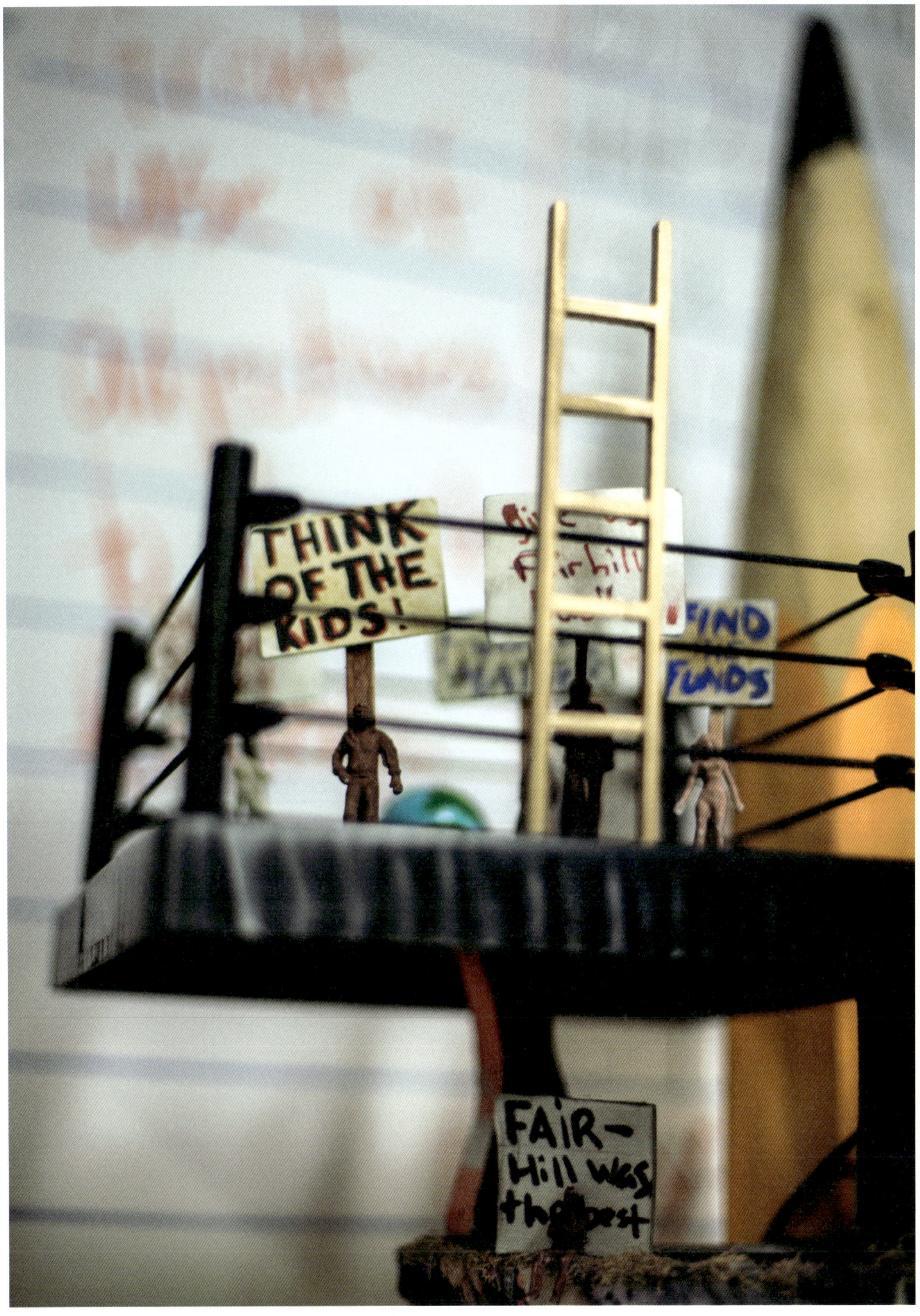
THINK OF THE KIDS!
FIND
FUNDS
FAIR-Hill was the best

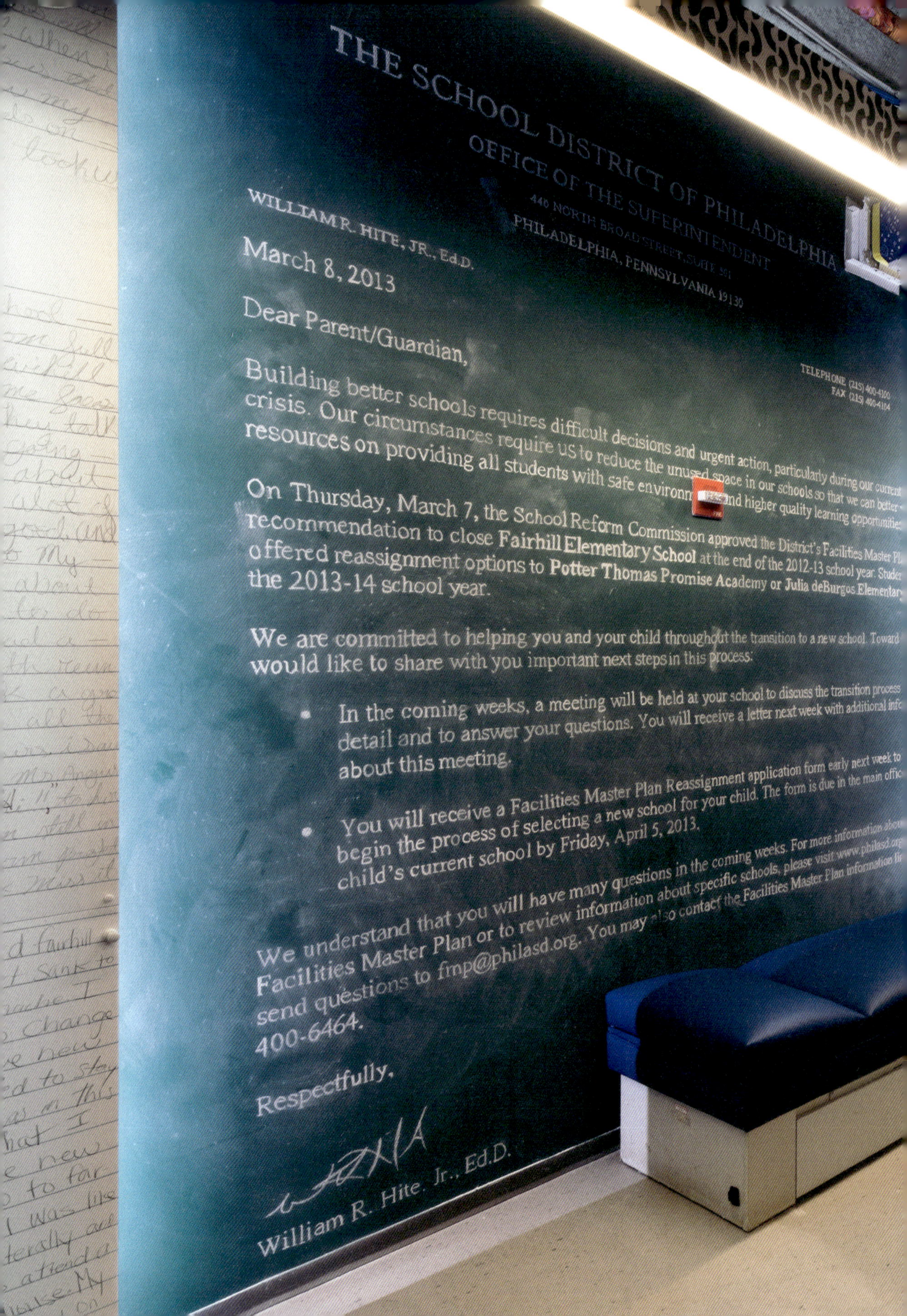
THE SCHOOL DISTRICT OF PHILADELPHIA
OFFICE OF THE SUPERINTENDENT
440 NORTH BROAD STREET, SUITE 301
PHILADELPHIA, PENNSYLVANIA 19130
WILLIAM R. HITE, JR., Ed.D.
TELEPHONE (215) 400-4100
FAX (215) 400-4104
March 8, 2013
Dear Parent/Guardian,
Building better schools requires difficult decisions and urgent action, particularly during our current
crisis. Our circumstances require us to reduce the unused space in our schools so that we can better
resources on providing all students with safe environ and higher quality learning opportunities
On Thursday, March 7, the School Reform Commission approved the District's Facilities Master Pla
recommendation to close Fairhill Elementary School at the end of the 2012-13 school year.
offered reassignment options to Potter Thomas Promise Academy or Julia deBurgos Elementar
the 2013-14 school year.
We are committed to helping you and your child throughout the transition to a new school. Toward
would like to share with you important next steps in this process:
In the coming weeks, a meeting will be held at your school to discuss the transition process
detail and to answer your questions. You will receive a letter next week with additional
about this meeting.
You will receive a Facilities Master Plan Reassignment application form early next week to
begin the process of selecting a new school for your child. The form is due in the main office
child's current school by Friday, April 5, 2013.
We understand that you will have many questions in the coming weeks. For more information about
Facilities Master Plan or to review information about specific schools, please visit www.philasd.org
send questions to fmp@philasd.org. You may also contact the Facilities Master Plan information
400-6464.
Respectfully,
William R. Hite, Jr., Ed.D.

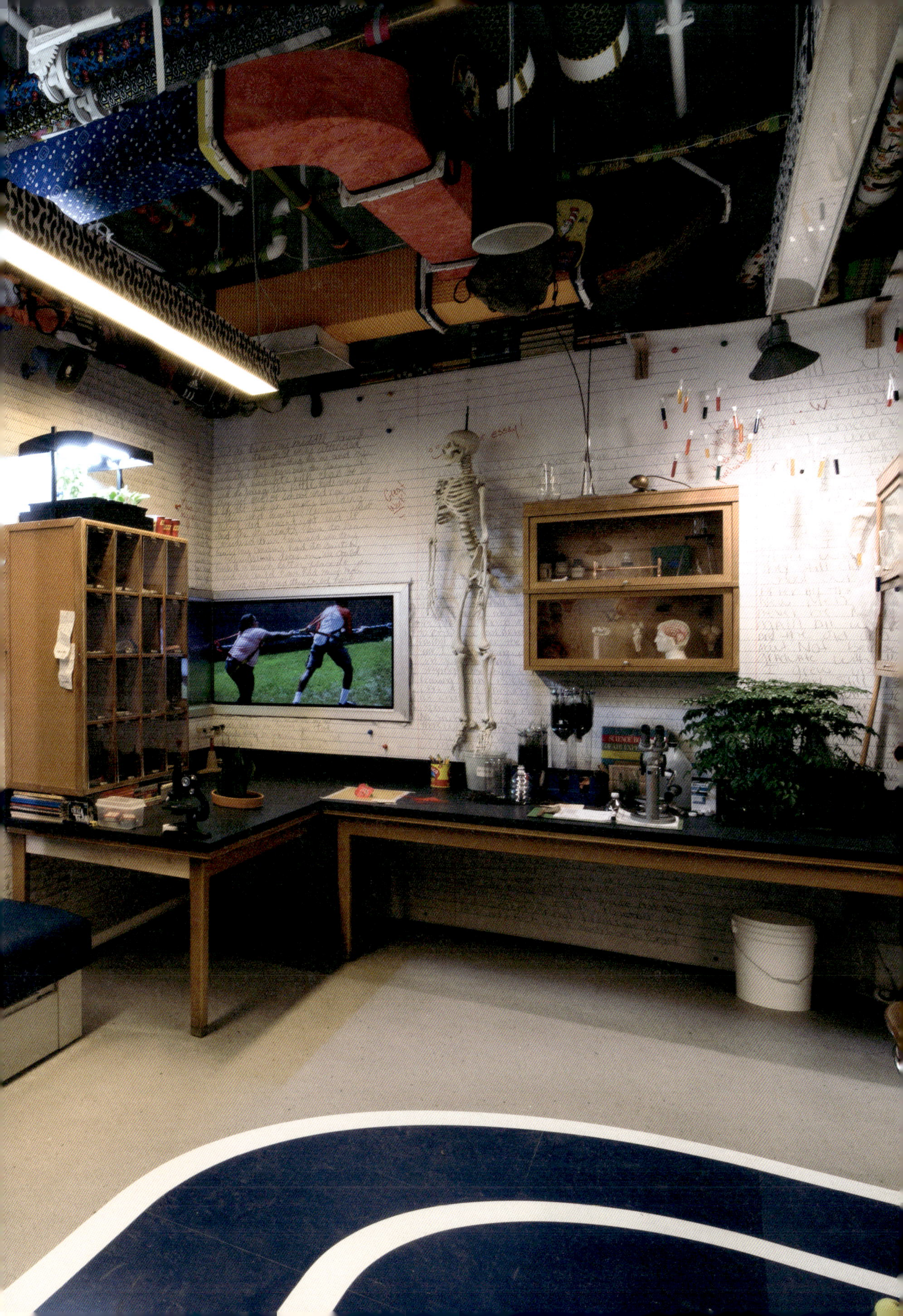

...experience everything over again. ... came out to share.

...d friends I had at Fairhill. I don't see them a lot and... ...e. I only see them sometimes. It's a shame to have seen our school closed. It's really upsetting. How can someone take a child's education away? We can't keep letting schools close down ...e Fairhill did. We need our education. Some students didn't get to graduate from Fairhill like I did. My brother and I got the chance to graduate from Fairhill but my sister did not. I was upset to see her sad because she ...ot graduate from Fairhill. I also miss the good teachers I had. We all miss Fairhill a lot. It would be great to see Fairhill open again one day. Maybe in the future it will. Who knows. My new school is not like Fairhill. My new school is ...ay different. I know that everywhere I go I always think of Fairhill. I know that most of us will. The closing of Fairhill affected a lot of people. Fairhill will always be a great school even if it closed down. Fairhill will always remain in our hearts. Forever! It's hard to say goodbye, but Fairhill will never ever be forgotten. R.I.P.

Looking forward to the final work! Great Start!

My feelings about my midle school closing down!! When I heard that my midle ...was about to close down I was upset! I told myself that I wasn't going to let them close down my midle school! I promised myself that I wasn't going to go down with out a fight. So I decided to join a program called Y.U.C that stood for (Youth United for Change). This program was to help stop schools from closing down. I was so determined that I had to stop ... so I could go to the school district and ...protested for our school. But at the end of ... down and their ... it was ...

... way we will ~~when~~ be ... going to be the same if they open back up our school. But I don't think that's going to happen. I wonder what they are going to do with our school. I miss Fairhill also. I miss cutting class and giving attitude to the teacher. We want our school back! Because When we speak you Listen! They took our school for no reason at all. Where the money going at cause their not going to our School! (R.I.P. Fairhill that school of mines!)

Excellent Work! Check your punctuation before your next Rewrite.

:) Can't wait to see the revisions! Very Emotional

I miss Fairhill school because My friends are now seperated from me. When I was in Fairhill I had the time of my life. My friends weren't the ~~best~~ ~~friends~~ but they were always there for me. I loved going to the after-school programs and playing ball with my friends for the team and for fun. I miss those days. Whenever I see the school and the mine, I want to break into tears. My second family was torn apart. I never thought this would ever happen to me or my friends.. I felt like I wouldn't be ok. When I was about to leave on the last day, I thought I wouldn't fit in anywhere else.

I went to a small school up the block and hated it when I first came and stood quiet and didn't talk to anyone at all.

I still wish Fairhill school was still open so I would visit it and see it improve from what I saw. When I found out why it was closed I was outraged! I was mad at the world and I tried to forget it over time when I went to my new school. ~~It~~ It left a scar in me mentality. My little sister was planning to go to Potter Thomas so there and my cousins had to go ... I almost felt devastated. In the end ... It was

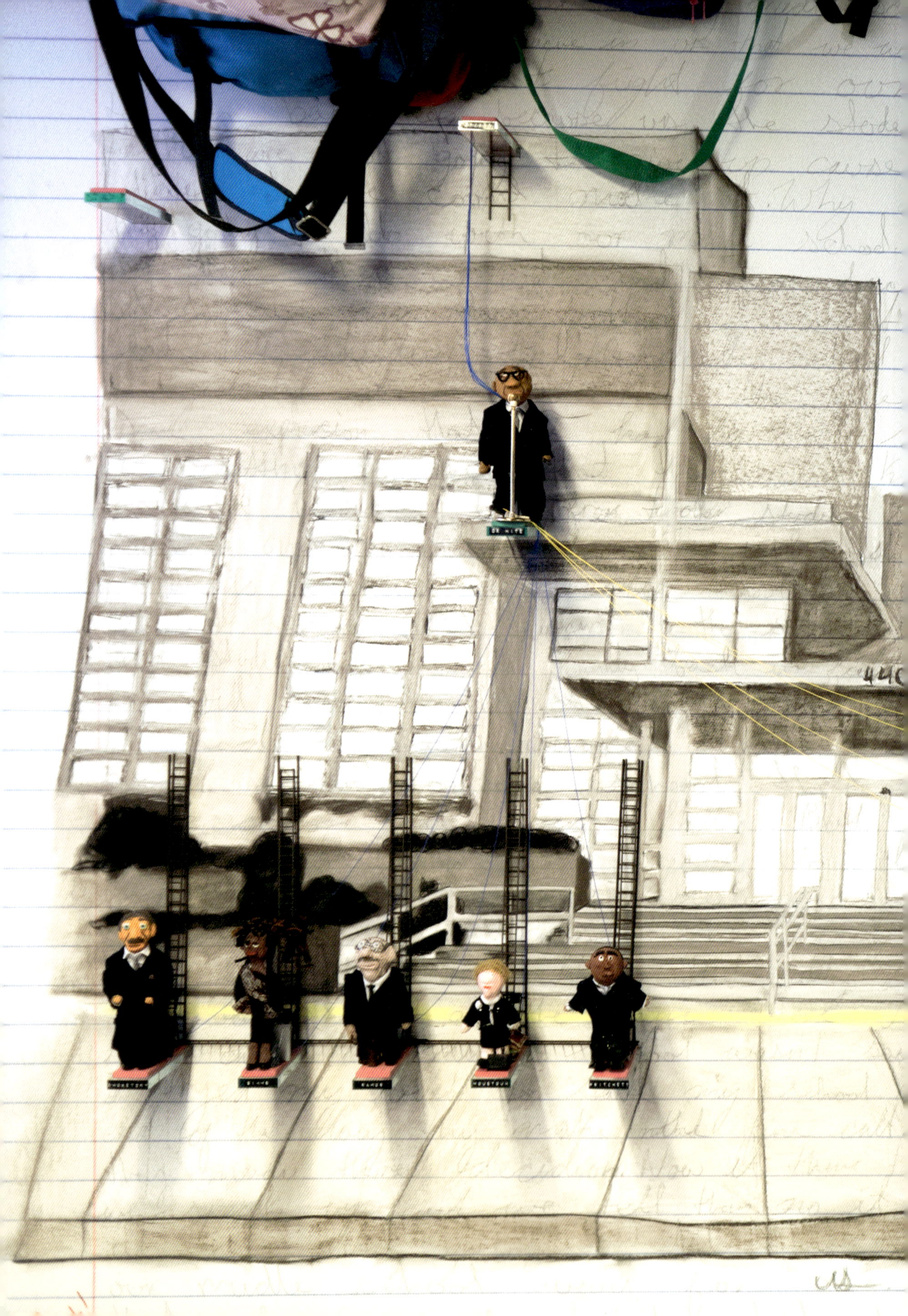

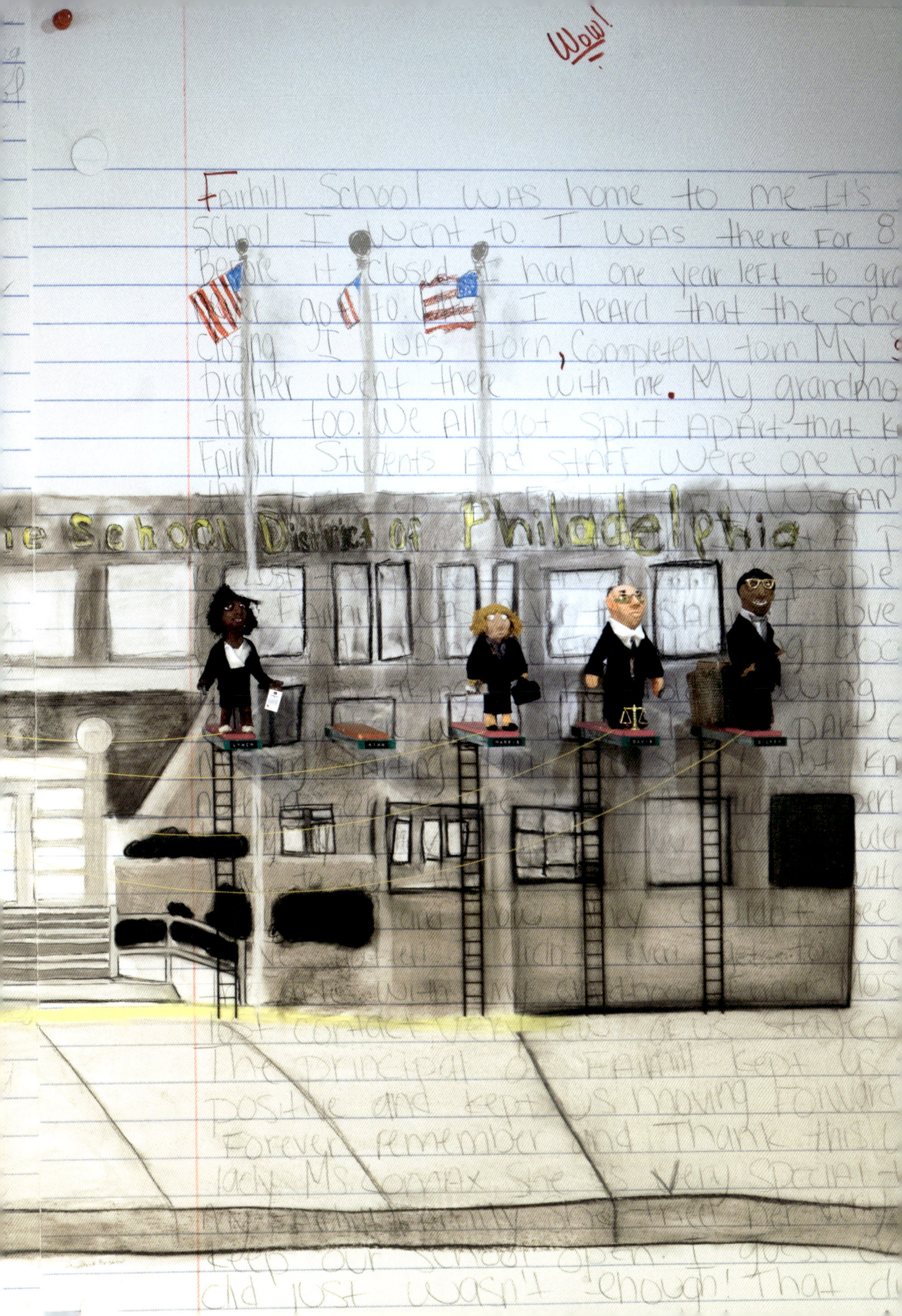

Wow!
School District of Philadelphia
Fairhill School was home to me.
School I went to. I was there for 8
Before it closed I had one year left to
I heard that the
closing I was torn, completely torn. My
brother went there with me. My
there too. We all got split apart,
Fairhill Students and Staff were one
The principal of Fairhill kept us
positive and kept us moving forward
Forever remember and thank this
keep our school open.
did just wasn't enough! That

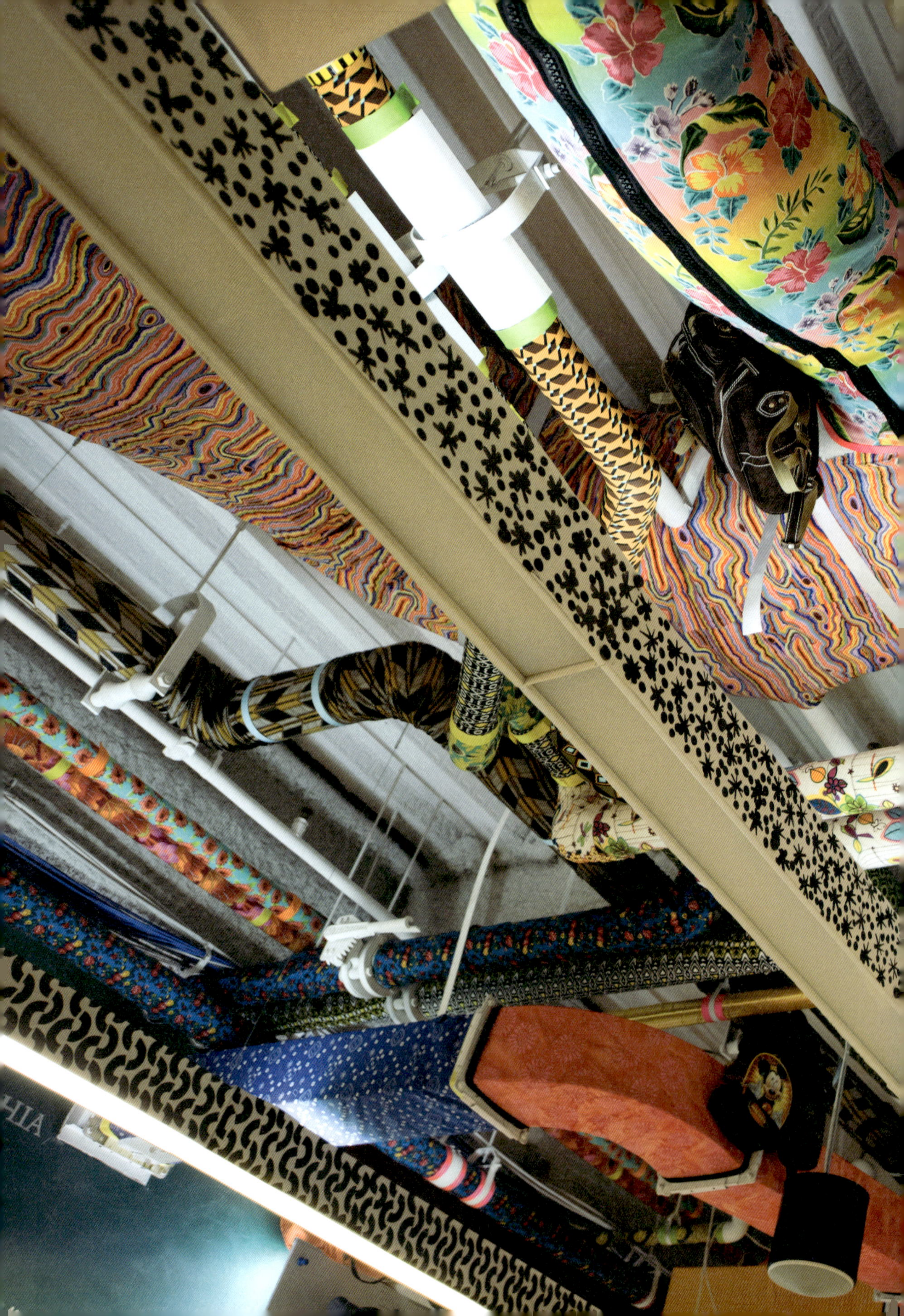

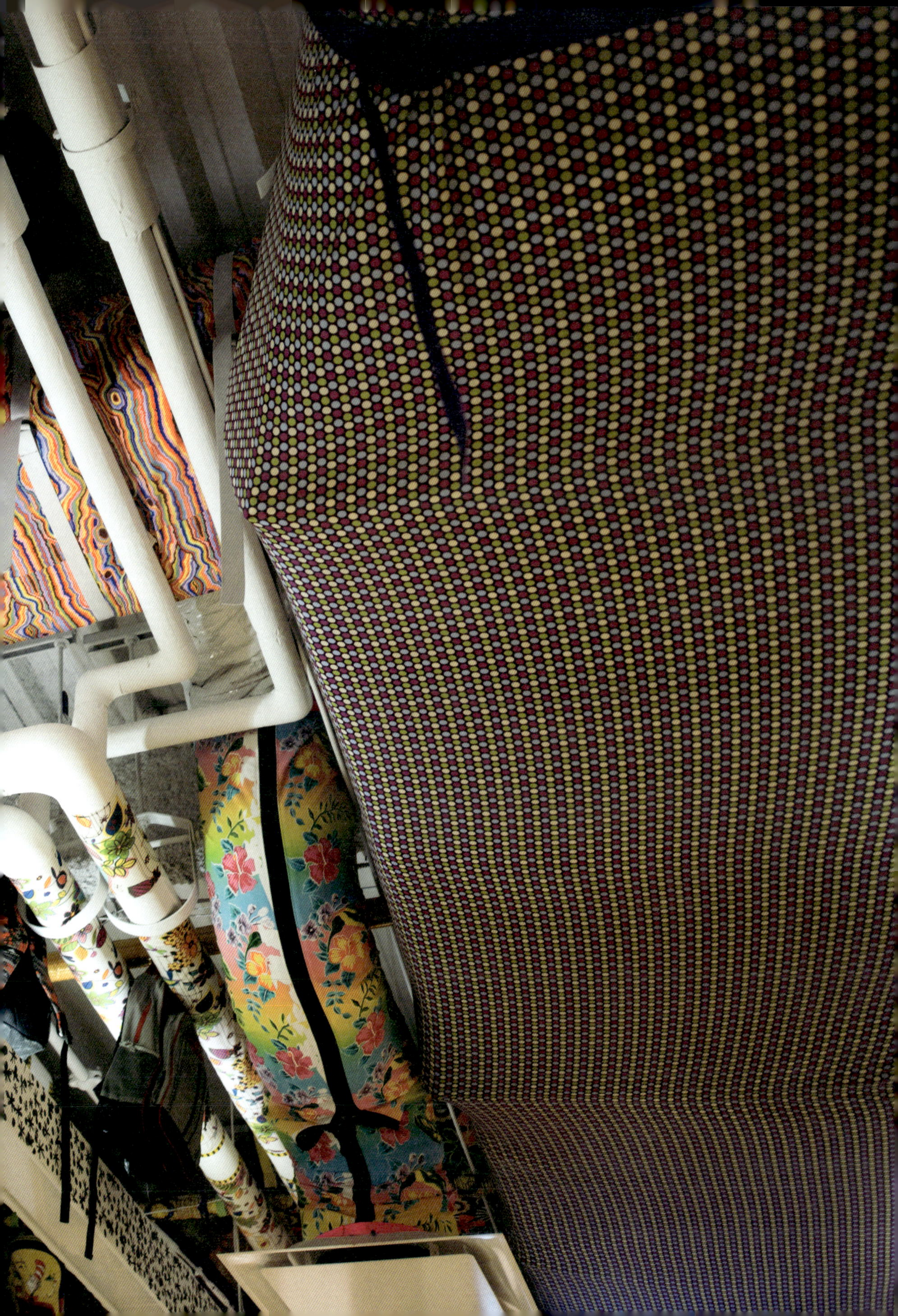

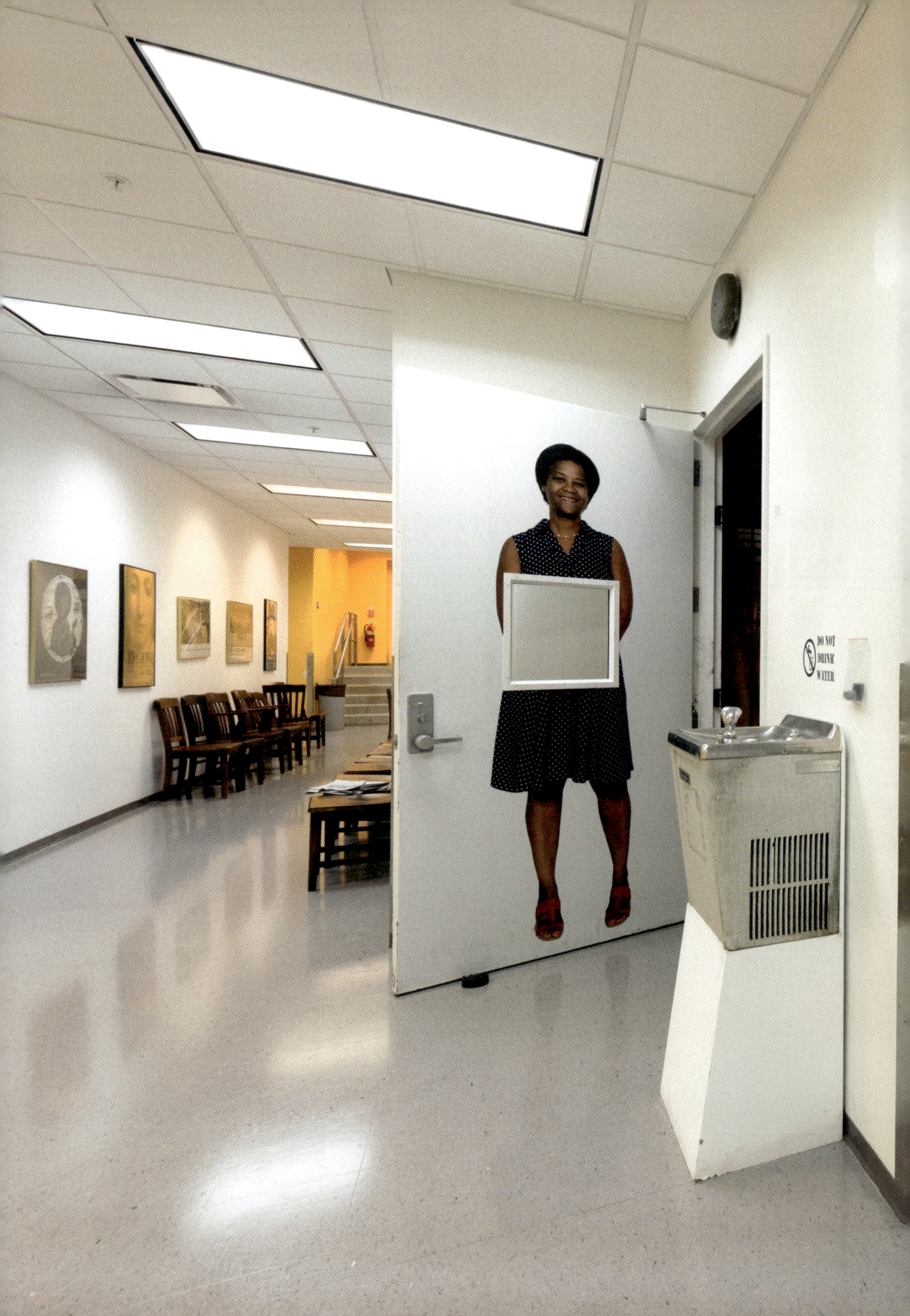
DO NOT
DRINK
WATER

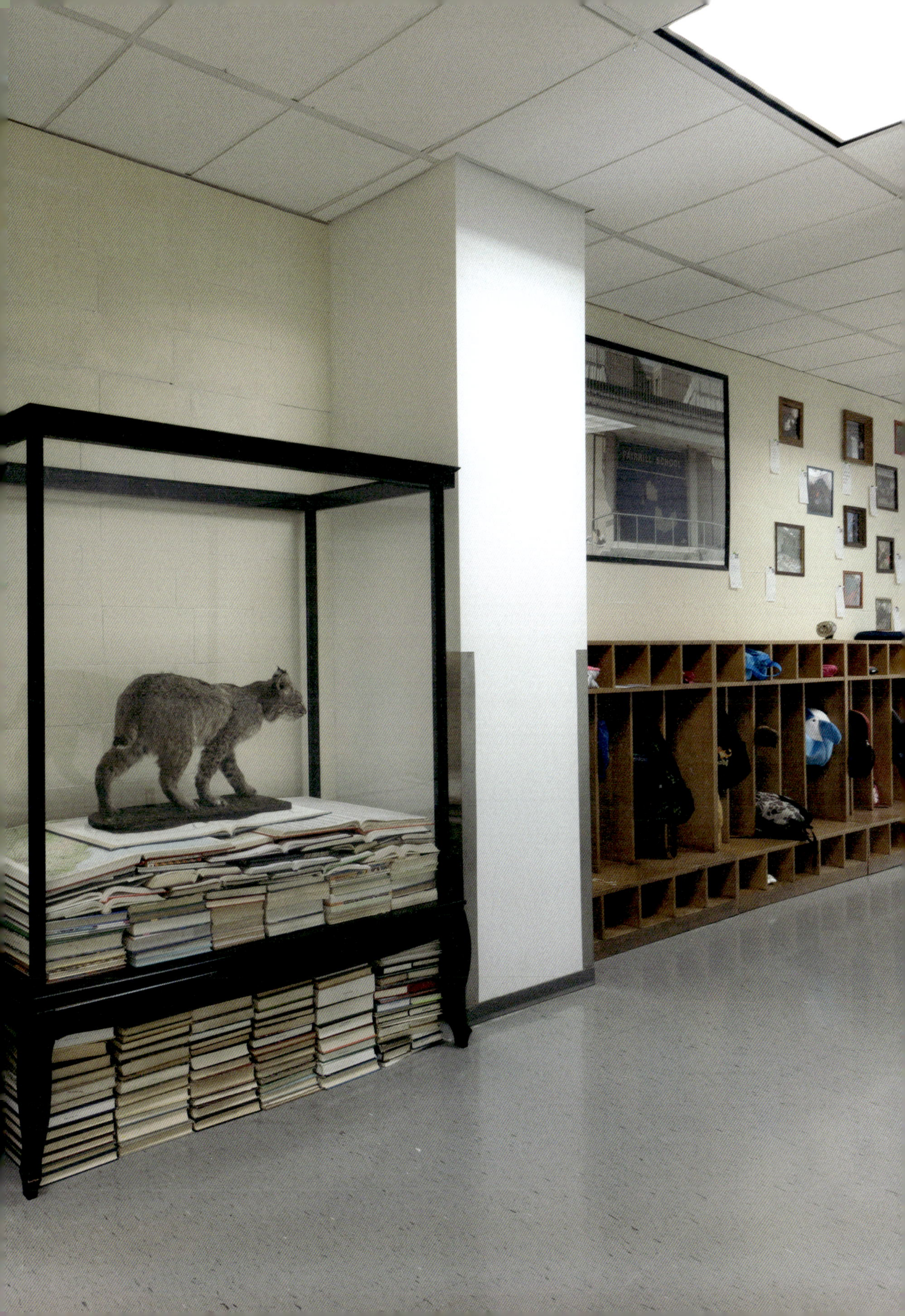

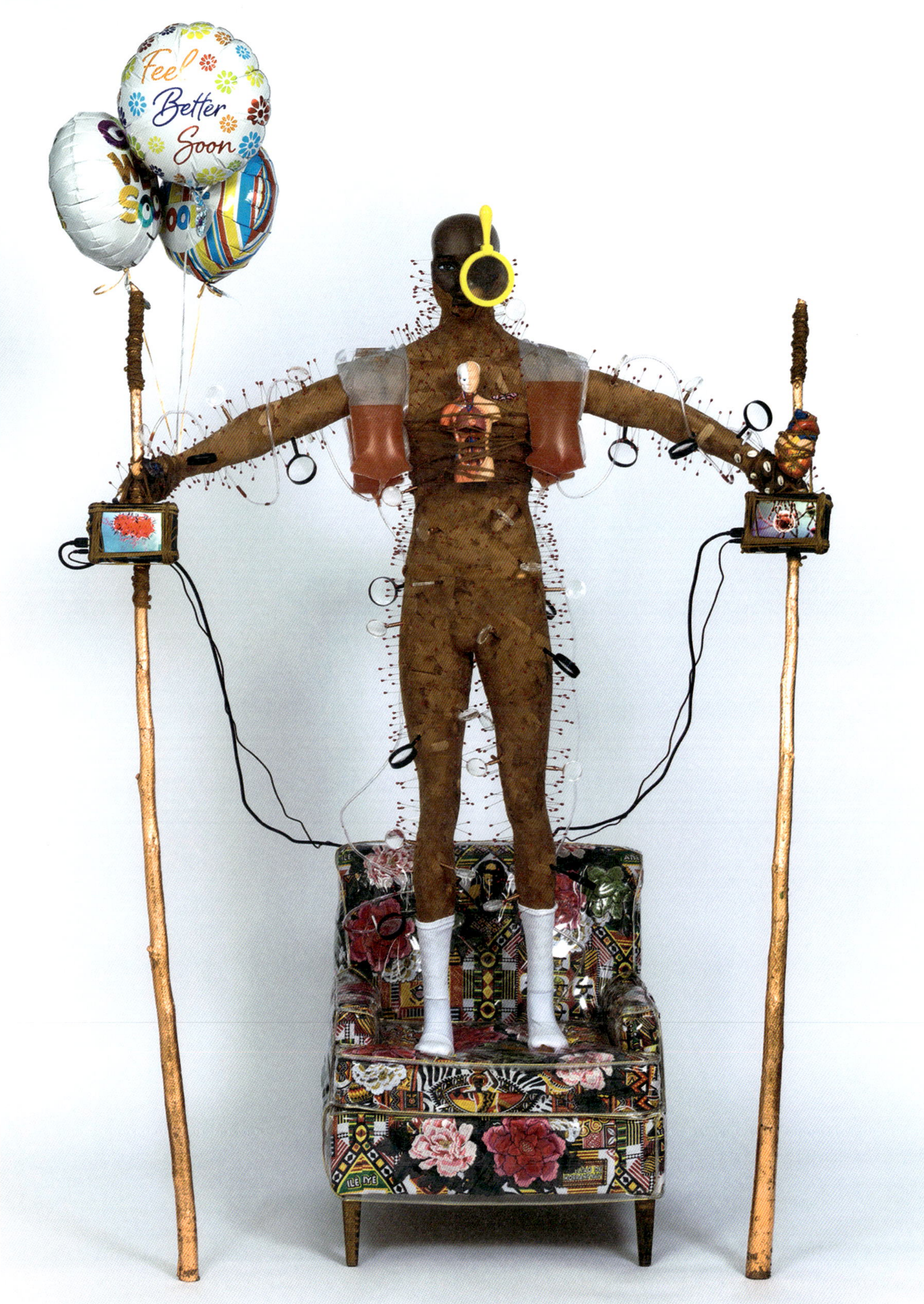
Feel Better Soon

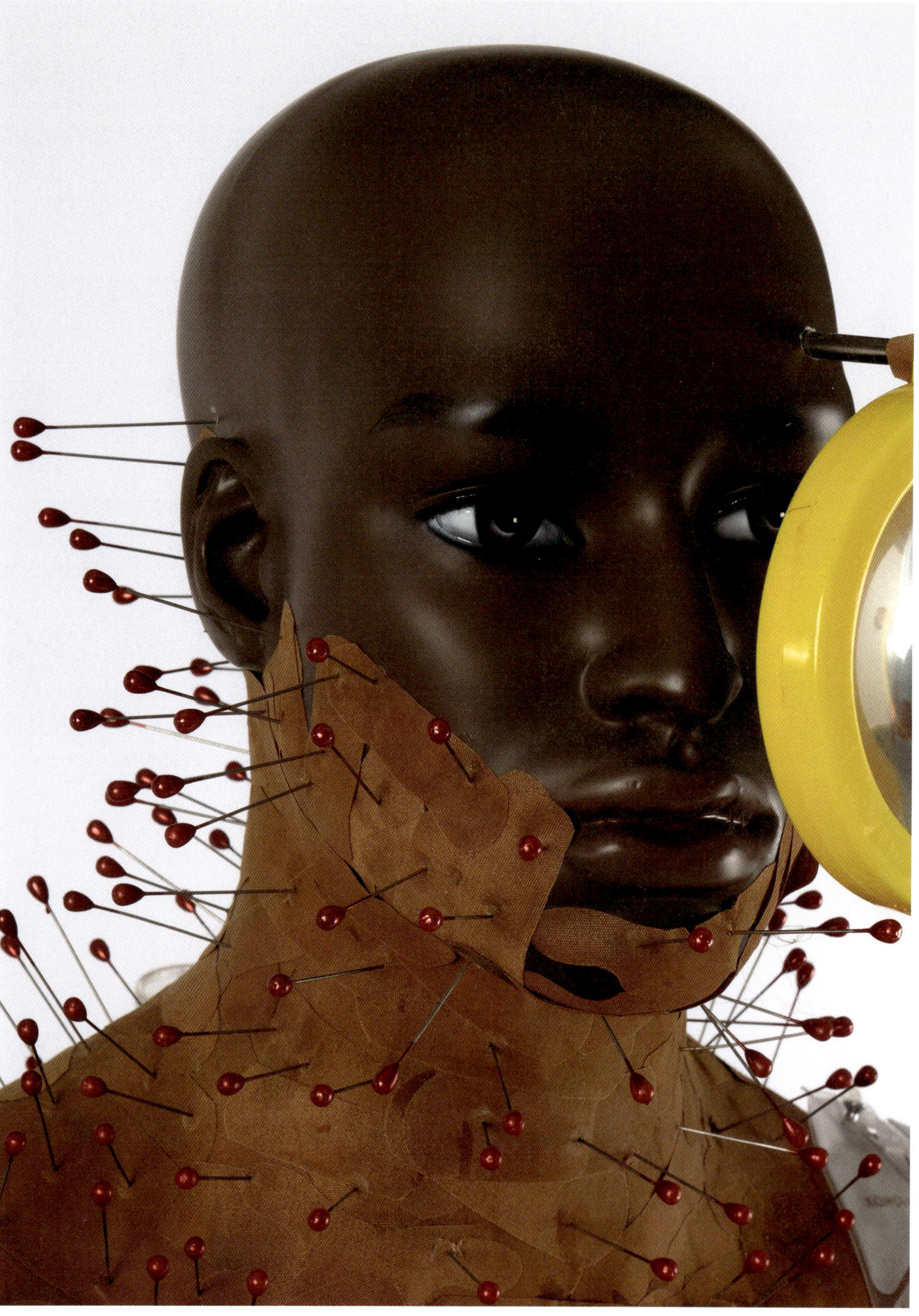

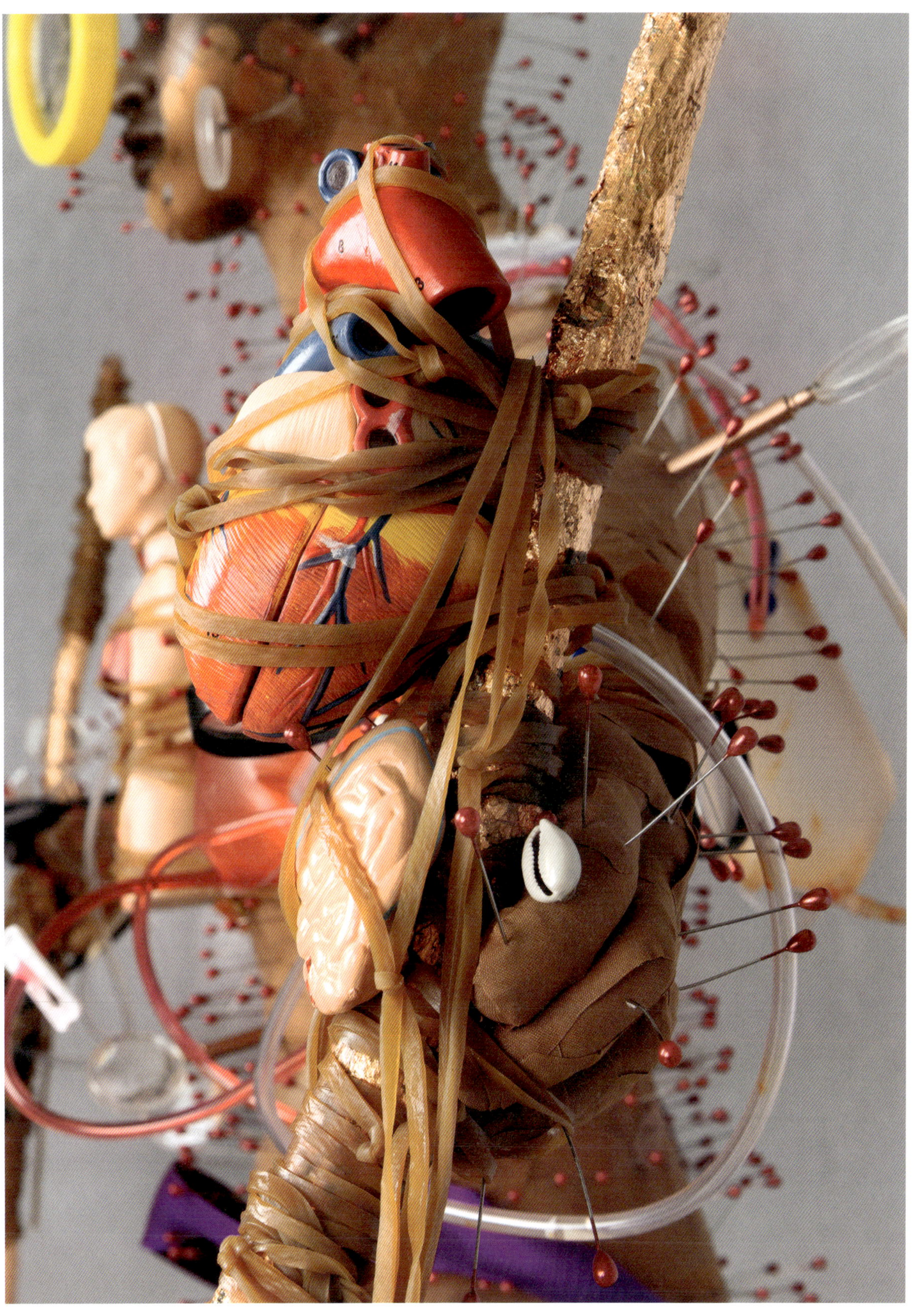

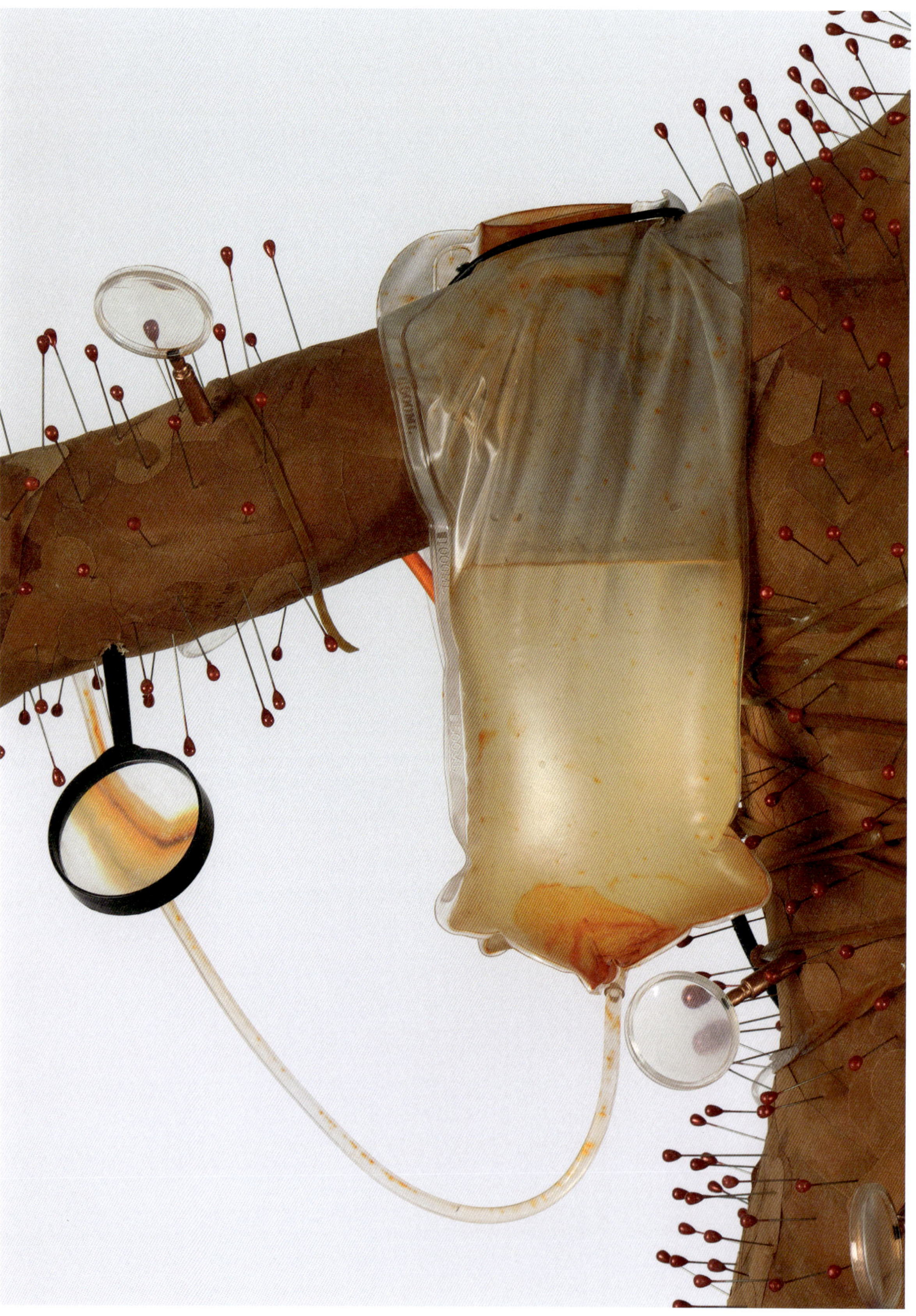

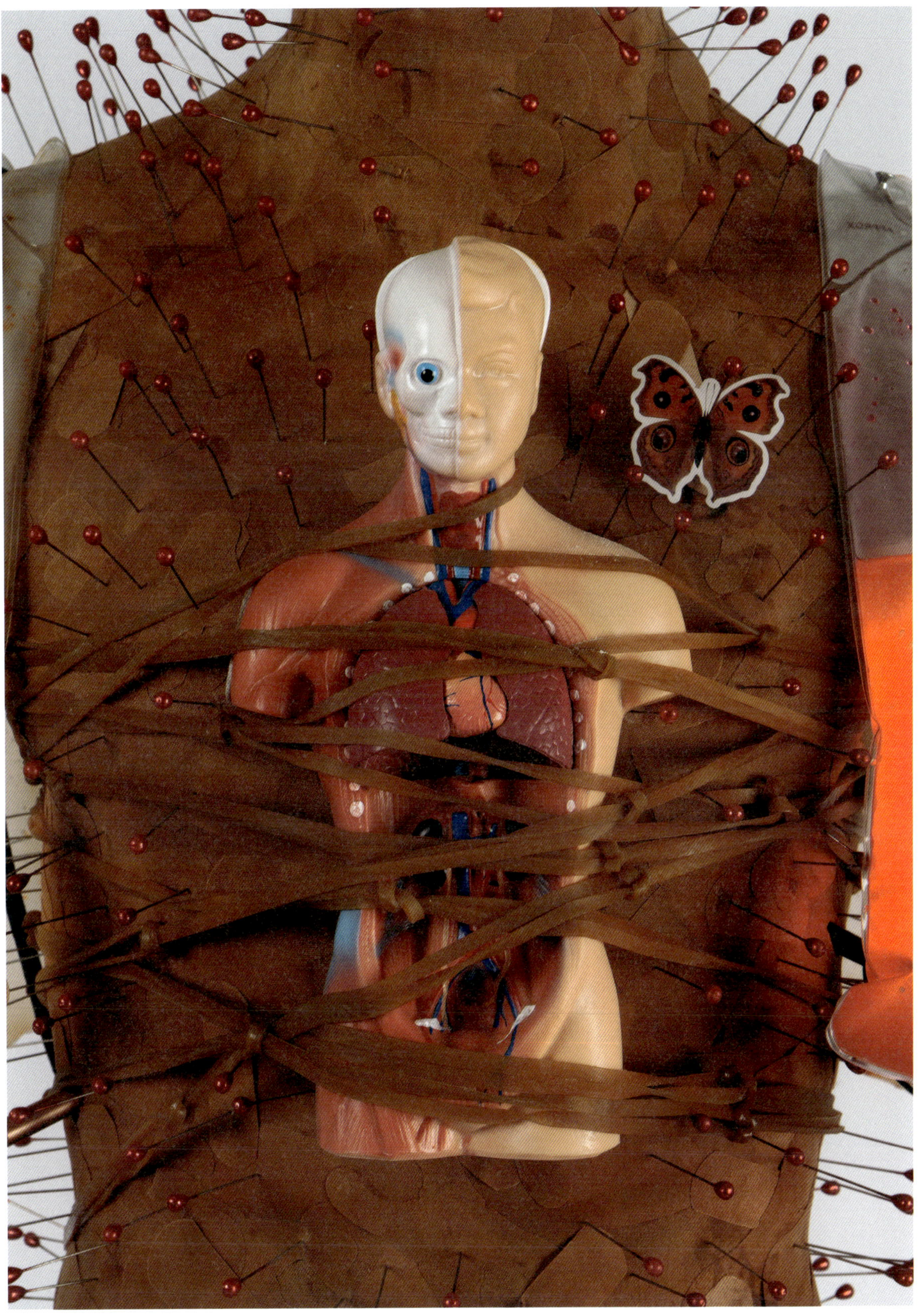

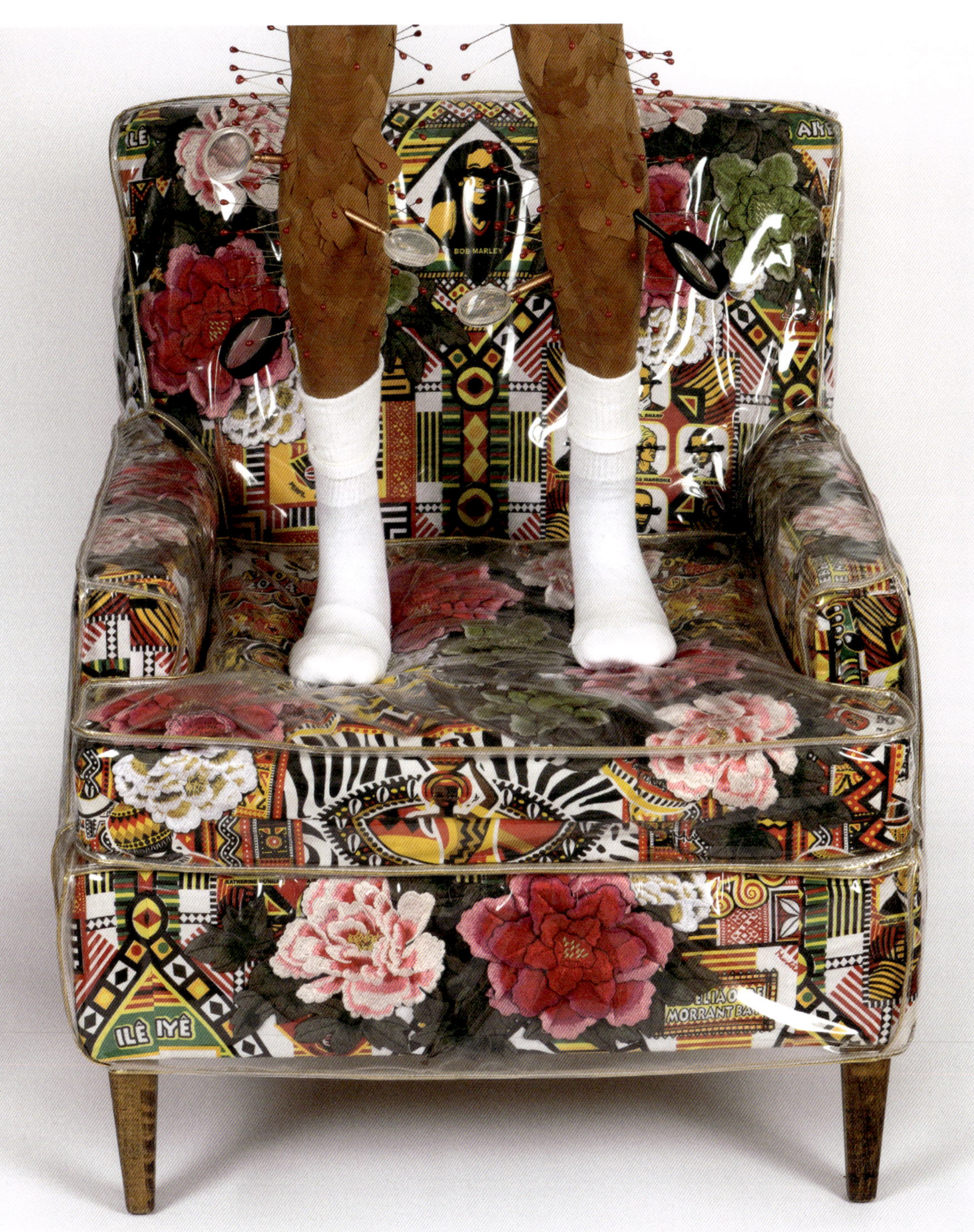
BOB MARLEY
ILÊ IYÊ

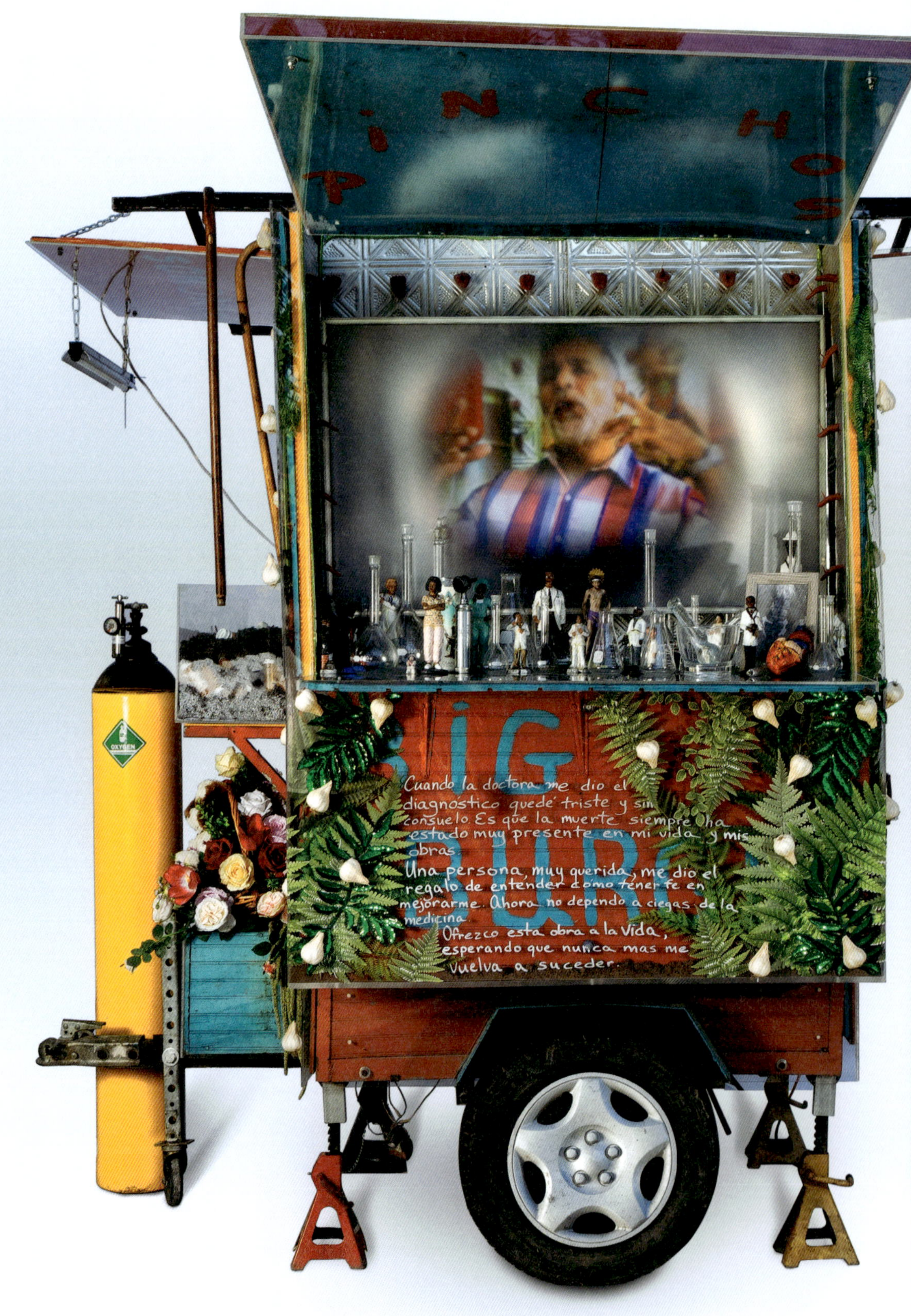
PINCHOS
OXYGEN
Cuando la doctora me dio el
diagnóstico quedé triste y sin
consuelo. Es que la muerte siempre ha
estado muy presente en mi vida y mis
obras.
Una persona, muy querida, me dio el
regalo de entender cómo tener fe en
mejorarme. Ahora no dependo a ciegas de la
medicina.
Ofrezco esta obra a la vida,
esperando que nunca mas me
vuelva a suceder.

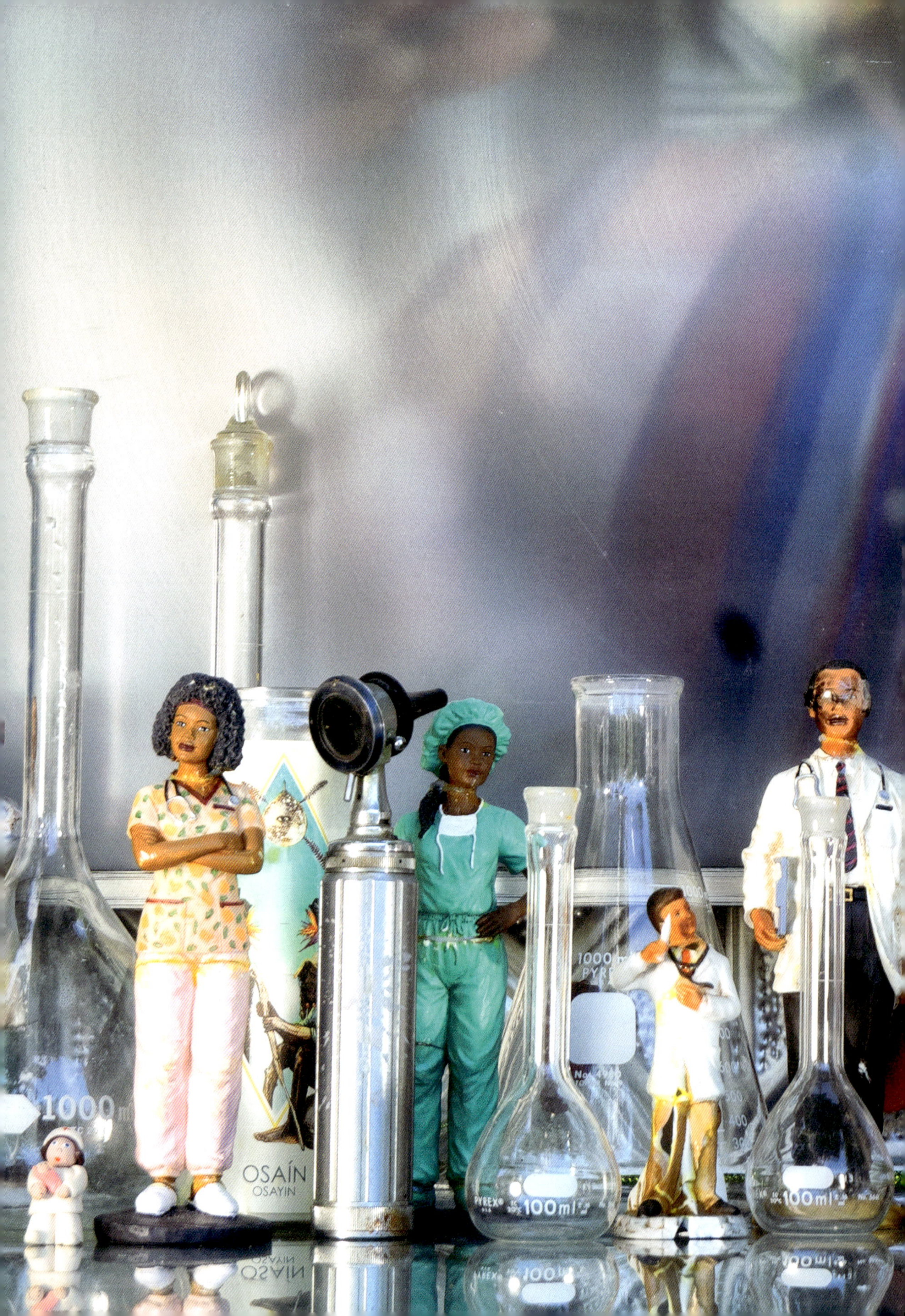

1000 ml
OSAÍN
OSAYIN
PYREX
100 ml
100 ml

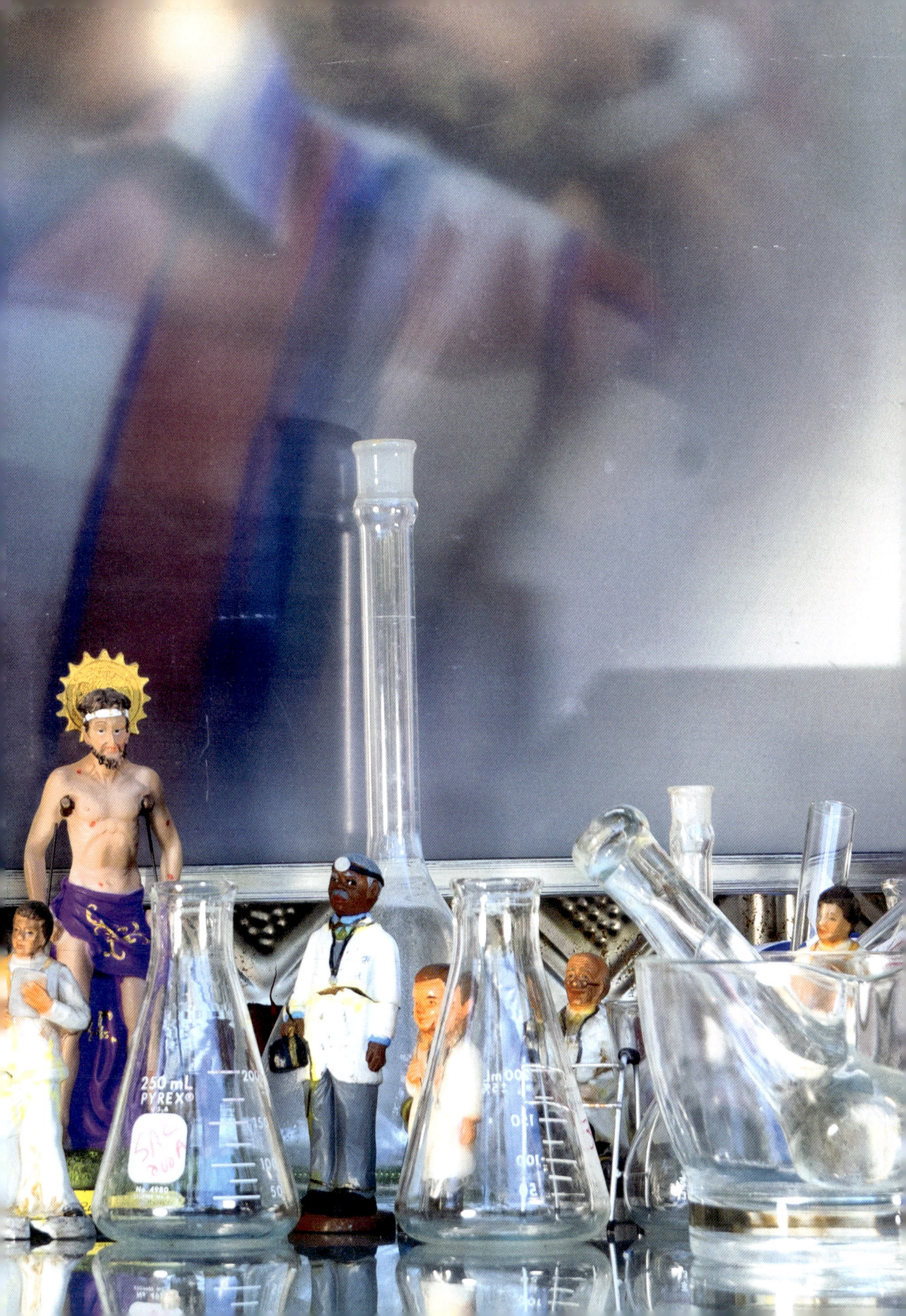
250 mL
PYREX

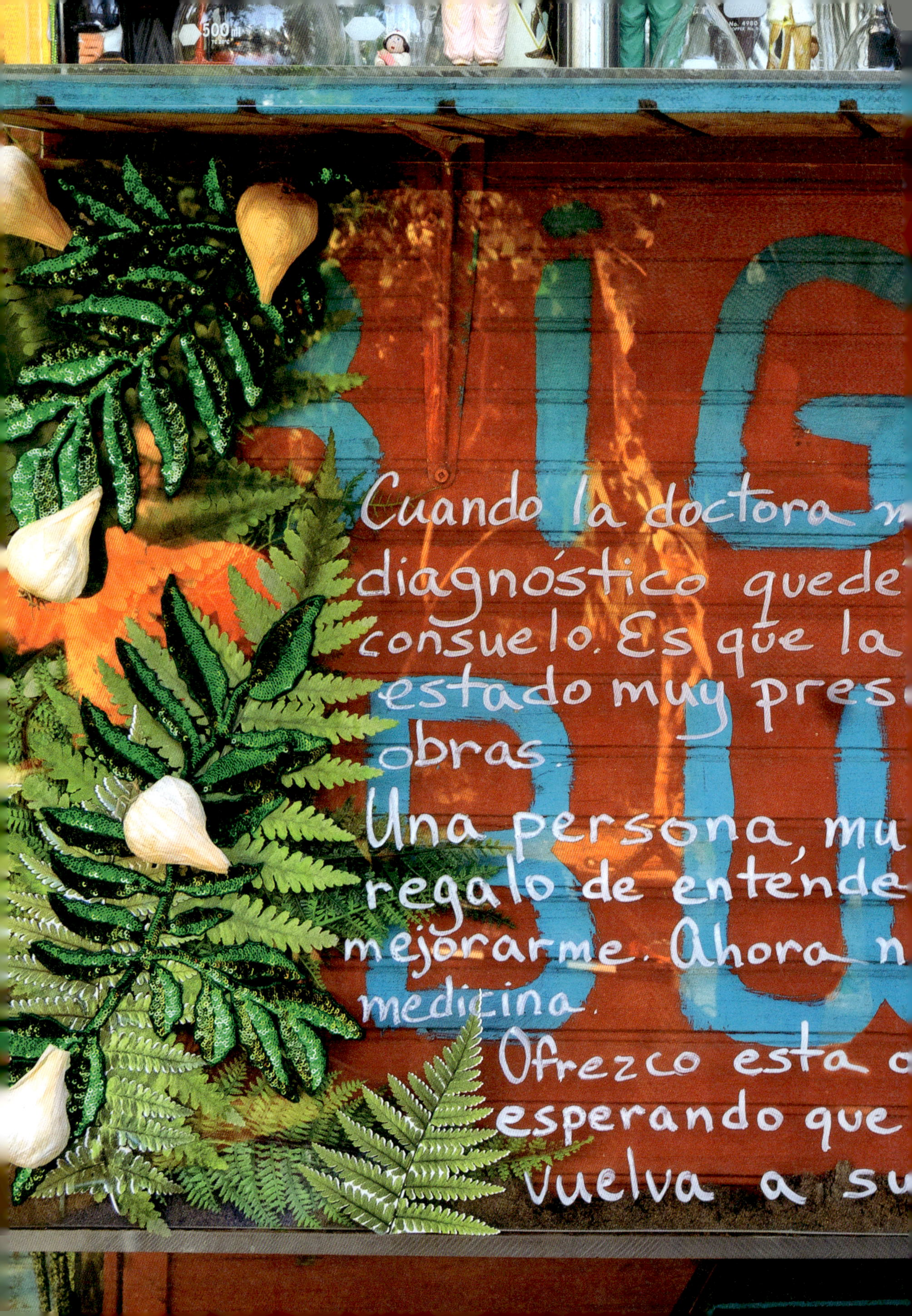
Cuando la doctora
diagnóstico quede
consuelo. Es que la
estado muy pres
obras.
Una persona, mu
regalo de entende
mejorarme. Ahora
medicina.
Ofrezco esta
esperando que
vuelva a su

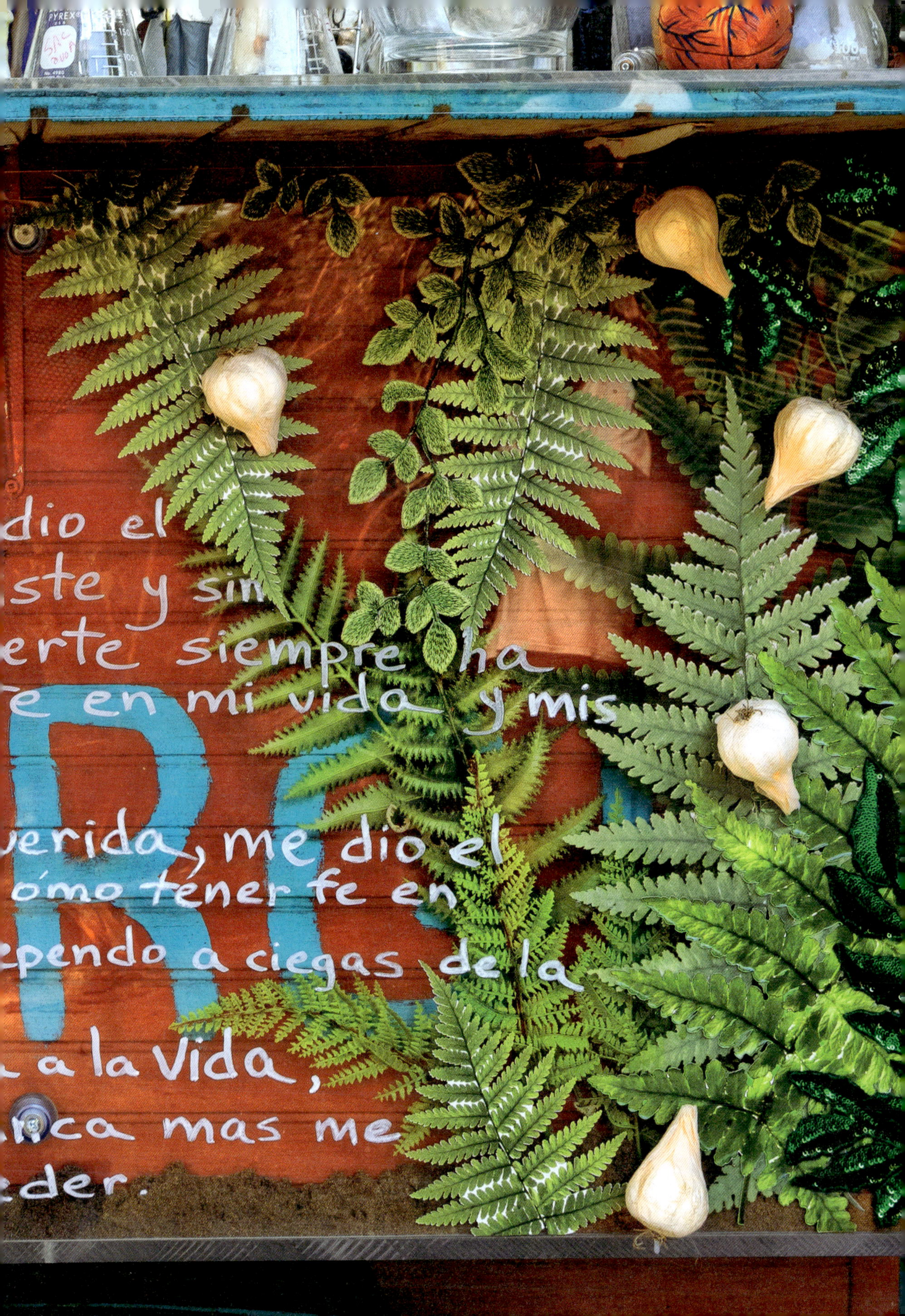

dio el
ste y sin
erte siempre ha
e en mi vida y mis
erida, me dio el
ómo tener fe en
pendo a ciegas de la
a la Vida,
nca mas me
der.

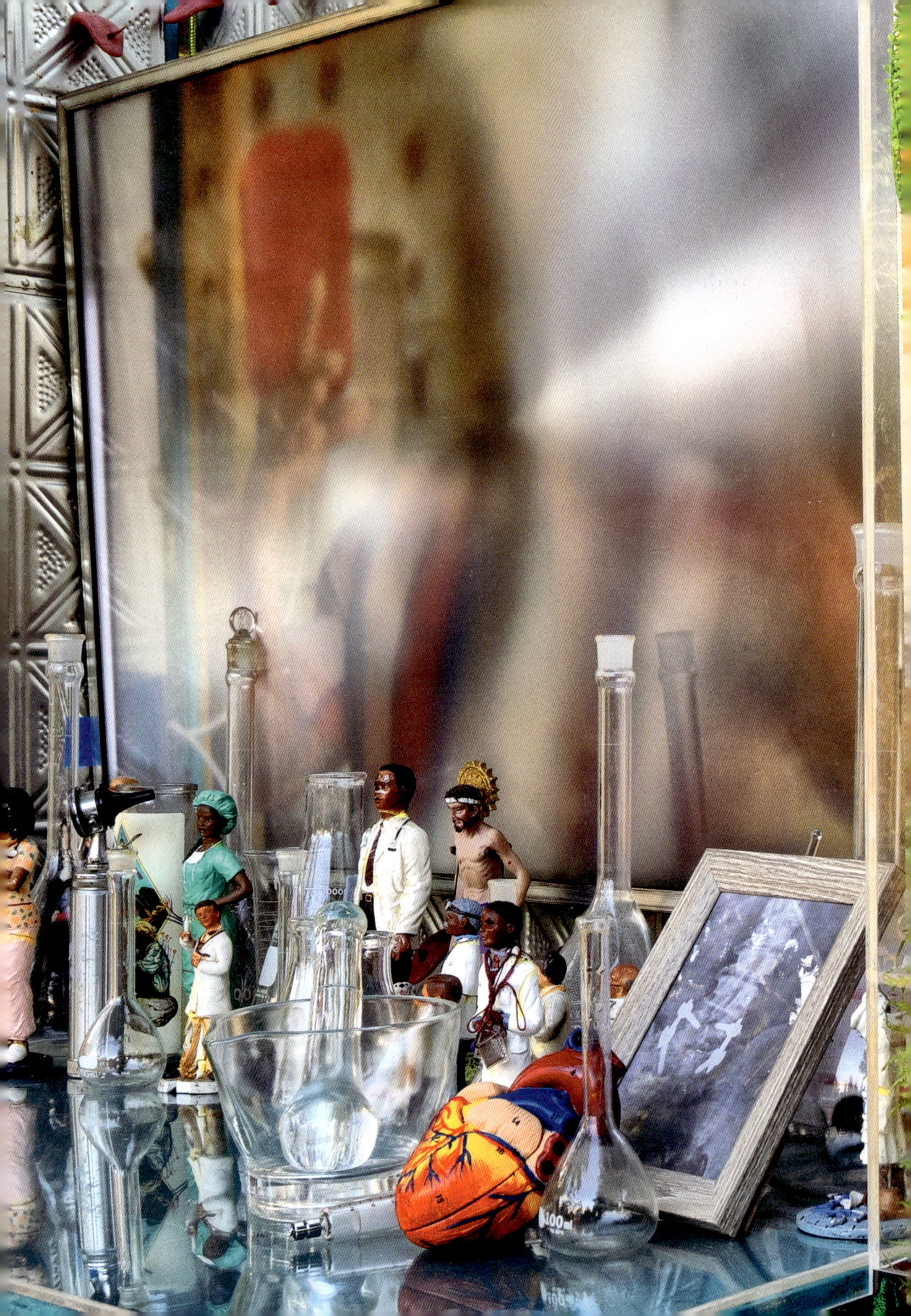

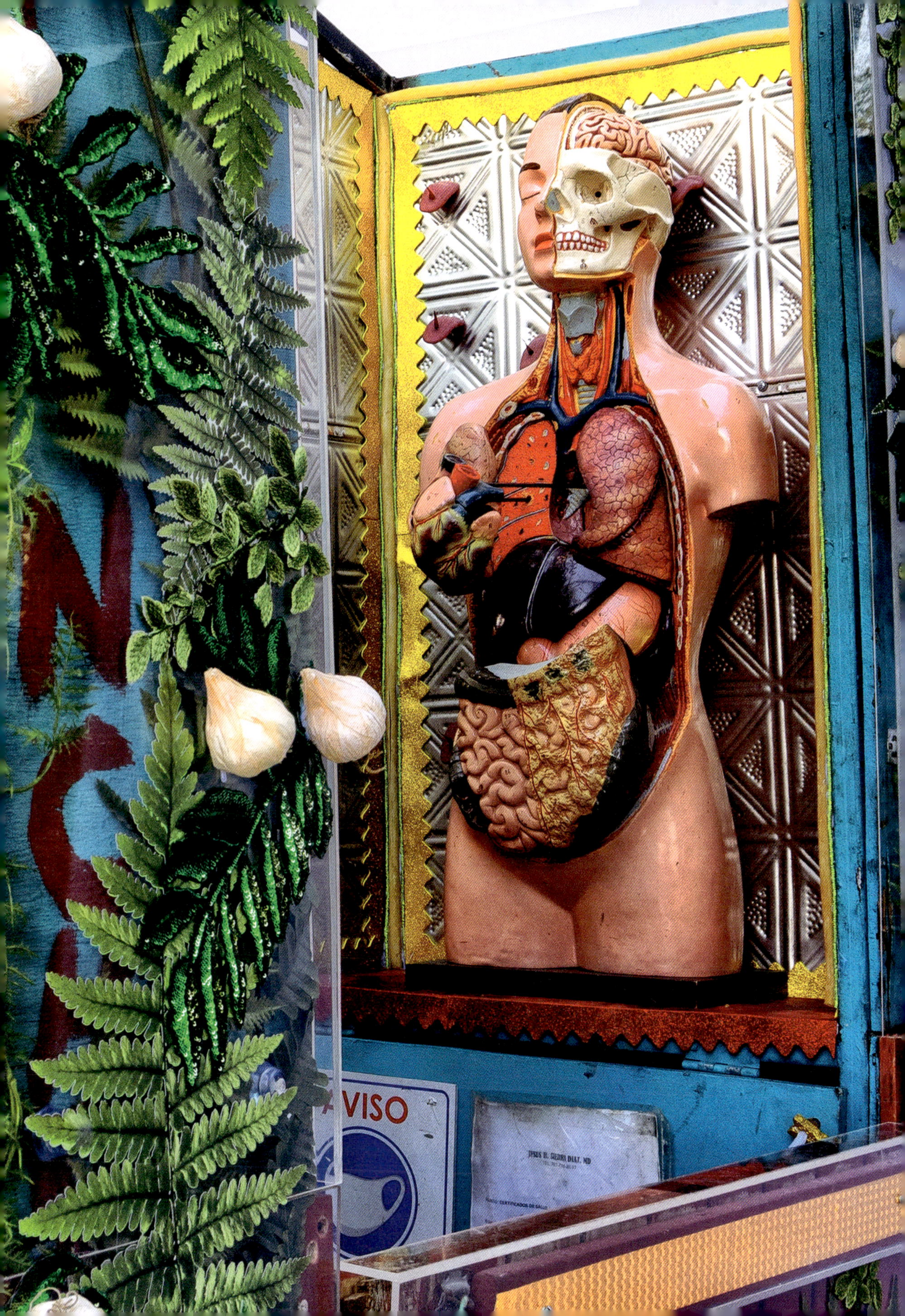
AVISO

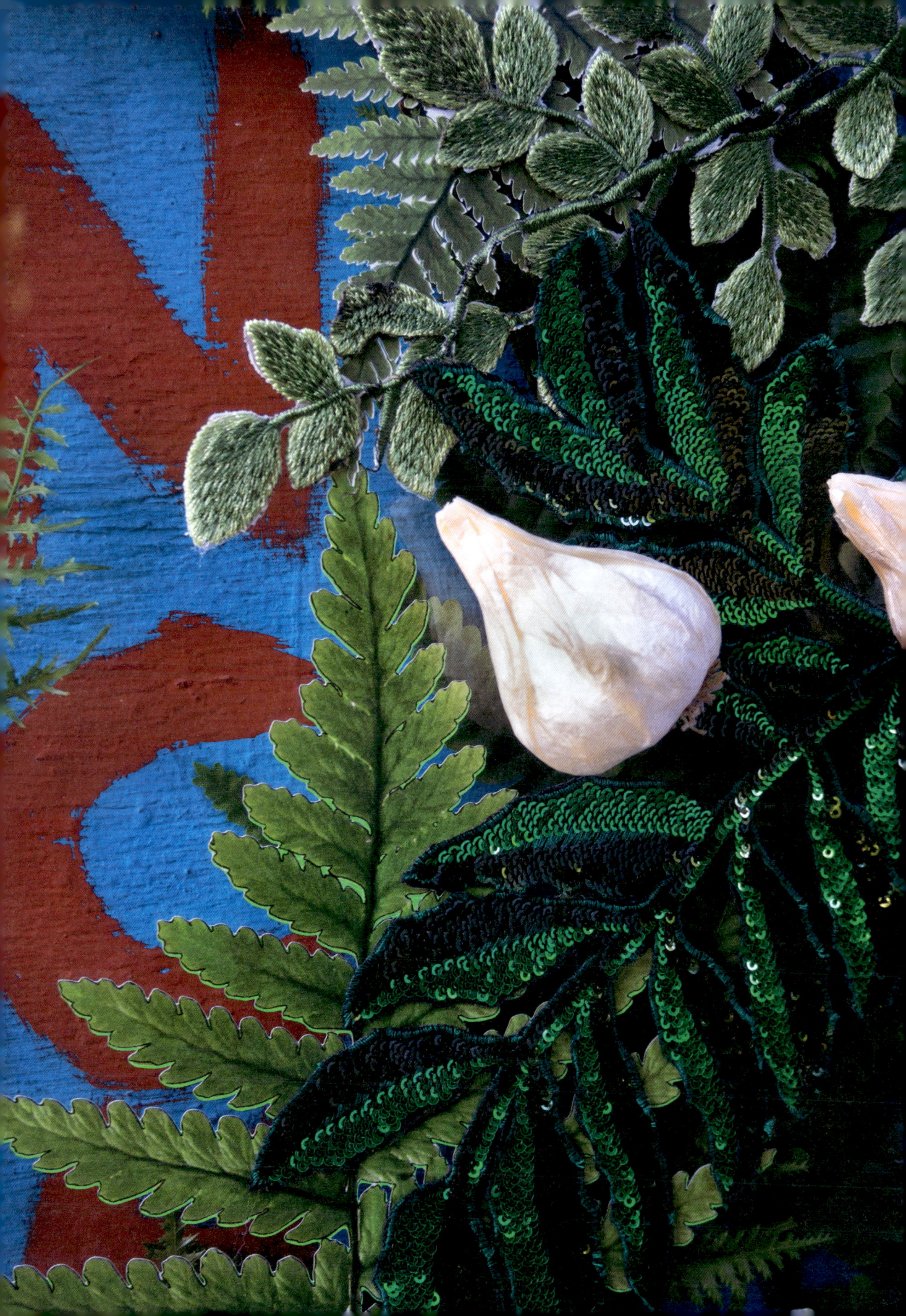

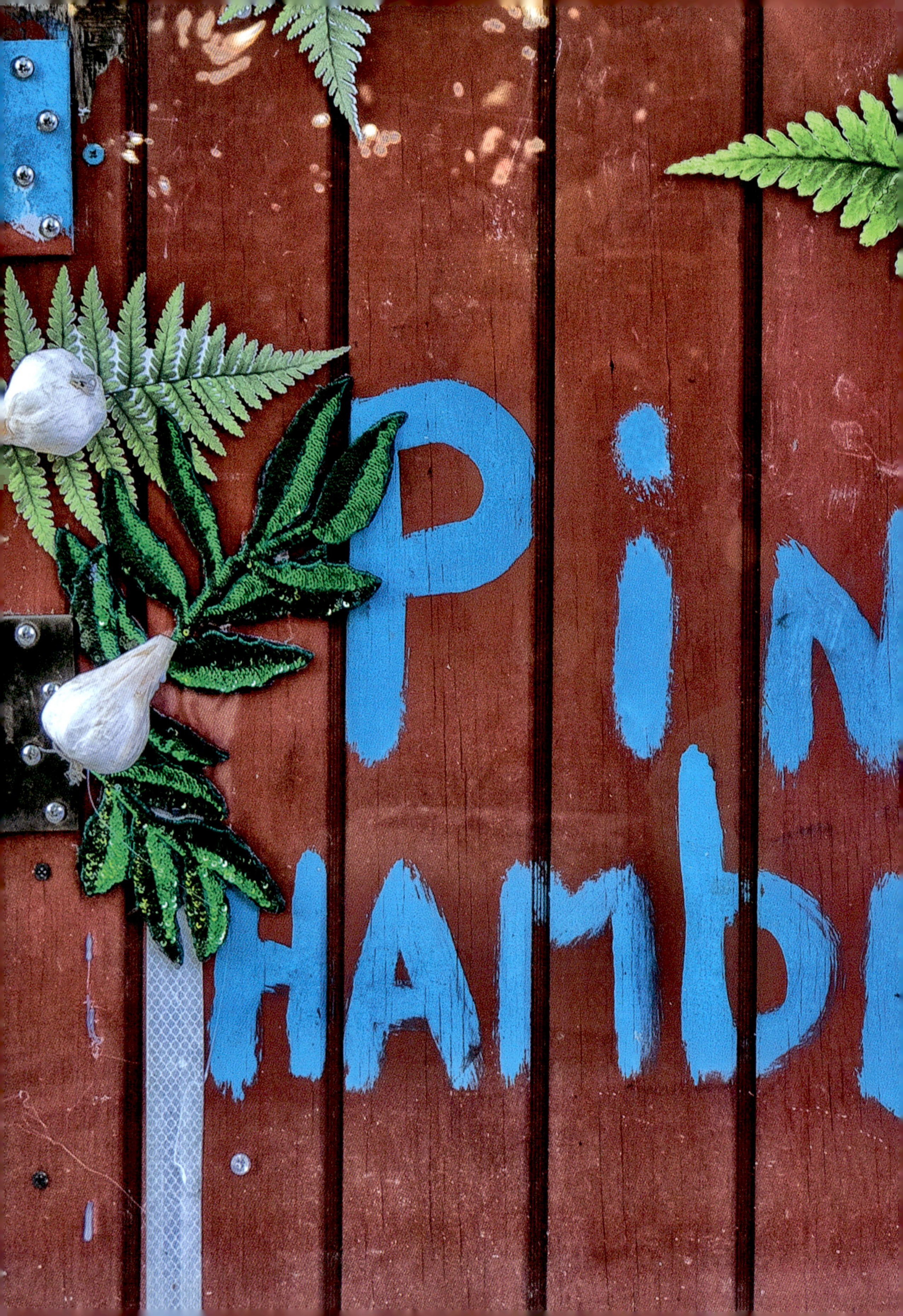

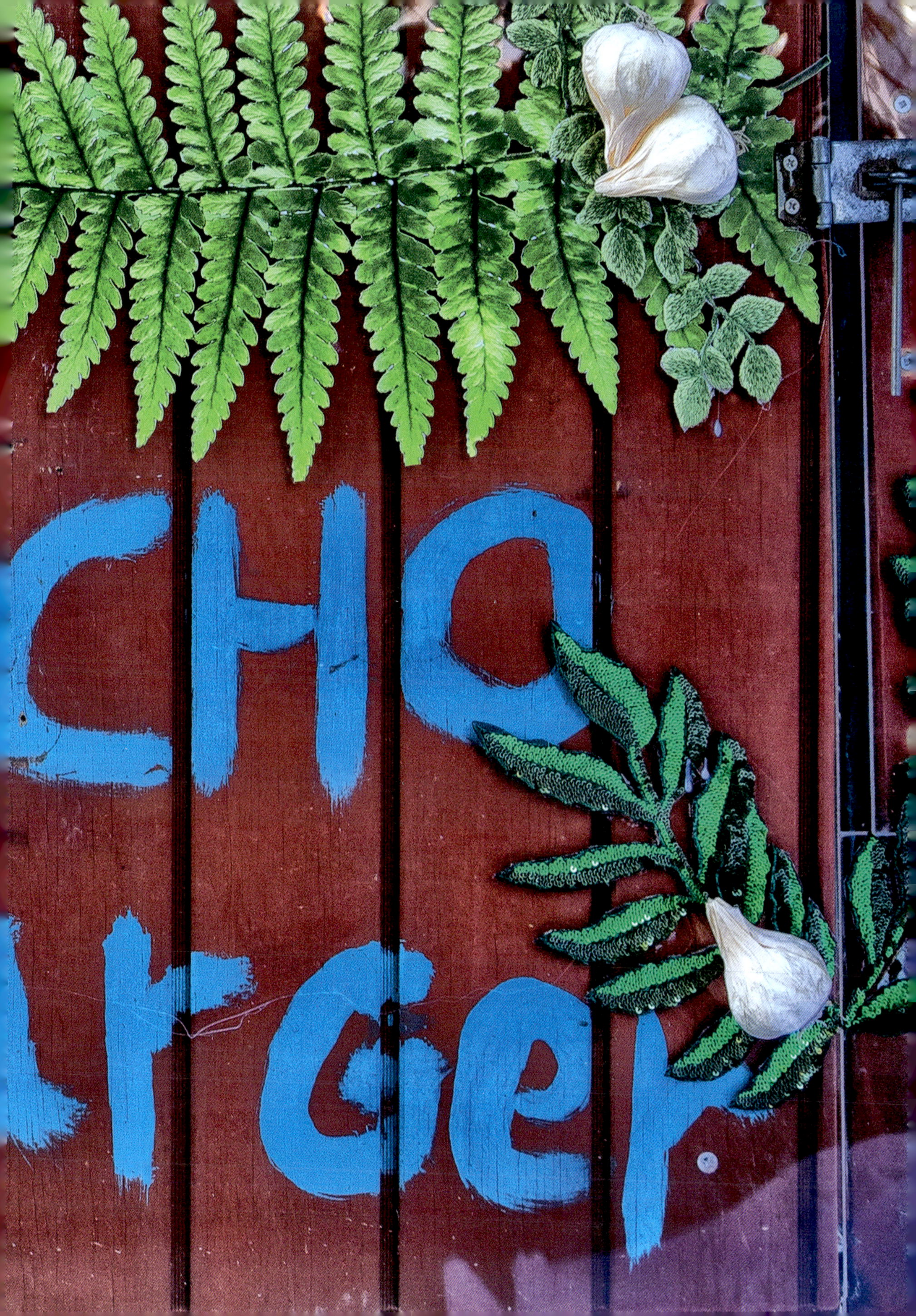

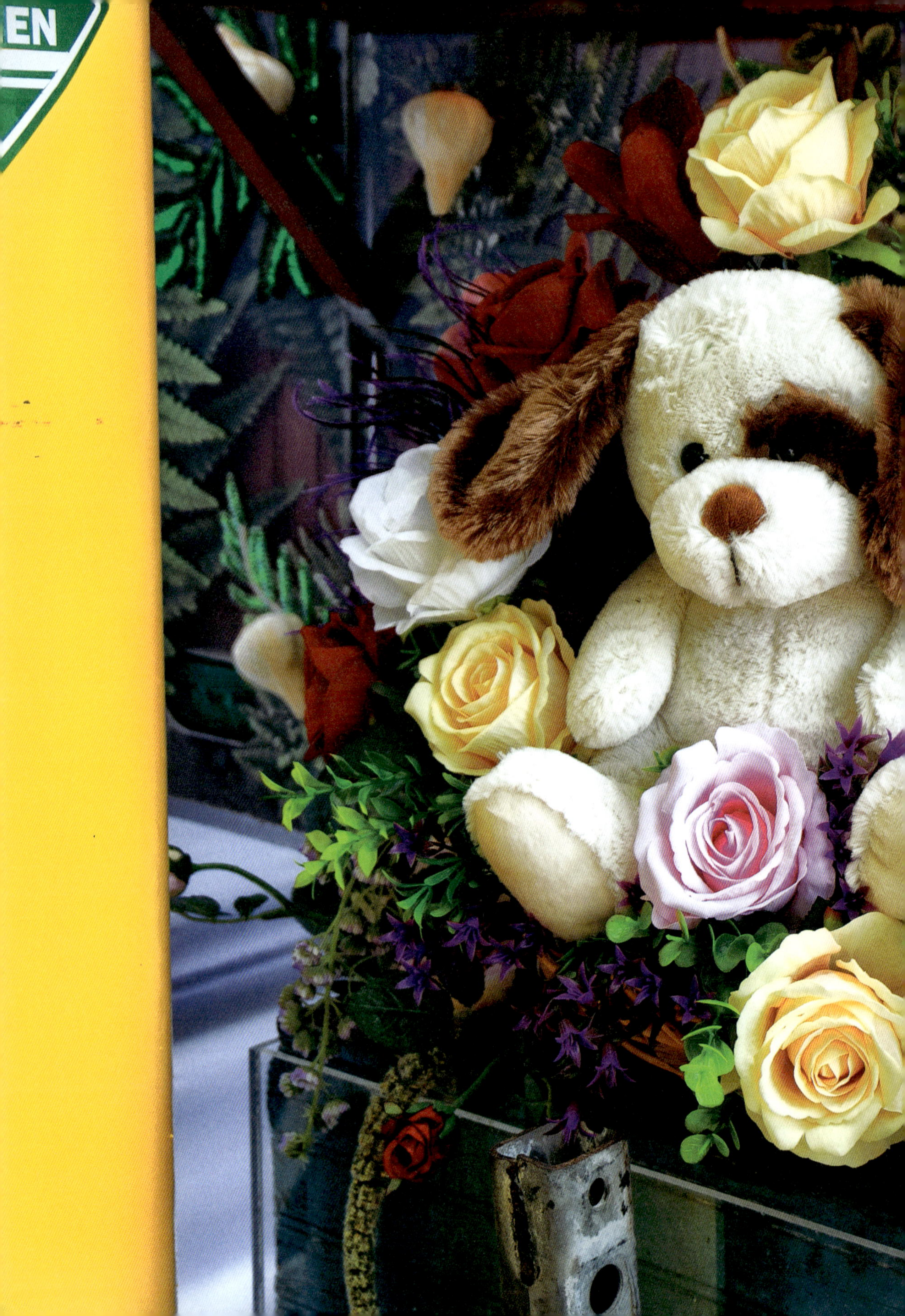

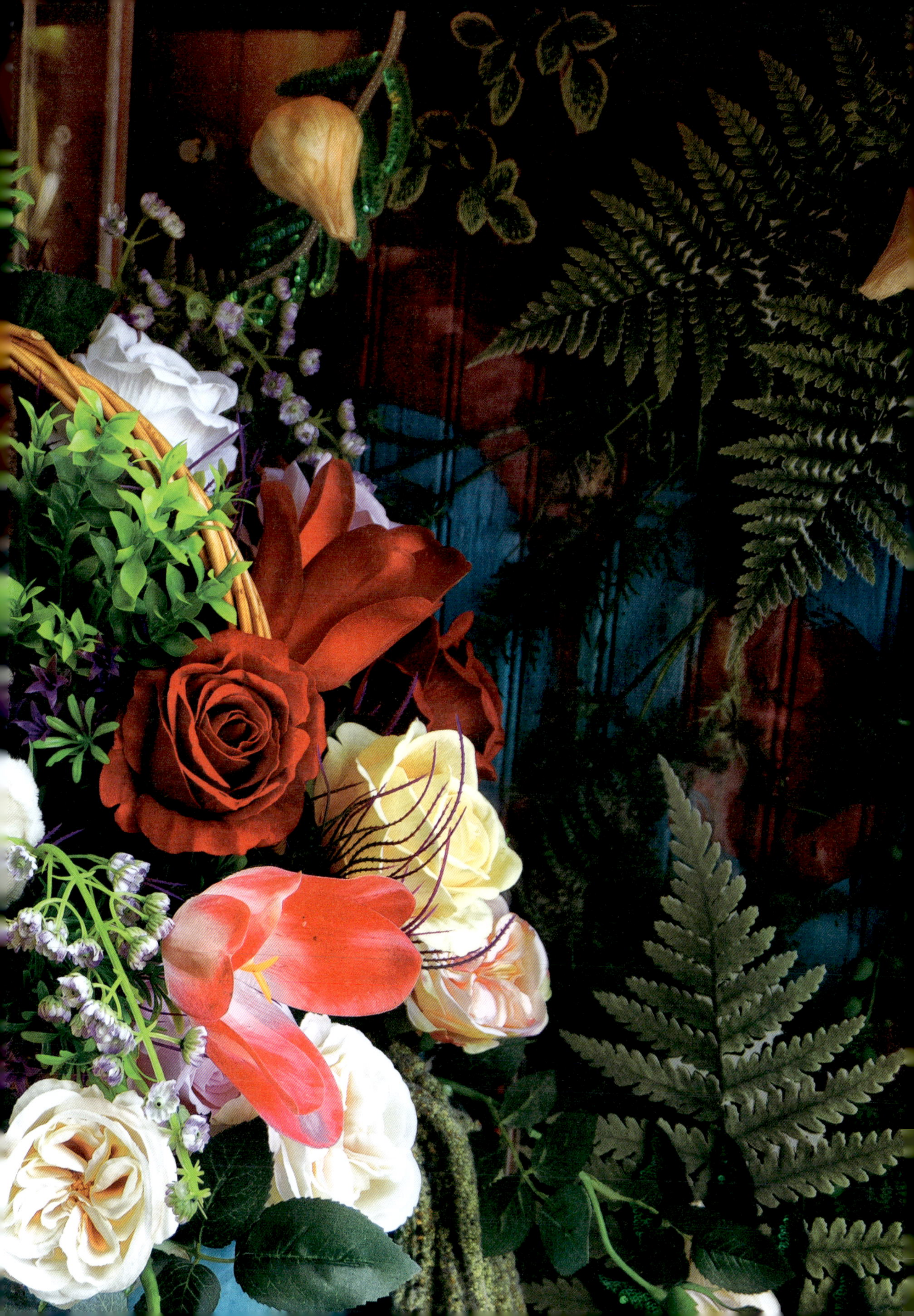

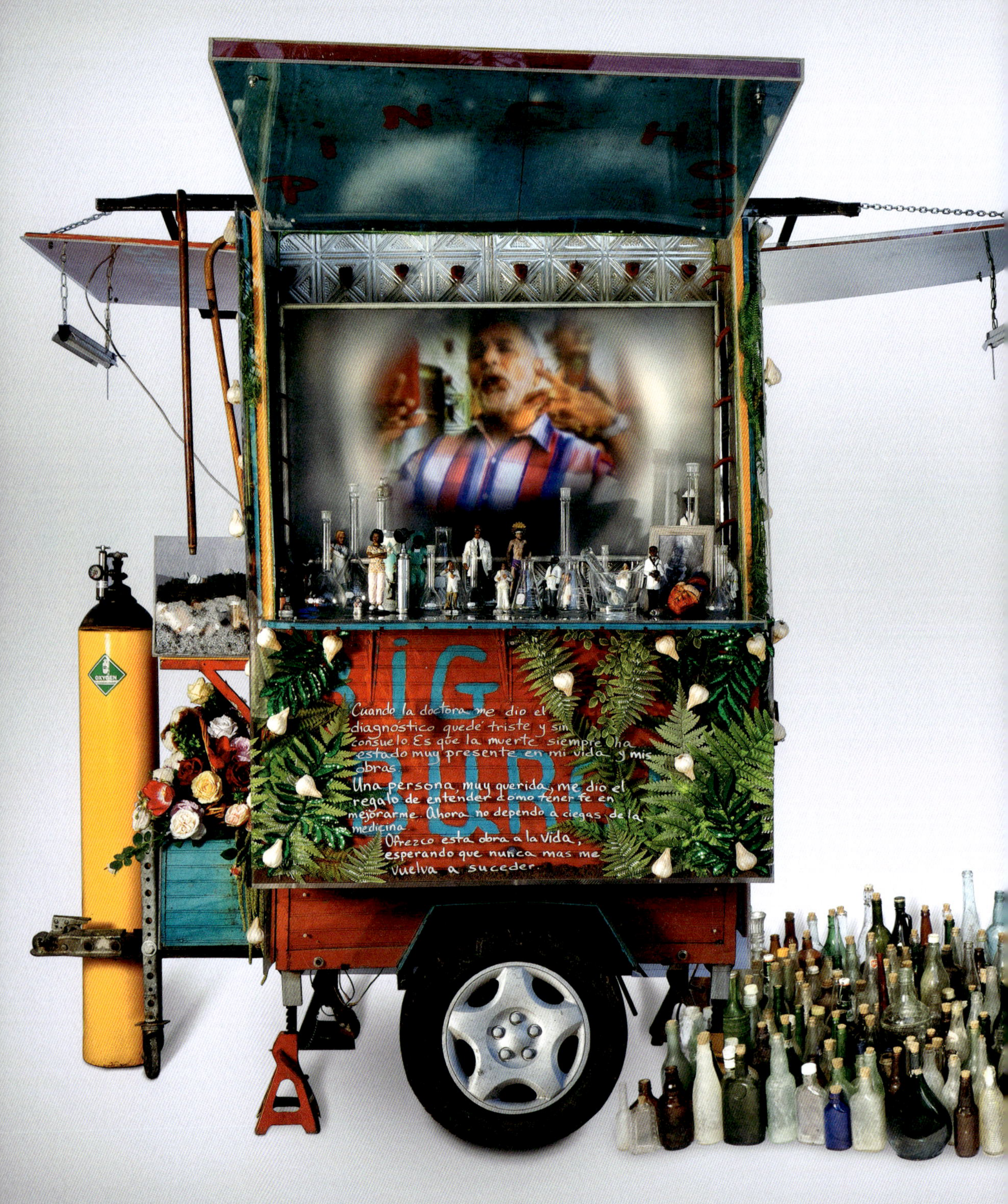
Cuando la doctora me dio el
diagnóstico quedé triste y sin
consuelo. Es que la muerte siempre ha
estado muy presente en mi vida y mis
obras.
Una persona, muy querida, me dio el
regalo de entender cómo tener fe en
mejorarme. Ahora no dependo a ciegas de la
medicina.
Ofrezco esta obra a la Vida,
esperando que nunca mas me
vuelva a suceder.

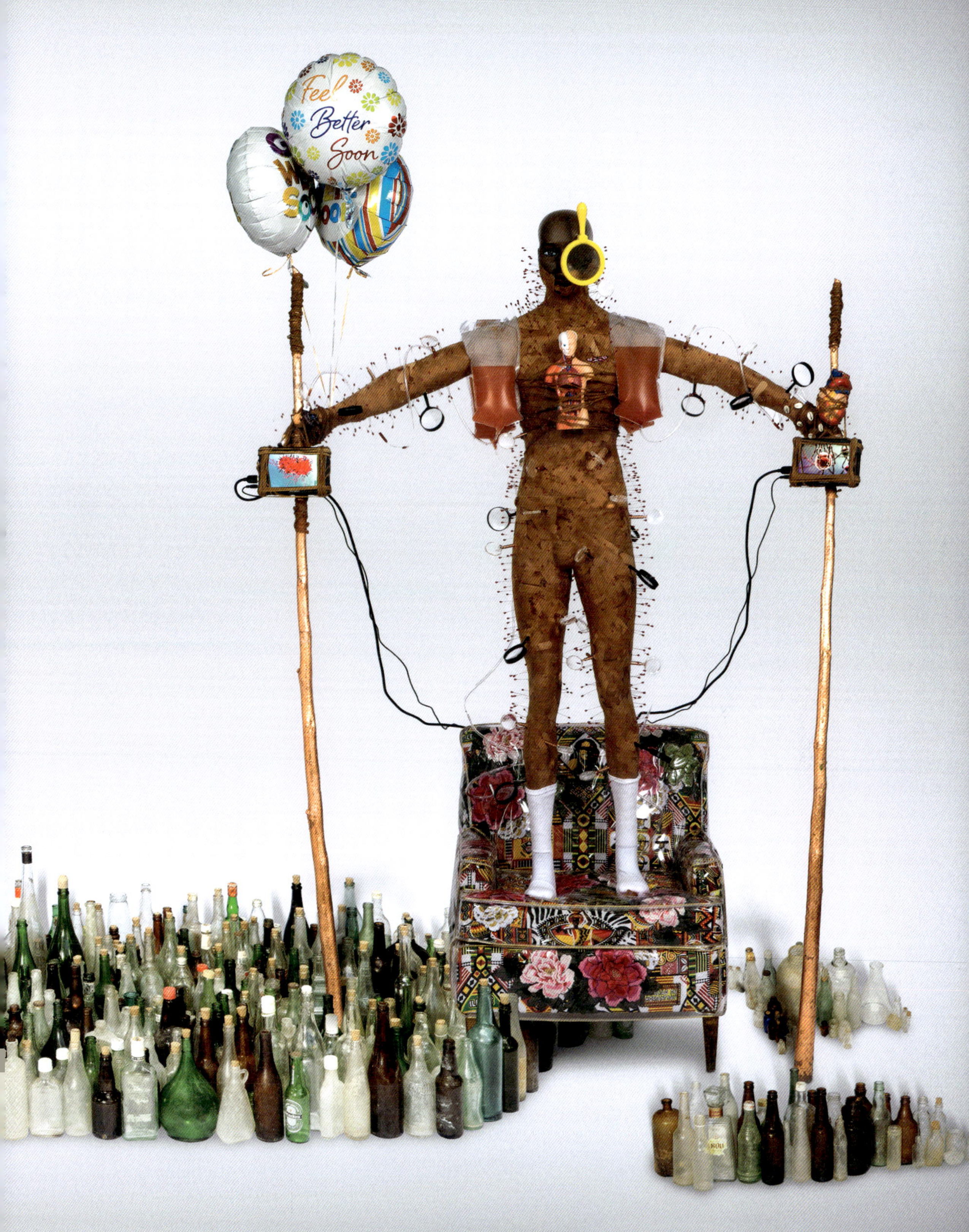
Feel Better Soon

List of Illustrated Works

Scene of the Crime (Whose Crime?), 1993
Mixed mediums and video installation
112 × 244 ½ × 146 ¾ in
(310 × 621 × 372.7 cm)
Bronx Museum of the Arts, New York. Purchased through funds from the H.W. Wilson Foundation and the National Endowment for the Arts, 1999.1.4

No Crying Allowed in the Barbershop (En la barbería no se llora), 1994
Mixed mediums and video installation
Dimensions variable
Museo de Arte de Puerto Rico, San Juan. Gift of Moisés and Diana Berezdivin

Badge of Honor, 1995
Mixed mediums and video installation
360 × 144 × 144 in
(914.4 × 365.8 × 365.8 cm)
Museum of Modern Art, New York. Acquired through the generosity of Heidi and Gregory Fulkerson, in memory of their parents, Dr. Samuel and Katharine Fulkerson, and in honor of Warren James

State of Preservation, 1996
Mixed mediums
Dimensions variable
Courtesy the artist

My Beating Heart (Mi corazón latiente), 2000
Mixed mediums, including: speakers with sound, archival paper, acrylic, and fiberglass
75 × 65 × 65 in
(190.5 × 165.1 × 165.1 cm)
Courtesy the artist

Lonely Soul, 2008
Wooden crutches, fiberglass, Styrofoam, wood, resin, photographs, metals, human hair, one thousand pins, hair clips, and wheelchair wheels
106 ½ × 83 × 77 in
(270.5 × 210.8 × 195.6 cm)
Courtesy the artist

Purifier, 2011
Glass, water, shelf, light
Dimensions variable
Courtesy the artist

Quinceañera, 2011
Mixed mediums
Dimensions variable
Courtesy the artist

reForm, 2014–17
Mixed mediums and video installation
Dimensions variable
Courtesy the artist

Reparación, 2021
Mixed mediums
8 × 6 × 6 in
(20.3 × 15.2 × 15.2 cm)
Private collection

Si mal no recuerdo (If I Remember Correctly), 2023
Mixed mediums
15 × 7 × 5 in
(38 × 17.8 × 12.7 cm)
Courtesy the artist

Convalescence, 2023
Mixed mediums
Dimensions variable
Courtesy the artist

About the Artist

Pépon Osorio (b. 1955, San Juan, Puerto Rico) lives and works between Philadelphia, Pennsylvania, and San Juan, Puerto Rico. He has had solo exhibitions at Williams College Art Museum, Williamstown, MA (2010); Institute of Contemporary Art, Philadelphia (2004); Museo de San Juan, Puerto Rico (2000); El Museo del Barrio, New York (1999); Contemporary Arts Museum Houston (1999); Museo Nacional Centro de Arte Reina Sofía, Madrid (1998); and Museo Alejandro Otero, Caracas, Venezuela (1998); among others. His work has been featured in group exhibitions in institutions such as the Museum of Modern Art, New York (2021); RISD Museum of Art, Providence, RI (2012); P.S.1 Contemporary Arts Center, New York (2008); Miami Art Museum (2008); São Paulo Biennial (2006); Center for the Arts at Yerba Buena Gardens, San Francisco (1997); Cuba Biennial, Havana (1997); Johannesburg Biennial (1997); Setagaya Art Museum, Tokyo (1997); Cleveland Institute of Art, OH (1993); and the Whitney Biennial, New York (1993). Osorio is the recipient of numerous awards, including Philadelphia's Cultural Treasure Artist Fellowship (2022), Guggenheim Fellowship (2021), United States Artists Fellowship (2018), Distinguished Artist Award for Lifetime Achievement from the College Art Association (2018), Skowhegan Medal for Sculpture (2001), MacArthur Fellowship (1999), and the Alpert Award in the Arts—Visual Arts (1999). In 2006, Osorio was nominated by former President Barack Obama to the National Council on the Arts, an advisory committee of the National Endowment for the Arts.

Board of Trustees

Photography Credits

All images courtesy the artist, unless otherwise noted.

Installation views: "1993 Whitney Biennial," Whitney Museum of American Art, New York (March 4–June 20, 1993). Photos: Frank Gimpaya (pp. 73–75)

Installation views: "NYC 1993: Experimental Jet Set, Trash and No Star," New Museum, New York (February 13–March 26, 2013). Photos: Benoit Pailley (pp. 76–83)

Installation view: "No Crying Allowed in the Barbershop (En la barbería no se llora)," Real Art Ways, Hartford, CT (1994). Photo: Cecilia Préstamo for the Hartford Courant (p. 85)

Installation views: "No Crying Allowed in the Barbershop (En la barbería no se llora)," Real Art Ways, Hartford, CT (1994). Photos: John Groo (pp. 86–89)

Installation views: Permanent collection, Museo de Arte de Puerto Rico, San Juan, 2022. Photos: Jose López Serra (pp. 90–105)

Installation view: "Badge of Honor," commissioned by the Newark Museum, NJ, 1995. Photo: Sara Welles (p. 107)

Installation views: "Collection 1880s–1940s," Museum of Modern Art, New York (October 30, 2021–April 24, 2022). Digital image: © 2022 Museum of Modern Art, New York. Photos: Robert Gerhardt (pp. 108–09; 120–21)

Installation view: "Home–So Different, So Appealing," Los Angeles County Museum of Art (July 11–October 15, 2017). © Pepón Osorio, photo © Museum Associates/ LACMA (pp. 110–11)

Installation views: "Home–So Different, So Appealing," Los Angeles County Museum of Art (July 11–October 15, 2017). Photo: Elon Schoenholz. © 2017 UCLA Chicano Studies Research Center (pp. 112–19; 122–25)

Installation views: "Pepón Osorio," Ronald Feldman Fine Arts, New York (September 9–October 21, 2011; pp. 126–29; 149)

Courtesy Ronald Feldman Fine Arts, New York. Photo: John Lamka (pp. 130–31)

Photo: Jose López Serra (p. 133)

Photos: Sam Fritz (pp. 135–37; 140–45; 169–77)

Photo: Carlos Avendaño (p. 139)

Courtesy Ronald Feldman Fine Arts (p. 147)

Installation views: "reForm," Tyler School of Art, Temple University, Philadelphia, PA (August 21, 2015–May 18, 2016). Photos: Constance Mench (pp. 150–67)

Photos: José Arturo Ballester-Panelli (pp. 178–91)

Published by
New Museum
235 Bowery
New York, NY 10002

On the occasion of the exhibition
"Pépon Osorio: My Beating Heart/
Mi corazón latiente"
June 29–September 17, 2023

Curators: Margot Norton, former Allen and Lola Goldring Senior Curator, and Bernardo Mosqueira, ISLAA Curatorial Fellow

Contributors:
Robert Blackson
Rita Indiana
Bernardo Mosqueira
Margot Norton
Pépon Osorio
Ramón H. Rivera-Servera
Guadalupe Rosales

Copy Editor: Sarah Stephenson
Design Template: An Art Service
Design Production: Nicholas Weltyk
Printing: SPC, Poland

Translation of "Perhaps Atomic: Pepón Osorio in Conversation with Rita Indiana": Nathan Osorio

Front and back covers: *Badge of Honor*, 1995. Mixed mediums and video installation, 360 × 144 × 144 in (914.4 × 365.8 × 365.8 cm). Photo: John Sciulli

ISBN: 978-0-915557-32-5

Major support for "Pepón Osorio: My Beating Heart/*Mi corazón latiente*" is provided by the Mellon Foundation.

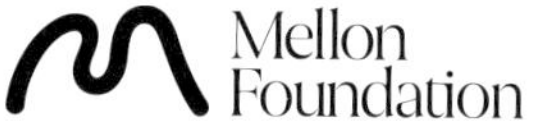

Artist commissions are generously supported by the Neeson / Edlis Artist Commissions Fund.

Generous support is provided by:
Liza Mauer
Ronald Feldman Gallery, New York, in memory of Ronald Feldman

We gratefully acknowledge the International Leadership Council of the New Museum.

Education and community programs are supported, in part, by the American Chai Trust.

Support for the publication has been provided by the J. McSweeney and G. Mills Publications Fund at the New Museum.

NEW MUSEUM